BIG ENERGY POETS:

ECOPOETRY THINKS CLIMATE CHANGE

BIG ENERGY POETS:
ECOPOETRY THINKS CLIMATE CHANGE

EDITORS:
HEIDI LYNN STAPLES & AMY KING

BlazeVOX [books]
Buffalo, NY

Big Energy Poets: Ecopoetry Thinks Climate Change
Editors: Heidi Lynn Staples & Amy King
Copyright © 2017

Published by BlazeVOX [books]

Printed in the United States of America

Interior design and typesetting by Geoffrey Gatza
Cover Art: Julie Patton

First Edition
ISBN: 978-1-60964-103-0
Library of Congress Control Number: 2016955115

BlazeVOX [books]
131 Euclid Ave
Kenmore, NY 14217

Editor@blazevox.org

publisher of weird little books

BlazeVOX [books]

blazevox.org

21 20 19 18 17 16 15 14 13 12 01 02 03 04 05 06 07 08 09 10

BlazeVOX

Acknowledgments

Thank you Geoffrey at BlazeVOX, your enduring generosity

& thank you to the University of Alabama, your grant support

& thank you to Sammi Bryant, Michael Lambert, Andrew Stevens, Meredith Ramella, your organizational and imaginative brilliance

& thank you to all these poets, your daring love

& thank you to you, for you, Dear Reader

Table of Contents

INTRODUCTION

In a time when politicians still either thumb their noses at the idea of climate change or simply put a pin in it because they don't know how to address or deal with the sense of urgency that is actually upon us, we look to the poets.

We look to the poets because poets historically are not beholden to the money-making apparatuses that use words to persuade lands away from Native Americans and to persuade permissions to continue to break terra firma for here-today-pollution-tomorrow fuels.

Poets make the connections between the treatment of lands and peoples; poets can see the intersections of how abuses and phobias extend from persons to animals and environments. Poets use words to enable us to make those sometimes conceptually-difficult leaps and articulate realities many sense and feel on the tips of our tongues. They give us ways to speak on such topics that might seem removed if we aren't scientists. They give us permission to make connections that seem unrelated on the surface. They interrogate and challenge what power says is off limits.

Just as we have shifted from "global warming" to "climate change", we know these understandings and urgencies are upon us and still becoming. We know that the feminization of the planet has left many of the harsh actualities of bankrupting the planet pushed to the side. We see droughts and depletion of soils and so much more in countries where people have lost their lives due to the effects of climate change. Only fools of certain political stripes deny the existence of such phenomena now.

Within these pages you'll find work that I have already been using on panel presentations and in classrooms. Much of what Heidi has outlined has proven to be material of a fecundity from which conversations grow and touch on complexities that our leaders who should be enacting policies to address perhaps cannot grasp yet. Just as we long ago suspected gender imbalances and racial inequities without concrete evidence, the poems on these pages give voice to and illustrate concepts and experiences that, in turn, allow us to compartmentalize and shut down "climate denial." The exercises unlock, open and give permission to develop our own understandings. Suppression and shame are no longer the dominant modes of address, thanks to scientists, activists and culture workers who would not be silenced.

I've known many of these poets for decades now and feel privileged to learn from their experiences, insights and growing bodies of knowledge when it comes to, not just addressing concepts, policies and practices that may affect our present day circumstances, but to considering how we might see what we have been conditioned to overlook, how we might reach out to and support communities that seem unlike our own, and how to begin mapping ways to possibly interact with communities without harming or taking from them. This kind of poetic work is the foundation fomenting the groundwork that will enable developments in ecological and cultural protections and environmental restorations far into the future.

If we can utilize these poets to help us break the mold of hierarchical thinking, of imperialistic impulses and approaches, and if we can move past the distractions of who will be in power next and let these poets help us see and interrogate the structures that support the continued denigration of the planet and people who are dubbed "expendable", the effects of which can be seen in places like Syria and India, then we just might have a chance at possibly impeding the increasing scarcity of resources and destruction for pleasure and profit. With these voices and ideas, we might also upset the routines and beliefs that sustain structures committed to harm.

As always, we look to the poets for insights into such power struggles and to help shape the conversation by articulating realities and ideas the media and politicians ignore and by pressing upon us the needs and urgency of what is at hand, what we may not be fully conscious of yet, laid out before you on these pages now with gratitude and care.

—Amy King

Big Energy Poets: Ecopoetry Thinks Climate Change provides those who may come after us with some answer to the question, as Anne Waldman writes in *Manatee/Humanity*, "what were they thinking, stupid fuckers?" Did those of us situated within cultural denial give a damn? Yes—perhaps we cannot dam the genocidal catastrophes of climate change, but these pages do record affective response.

The collection emerges from *Poets for Living Waters*, a similarly co-edited, online international poetry response to the 2010 BP oil disaster in the Gulf of Mexico—the biggest manmade environmental disaster in U.S. history, that monumentally farcical botch with implications unto geologic time. This book is not an excerpt of that anthology. Instead, it is a diverse sampling of twenty-one contemporary writers, several of whom are published in *Poets for Living Waters* and several whose work fit with this particular anthology's purposes: Stephen Collis, Matthew Cooperman, CAConrad, Adam Dickinson, Suzi Garcia, Aby Kaupang, Anna Lena Phillips Bell, Brenda Hillman, Lucas de Lima, Brenda Iijima, Eric Magrane, Joyelle McSweeney, Julie Patton, Craig Santos Perez, Evelyn Reilly, Linda Russo, Metta Sama, Kaia Sand, Kate Schapira, Jonathan Skinner, and Cecilia Vicuña. Each poet offers a representative sampling of poetry, a description of the writing process, an ecopoetics statement, a perceptual challenge, and a suggested reading list. The perceptual challenges and reading lists are written as invitations into the collective yet individual process of cultivating wholistic attention to our ecological predicament while situated within large-scale popular denial.

These pages include an agony so intense it results in self-harm, described in a process statement and attendant poem by CAConrad, who inserts a catheter into his penis as reminder of military-industrial horrors. These pages include referral to a suicidal plea by an indigenous people under colonial attack, suggested reading by Lucas de Lima. These pages include a grappling despair, as Kate Schapira reports in her process statement: "I cried through the winter of 2014 about the effects of climate change, present and possible future." These pages include emotions ranging from what Stephen Collis describes as "something between an animal's howl of terror and rage, and the philosopher's contemplative drive to 'know thyself'."

The anthology's title asserts that these poets "think climate change;" yet, how can we use an inherited logic to prevent its legacy? The articulation of climate change as part of the Anthropocene is a case in point. The scientific idea of the Anthropocene is from geography, a claim that, as described, for example, in the *Smithsonian* article "What is the Anthropocene and Are We In It?," "human-kind has caused mass extinctions of plant and animal species, polluted the oceans and altered the atmosphere, among other lasting impacts." While the exact date of the Anthropocene's beginning is argued—from either unsustainable agricultural practices in Europe 900 AD, the industrial revolution, or atomic-bomb testing—the basic formulation of the term asserts that 'humanity' is altering the entire planet, the greatest crisis of which is climate change—"We're the first species that's become a planet-scale influence and is aware of that reality. That's what distinguishes us."

Holding species accountable--rather than particular economic systems or philsophical systems--for planetary-wide systemic collapse implies that the lack of a parasitic relationship to our living Earth is, in fact, nonhuman— dominion: "that's what distinguishes *us*" (emphasis mine). Societies defined by a "planet-scale influence" of sustainable practices that effectively "leave-no-trace" are not part of the 'Human' implied in the idea of the Anthropocene. This distorted definition of collective Humanity arises from racist Enlightenment definitions of the Human, that understanding of Human subjectivity defined as rational, ordered, clarifying, objective, immutable, boundaried—a definition invested in, as de Lima says, "valorizing human-centered mastery where the epistemologies of other societies—the "rest" to the West—do not."

The way of knowing "valorizing human-centered mastery" is often traced to Descartes' famous formulation, "I think therefore, I am—" Descartes, father of science, who slit the voice box of his subjects to silence their protest as he performed experiments on their tortured bodies. A Cartesian perspective produces the same denial of embodied reality that allows us to believe we might abandon our physical form, downloading our consciousness onto a server; allows us to believe we might rapturously destroy the material palpable Earth, moving on to dwell intact happily forever in some remote invisible paradise. The silencing of bodies produces the same disassociative stance that has us gleefully projecting into virtual 'realities' while we inhabit a mass extinction. Knowing ourselves primarily through a disruption of mind/body connection, inherited from Descartes, is the anthropocenic capital-letter 'Human', a way of knowing and thusly, doing, manifesting climate change.

The poets selected for inclusion in this anthology imply that the 'Self,' the Cartesian 'Human' is, to a certain extent, performative, as considered through Judith Butler's widely known theory on gender performativity. Butler describes "One is not simply a body, but, in some very key sense, one does one's body." Many of the works here extend by implication performativity to the social construct of the Human. One's experience as an anthropocenic 'Human' "cannot be understood as a role which either expresses or disguises an interior self." Rather, a performative capital-letter "I", as in the formulation of "I think, therefore, I am," is "an act, broadly construed, which constructs the social fiction of its own psychological interiority--" to which may be added, the social fiction of its impermeability.

The hegemony of dominion requires our perpetual, unreflective repetition of Human knowing—the performance of a stable, boundaried, objective self. The works in *Big Energy Poets* all suggest that to "think climate change" in an activist sense requires "unthinking" Enlightenment notions of personhood, actively undoing Human. At the same time as undoing the inherited notion of Human, these writers engage in a scientific empiricism acknowledging the permeability and constitution of the self within systemic exchanges. They perform what ecotheorist Timothy Morton calls "the ecological thought," singing songs of the "nonself"—that is an evolving participant within highly complex mutually constitutive material exchanges.

Songs of the nonself make for maximum possibility. In addition to extending the historical document, as Muriel Rukesyer suggests, poetry has political power in its generative ability to create new material realities--as Cecila Vicuña writes, "History is not just 'written', it is performed in a cosmic field, the quantum memory of Earth." The collection begins with the work of Stephen Collis, including his "Manifesto of the Biotariat," in which he provides a definition of "the biotariat," calling for action on behalf of a collective "we" engaged in class struggle—all "life, in all its manifold aspects (from boreal forests to sea turtles...to sex workers to precariously employed adjunct professors to coral reefs and honey bees and so on and so forth)." Suzi Garcia responds to *The Sexual Politics of Meat: A Feminist-Vegetarian Critical Theory* by Carol J. Adams with a series of poems, thinking about how the cultural practice of meat production and consumption informs her sense of self, —reminding us scholars have claimed widespread vegetarianism would reduce greenhouse gases dramatically—"Even my food is a reminder that I am oppressor and oppressed, that it is not a straightforward, top-down life, and sometimes it doesn't even make sense. My body is a destroyer, my joy is a destroyer, even as I am destroyed." Joyelle McSweeney's excerpt from "Necropastoral" describes a nonself "where avian flu...toxic contamination via industrial waste...mass graves which double as classrooms, have destroyed the idea of the bordered or bounded body and marked the porousness of the human body as its most characteristic quality." Matthew Copperman & Aby Kuapang in their collaborative work "*Whether Underground*" explore how the body of their daughter and of their marriage is permeated by relations with Big Pharm and its queen, plastics. Craig Santos Perez includes a poem written on the subject of plastic and discusses his course on Ecopoetics. Adam Dickinson sings of his nonselves metabolic in a "metabolic poetics" project, wherein he examines "the way oil has become a form of writing in human biological and metabolic contexts by researching and writing...poetry...based on a toxicological and symbiotic map of my own body (obtained through blood, urine, and microbiome testing)."

Evelyn Reilly invokes the micro-muses in her process statement:

> What might happen if the multitudinous, utopian-
> democratic, polymorphically-erotic Whitman poetic "self"
> were re-constituted within the context of our post-colonial,
> post-humanist, globally inter-tangled and genderly
> profusional era? Could there be a new "song of ourselves"
> that expands to include many more kinds of permeable
> relationality, including cross-species relationality? And
> what kind of language critique, experimentation and
> innovation would that require?

The works we've gathered for you answer Reilly's question, demonstrating a commitment to what feminist science philosopher Donna Haraway describes as "feminist empiricism" through "situated knowledges." They pursue ecological awareness through engagement with unique situations grounded in "partial, locatable, critical knowledges sustaining the possibility of webs of connections called solidarity in politics and shared conversations in epistemology." What they "do" with their bodies, is enact "feminist objectivity," generating a wide range of projects whose topics are about "limited location and situated knowledge, not about transcendence and splitting of subject and object." CAConrad's somatic exercises self-generate defamiliarizing situations out of which, as William Blake describes it, "the doors of perception are cleansed." Poet and geographer Eric Magrane engages in what he calls "site-based geopoetics," writing "pieces arrived from a site-based practice," in which the poet inhabits the "Biosphere 2 (B2)...a site that blends big science—climate and systems research—with tourism." Linda Russo engages in what she calls "resurgent poetics," composing during regular walks surveying the site of a Walmart construction on the Palouse Prairie to "invoke freely a culture of interspecies inhabitance." Julie Patton's collages are "compost, improvisations live fermentation, visual trash heaps. I don't set out to make 'art'. Rather the art of living makes me." Kaia Sand discusses the multiple iterations of "Tiny Artic Ice," explaining that "with so much distraction, attention takes tending, which seems redundant—'tending' rooted in 'attending,' 'attention'." The emphasis on situation asks readers to become attentive to their own contexts, to engage their relationships imaginatively.

Full attention within the contemporary context necessitates inhabiting what African American studies scholar Daphne Brook describes as a "particular and dark position." The trope of darkness can serve as "an interpretative strategy," and the performance of nonself by many of these writers includes this way of reading realities and inhabiting difficult more typically repressed emotions like anger, despair, fear, and hopelessness. Such a stance includes Brenda Hillman rising in a protest with her students, facing into what "will be called batons, nightsticks or truncheons, clubs— are certain in the angle of the hitting $OOOOOO$." We're in the toxic dark when Brenda Iijima imagines radioactive waste, dead soils, and "a certain resilient worm that has migrated to the hot spots." We're in the dark arts with Anna Lena Phillips Bell, who applies language charms for staving off a deadly fungus killing her native Hemlock groves. Brooks also describes an "aesthetics of opacity" in which textual darkness works as a "trope of narrative insurgency, discursive survival, and epistemological resistance" (108), as Metta Sama writes in her poem: "how can I look at these petalled trees / and the glittery wings of these so black / they're blue birds in the South and not see / unmerciful white hands strangling them." Jonathan Skinner, who focuses on sound and vibration, offers us a trope for understanding poetry as a type of invisible subterranean communication creating change in the dark. Skinner's emphasis on vibrations, particularly bat and insect communication, evokes Charles Olson's emphasis on proprioception.

Join the movement and transfer of energy from the human body onto the page and into the reader—the power of invisible connective collective corporealities embedded in this collection's title *Big Energy Poets*. Read the singular work collected here by some of the most profoundly ambitious poets alive, poets answering Rilke's imperative, "You must change your life." Swarm with them in their perceptual challenges. Thrum in the wisdom of their suggested readings. Dance in your beings as the ground moves beneath our feet.

—Heidi Lynn Staples

References

Adams, Carol J. *The Sexual Politics of Meat: A Feminist-Vegetarian Critical Theory.*
     Bloomsbury Academic: NY, NY. 2010.

Brook, Daphne, *Bodies in Dissent: Spectacular Performances of Race and Freedom,*
     1850-1910. Duke University Press Books. 2006.

Butler, Judith. *Gender Trouble.* Routledge: NY, NY. 2006.

Harvey, Fiona. "Eat less meat to avoid dangerous global warming, scientists say,"
     Guardian. March 21, 2016.

Haraway, Donna. *Simians, Cyborgs and Women: The Reinvention of Nature.*
     Routledge: NY, NY. 1990.

King, Amy and Staples, Heidi Lynn. Poets for Living Waters,
     https://poetsgulfcoast.wordpress.com/

Morton, Timothy. *Ecology Without Nature.* Harvard University Press: Boston,
     MA. 2009.

Olson, Charles. "Projective Verse," *Poetry Foundation.*

Rilke, Maria Rainer. "Archaic Torso of Apollo," *Ahead of All Parting: Selected Poems of*
Rainer Maria Rilke. Modern Library: NY, NY. 2015.

Rukeyser, Muriel. *Collected Poetry of Muriel Rukeyser.* University of Pittsburgh Press:
Pittsburgh, PA. 2005.

Sanders, Laura. "Microbes can play games with the mind," *Science News.*
     March 23, 2016.

Stromberg, Joseph. "What is the Anthropocene and are we in it?,"
     Smithsonianmag.org. July 2013.

Waldman, Anne. *Manatee/Humanity.* Penguin: NY, NY. 2014.

BIG ENERGY POETS:
ECOPOETRY THINKS CLIMATE CHANGE

Stephen Collis

Stephen Collis's many books of poetry include *The Commons* (Talon Books 2008; 2014), *On the Material* (Talon Books 2010—awarded the BC Book Prize for Poetry), *DECOMP* (with Jordan Scott—Coach House 2013), and *Once in Blockadia* (Talon Books 2016). He has also written two books of literary criticism, a book of essays on the Occupy Movement, and a novel. In 2014 he was sued for $5.6 million by US energy giant Kinder Morgan, whose lawyers read his writing in court as "evidence." He lives near Vancouver, on unceded Coast Salish Territory, and teaches poetry and poetics at Simon Fraser University.

Works

Hockey Night in the Anthropocene

People's Climate March, New York, September 21 2014

And then we extend the climate of our unknowing
Despite false colour views and massive stacks of data
The moment wasn't about the symbolic after all
The moment followed a bee
Through the streets of Manhattan

The earth spinning hot on its axis
Was—or wasn't—more like a tree falling in a forest
Than it was like an instrument measuring CO_2
On a mountain in Hawaii—but if a tree falls in a forest
And everyone is already in that tree

Having climbed there to get above rising waters
Does it make any sound? Or is that
Just the noise our limbs make—wind-milling in space
As we launch—indexical of our own distraction—
Off the ends of our two hundred year old hockey sticks?

But tell me, Cecilia Vicuña, if you can
Is that bee the last fluttering index
Of an animal cognition undone by our too many doings?
Or will the herd of boreal caribou coming behind us
Sweep us round Columbus Circle one too many times?

I know—it's hard to stop coming to America—
The waiting room is the size of the world
Has a sign that says Welcome to the Anthropocene
And all the exits are jails furnished with
Unassembled Ikea furniture, and nary an Allen Key in sight.

Take Oil & Hum

The body is liquid what I'd send back to
Seas we swam out of or plied oars over
Seeking fleece the thunder of islands lakes squalls
A point beyond lighthouses species I pour down a
Mere factor in hydrology which is the subject now

What is this piping welter things with fences
Round them and things unfenced the fires in
Backdoors flood of crows from chimneys tract of land
Or water blacked lake through trees no limits
To the berries growing in great clots all over suburbs

Measured as lack euphemism for quaint topiary
And diesel fumes from gulfs terminal terminals the rinse
Cycle sea Northern Gateway Trans Mountain coastal
Viaducts an asterisk beside corporate stats and unopened
Grail castles where we wanted causes and plunder's liquid end

Driven snow west fleece over ocean tanker
Turned sound locked piracy over coal dock sulphur
Spilt wrath not west not first last peoples animals
Tuned ruin broken being you become all mouth all appetite
Swallowing appetite go wolf go devourer the planet is your plate

More and more sources of anxiety—oil and gas
Absorbed social environment—kill floor & tailings pond
More cunning container cuckold culture more Alberta
More like Mordor—But that's—retorted the lawyer—economics
An ordinary war run short of thieves and the curious? Curiouser

Stand amidst pines beetle laden carpet smell
Of brown needles welcomed into nostrils try ignoring
Pipelines try walking on berber as something insatiable
Explodes ghost bottom of a ship passing overhead plume of oil
Clouding the undersea diving birds and their nests in the plastic trees

What do we do throw our bodies out on the water in plastic
Kayak it's not the problem throw Burnaby at Grasmere Grasmere
At Burnaby I've given up on quests and literature the book
In the night rustles its leaves I ignore it and turn to the sea
Burying my cock in a wooden box afloat for endless days of slick rain

Then dark rains come sheeting ashore new conquests black gold
Cause of all this and all those barricades made out of burning tires
In the streets of Bangkok black smoke billowing into
All our screens as whales beach or Tiananmen or Tahrir and the
Animal territories of nether light we've lit out for once again

Poetics

Manifesto of the Biotariat

that which is excluded comes back to haunt the excluder... the shadow of animality becomes constitutive of the human.[1]

1. When we compare humans to animals in terms of mistreatment ("they were treated like animals"), we mean no disrespect to animals; we mean only that animals, including human beings, are often mistreated, exploited, and accorded no dignity. These processes are increasingly systematized and totalized across the biological spectrum.

2. First, a provisional definition. The biotariat: that portion of existence that is *enclosed* as a "resource" by and for those who direct and benefit from the accumulation of wealth. So: labouring human beings generally; most animals and plants; forest, wetland and grassland ecosystems; water; land itself, as it provisions and enables biological life broadly; minerals that lie beneath the surface of the land; common "wastes" and "sinks" too, into which the waste products of resource extraction and production and use are spilled—primarily the atmosphere and the oceans, primarily in the form of carbon and petroleum products. The enclosed and exploited life of this planet.

3. Is it possible to politicize *life as such*? To—even conceptually—imagine its "class composition"? To read it—cross biotically—as *social*? I believe that current world conditions push us in this direction—make this an unavoidable move. If the Anthropocene (a term that possibly obfuscates as much as it clarifies) is coterminous with the scientific foundation of "life" as a general category (Larmack, 1801, introducing the idea of "biology" as a unified science of all cellular life)—as well as with the historical development of capitalism—then the biotariat comes into being as a response to the fluorescence of the Anthropocene—as a reminder of its biopolitical foundations. Once we can perceive the *total* impact of capitalism on *life itself*, just then does it become necessary to develop a new political consciousness and new revolutionary subjectivity *on the basis of life as such*.

4. This is the reason to propose the biotariat: the enclosure and exploitation of life, in all its manifold aspects (from boreal forests to sea turtles to Bangladeshi garment workers to the homeless of the world's major cities to sex workers to precariously employed adjunct professors to coral reefs and honey bees and so on and so forth),

---

[1] *Ron Broglio. "Incidents in the Animal Revolution," in Beyond Human: From Animality to Transhumanism. Ed. Charlie Blake, Claire Molloy, and Steven Shakespeare. London: Continuum, 2012.*

has reached a stage in which "we"—all of life—are in the same desperate and drunken boat—constrained there by a system of total and planetary accumulation that even the term "capitalism" perhaps cannot adequately capture anymore. In what sense is this "economics"—this means of the production of financial inequality that systemically impacts and imperils life itself?

5. Enclosure, Peter Linebaugh notes, involves at once the "taking of land and the taking of bodies."[2] Linebaugh is noting the historical convergence of the enclosure of common lands and the "body snatchers" who stole and murdered commoners and other poor people to provide cadavers for the burgeoning medical schools of early nineteenth century England. But we can extend this analysis to the "taking of land" from indigenous people under colonization (and the extension of colonization into the current era of extreme resource extraction) and the "taking of bodies" evident in both the Residential School System and the vast numbers of murdered and missing indigenous women in Canada. Going even further, the "taking of land" becomes almost total under current conditions, where the entire surface of the Earth and its atmosphere too functions either as "productive resource" or sink for waste products (including carbon emissions), and the "taking of bodies" includes the capture of nearly all animals in factory farms, zoos, or "nature reserves."

But again—how can we politicize *life as such*? What might this look like as an *organizational practice*?

6. The Gaia hypothesis proposes that the Earth is a single, self-regulating complex system, integrating biological, atmospheric, and inorganic subsystems. With the biotariat, I would imagine a "socialized" version of this hypothesis—the Earth as planetary commons, all life as constituting a realm of communing which depends upon shared access to the planetary commons. This would be to project not a divine goddess (Gaia), but Earth itself as a repressed, enclosed commons—lowly, levelled, and exploited. Earth not as singularity, but as the complex multitude of life, coming, under the impetus provided by globalization and climate change, into a new and necessary bio-solidarity. We need to take the snatched body of the Earth back—for all the beings on the Earth.

7. The politicization of life as such, and thus the calling to arms of the biotariat, depends upon a willingness to accept "a definition of politics as a political *ecology* and a notion of publics as human-nonhuman collectives that are provoked into existence by a shared experience of harm." This is Jane Bennett, from her book *Vibrant Matter*. The perspective of the biotariat requires "taking the side of things" (*parti pris des choses*—Francois Ponge), or what Bennett describes as

---

[2] *Peter Linebaugh. Stop Thief! The Commons, Enclosure, and Resistance. Oakland: PM Press, 2014.*

Dogged resistance to anthropomorphism.... I will emphasize, even overemphasize, the agentic contributions of nonhuman forces (operating in nature, in the human body, and in human artifacts) in an attempt to counter the narcissistic reflex of human language and thought.[3]

Similarly, biologist Scott Gilbert suggests that there are significant interactions of animals and plants with symbiotic microorganisms that disrupt the boundaries which heretofore had characterized the biological individual. Animals cannot be considered individuals by anatomical, or physiological criteria, because a diversity of symbionts are both present and functional in completing metabolic pathways and serving other physiological functions.[4]

8. Thus we need to frame struggles not exclusively on the ground of human rights, but more broadly, in terms of inter-systemic responses and responsibilities. To recognize that the commons is more than a system of social reproduction—that it in fact is a system of ecological sustainability, writ large, into which human social reproduction fits. Or—to be itself sustainable—*must fit*. So—communing, as a verb, is what all life *does*—a process and an action upon which all life depends—the radical sharing of the means and material of existence. The proposition of a biotariat calls a new collective identity into being, a new common subjectivity formed by life itself, which we are only beginning to find out how to access and enable agentically.

9. Ron Broglio roots around the foundations of the biotariat when he asks of "emancipatory projects" which "mesh across human and nonhuman boundaries": "To what mutuality could we appeal?"[5] The source of such "mutuality," and thus for a potential biotariat, Broglio argues, is the shared fact of embodiment, and thus the shared corporeal vulnerability of all of life. All bodies convey the fact of their impermanence. All bodies convey their dependence on, and openness to, other (animal or plant) bodies. Broglio writes, "the animal revolution finds a hole in the social system which keeps the animals at bay." This "hole," he argues, is the shared fact of vulnerable embodiment. I would only add that the "hole" now is blown wide open, so that the entire planet is marked by this embodied precariousness—that in

---

[3] Jane Bennett. *Vibrant Matter: A Political Ecology of Things.* Durham: Duke University Press, 2010.
[4] Scott Gilbert. *"We Are All Lichens: How symbiosis research has reconstituted a new realm of individuality."* http://scijust.ucsc.edu/we-are-all-lichens-how-symbiosis-research-has-reconstituted-a-new-realm-of-individuality/
[5] Broglio, *"Incidents in the Animal Revolution."*

the Anthropocene the entire biosphere is revealed as an imperilled and vulnerable *body*.

10. What can "we"—the biotariat—do? How can you "organize" *life as such* in resistance to totalized, planetary capitalist exploitation? This isn't *Animal Farm, The Rise of the Planet of the Apes*, or a Tolkien tale in which an army of trees will join us on the battlefield. I don't have an answer to these pressing questions; for now, I will only suggest that organizing on a common ground with all of life—resisting capitalism from the position of life itself (rather than one species or one human class or social subsection)—draws together a number of strands of current global resistance—from indigenous land resistance through climate justice movements to new urban occupations and the organization of migrant rights—all of which might be reconceived and reinvigorated as the resistance of the commons of life to the new and massive enclosures of total subsumption and totalized global capitalism.

11. Walking on many large climate marches in 2014, what struck me was the almost total absence of other life forms. We were human—all too human—all too many and exclusively, mirroring our manufactured humanity to each other—moving across spaces we had made (the tar sands/New York City) and from which we had eliminated much of the rest of life. These were human events in decidedly man-made spaces. I was left hungering for what Kathryn Yusoff, in "Project Anthropocene," calls "a geologic social and body politic." Yusoff writes:

> if we hold a certain *fidelity* towards the issues the Anthropocene raise; i.e. a fidelity to the future promises of the Anthropocene and the reconceptualization of social relations that are released by holding with its promises, then we must grapple with a different sort of politic than the one we've been doing so far in social theory.[6]

This "grappling" is the biotariat—of and by and for the biotariat—that *office, function*, or *collective body* life now necessarily forms. We politicize life anew when we face the fact of the Anthropocene, and see that this misnames something we desperately need to name (and in the face of which the biotariat rises). "Capitalocene" is too clumsy/awkward. But life is rising, in new interspecies ways, in geophysio-social ways, at the moment the impact of human beings on the rest of life has become total.

12. So what is left to say but—*biotarians of the world unite—the only thing you have to lose is your chains!*

---

[6] *Kathryn Yusoff. "Project Anthropocene: a minoritarian manifesto for reoccupying the strata." http://www.geocritique.org/project-anthropocene-minoritarian-manifesto-reoccupying-strata-kathryn-yusoff/*

Process

I write towards something I do not yet know how to realize. In the poem "Take Oil & Hum"—in the face of several massive pipeline proposals (the Enbridge Northern Gateway Pipeline and Kinder Morgan's Trans Mountain Pipeline), both projected to cross British Columbia, from the Alberta tar sands, over many rivers to the deep inlets of the west coast—it is proposed that "hydrology" be the "subject" of the poem. I mean here, I think, the "agent," the poem's main *actor*. The human/poet rides shotgun, trying to divest itself of anthropocentric control. It is not easy, when all we can really do as poets is wander in a worded wood.

This is writing towards the rise of what I have called the *biotariat*, a new collective social/animal subject of the Anthropocene whose poetry does not yet exist. I see glimmers of its potentiality in Oana Avasilichioaei's *We Beasts* (especially in the book's title poem) or Angela Rawlings' *Wide Slumber for Lepidopterists* and its sonic wing beats. Jordan Scott and I, in *DECOMP*, tried to de-compose a book, in the service of the soil—as all life serves life via the production of soils with our decaying bodies. These projects are yet mere harbingers of the rise of the biotariat, necessarily entropological explorations of what Jonathan Skinner has called "third landscape." For as Ron Broglio writes, "there is no calendar for the animal revolution"—it is always—at any moment—*yet to come.*

"Take Oil & Hum" and "Hockey Night in the Anthropocene" are both poems written via an extensive process of recycling and recoding—taking previously generated material and reworking it, taking draft poems apart and de- and recomposing them, shaping it in a series of potential forms, again and again. They are also written with Jacques Rancière's idea of a "double effect" in mind:

> Suitable political art would ensure, at one and the same time, the production of a double effect: the readability of a political signification and a sensible or perceptual shock caused, conversely, by the uncanny, by that which resists signification (*The Politics of Aesthetics* 63)

The shock of the "uncanny" is poetry's long-standing tendency to tell things slant—to aspire to take the top of the head completely off. Animals, like poems, "resist signification"—though they do so in oddly communicative ways.

The "readability of a political statement" relates in part to the context in which the poems were written and performed/distributed. Thus they are also poems written from within the context of engaged social struggle—from a position within the climate justice movement, in part intended as contributions to that movement. "Take Oil & Hum" has a long genesis and has cycled through many different forms. It appeared, in radically different form from its present arrangement, in *The Enpipe Line*—a collection of poems, edited by Christine Leclerc, written in opposition to the proposed Enbridge Northern Gateway Pipeline. Many of the poems in that collection were read at rallies and included in anti-pipeline publications. The book launch took place in the streets outside of Enbridge's Vancouver offices.

"Hockey Night in the Anthropocene" was composed from several fragments written around the People's Climate March in New York City, September 2014. I marched with Cecilia Vicuña, Anne Waldman, Marcella Durand and many other friends—right in front of a herd of boreal forest caribou puppets. There were some 400,000 of us. It still wasn't enough.

I was thinking through Eduardo Kohn's idea, from his book *How Forests Think*, that there are three main forms of communicating information: the iconic, the indexical, and the symbolic. All animals deploy the first two; possibly, only humans use the symbolic. It struck me that climate change, that content the entire biosphere is currently signalling, is an indexical piece of information: it is a pointing, a deictic marker of biospheric catastrophe. Fine then. Poetry is a deictic medium too—good for indexing (indicating), maybe not as good at discursively unravelling. Poetry's pointing (Stein: "a system to pointing") occurs at the point of maximum dialectical tension that Rancière names the marker of "suitable political art." So these poems attempt something between an animal's howl of terror and rage, and the philosopher's contemplative drive to "know thyself." Only now the knowing I am hungry for is the knowing of natural systems. How forests think. The subjectivity of the hydrological cycle.

Write so that you do not merely personify another species but so that you embody other species resistance to a world in which only the human might inhere. Write so that systems can themselves index grief outrage and desire through your writing.

Suggesteds

Oana Avasilichioaei. *We Beasts*. Hamilton: Wolsak & Wynn, 2012.

Jane Bennett. *Vibrant Matter: A Political Ecology of Things*. Durham: Duke University Press, 2010.

Charlie Blake, Claire Molloy, and Steven Shakespeare, eds. *Beyond Human: From Animality to Transhumanism*. London: Continuum, 2012.

Eduardo Kohn. *How Forests Think: Towards an Anthropology beyond the Human*. Berkeley: University of California Press, 2013.

Christine Leclerc, ed. *The Enpipe Line*. Smithers BC: Creekstone Press, 2012.- - - . *Oilywood*. Vancouver: Nomados 2013.

Angela Rawlings' *Wide Slumber for Lepidopterists*. Toronto: Coach House Books, 2006.

Jordan Scott & Stephen Collis. *DECOMP*. Toronto: Coach House Books, 2013.

Jonathan Skinner. "Thoughts on Things: Poetics of the Third Landscape." *((eco)(lang)(uage(reader))*. Ed. Brenda Iijima. New York: Portable Press, 2010.

CAConrad

CAConrad's childhood included selling cut flowers along the highway for his mother and helping her shoplift. The author of 9 books of poetry and essays, the latest is titled *While Standing In Line For Death* and is forthcoming from Wave Books (September 2017). He is a Pew Fellow and has also received fellowships from Lannan Foundation, MacDowell Colony, Headlands Center for the Arts, Banff, RADAR, Flying Object and Ucross. For his books, essays, and details on the documentary *The Book of Conrad* (Delinquent Films 2016), please visit CAConrad.blogspot.com

(photo credit: Dog Face Studio of Olympia)

Process/Works
(Soma)tic Poetry Rituals followed by resultant poems

Flying Killer Robots: The Renaming Project
for Mary Kalyna, artist, activist, and dear friend

To taste a word like a poet, not just to use it to construct sentences but to understand how it enters the body and what it does once it has made its way in us. This ritual is focused on one word and how it has altered human bodies in recent years.

OM is alive and well in the United States with people learning yoga and meditation. When chanted, OM vibrates through the body, quivering cells to attention, calming us, embracing a sympathetic frequency. In the Bhagavad Gita it is written, "There is harmony, peace and bliss in this simple but deeply philosophical sound." The Pentagon spends millions on research for quality language to sell us the newest, shiny products for the war machine: drone.

On a residency at Machine Project in Los Angeles I sat with eyes closed and chanted DRONE, DRONE, DRONE, feeling that ancient OM inside the word quiet me, moving me toward serenity. I went to the corner of Sunset and Alvarado to ask people, "Would you please join me in calling drones what they really are: Flying Killer Robots?" Some people wanted to talk and I invited them to chant DRONE with me on the busy street corner to feel how a soft sense of war quietly infiltrates our bodies, trading common sense of justice and love for annihilation. "Join me in the renaming project: Flying Killer Robots." I took notes for the poem.

The next ingredient of the ritual examined the sharp contrasts between the effects from hearing the word and the carnage drones create with their bullets and bombs. I walked a few blocks to Echo Park and drew a target on my left palm with red ink. Through headphones I listened to a recording of the Israeli-American military mission Pillar of Cloud, a fleet of drones buzzing over Gaza 24 hours a day, missiles exploding targets. With the volume turned up high I took my notes by the water's edge. At the sound of each explosion I screamed into the red target on my palm, screamed while writing notes for my poem. Each explosion snuffing out lives, the red target drawn through love line, heart line, life line; chanting, screaming, writing. Chanting DRONNNNE calmed me, but screaming with them in combat rattled me along the water. The recording is at this URL: http://bit.ly/2bzxy4V

I want every US-American reading this book to remember this: Before the use of drones my working-class military family was by the end of the Bush administration opposed to the wars, too exhausted from worrying about young family members fighting in Iraq and Afghanistan. Now that we are using drones they are at ease with our racist military bloodbath across the Middle East. In Pakistan alone our drones have killed over 1,000 civilians, 207 of them children. Yemen, Somalia, Syria, Libya, these are other countries being traumatized by our drones. We will never be able to apologize for our barbarism.

Eating Both Sides of What Is Left

in the midst of war
even our shyness
must cease
held inside a shudder
pressed into the dream
memory and their
graves not in
harmony today
stretching the vast sleep of this
world where
recent planetary
inventories show
more leopard-print
blouses than leopards
starvation's new life as
an accidental diet
poet on
board ship
making note of
who is looking at the sky
who is looking at the distant sea
who is looking at the churning turmoil shipside

Tarot as Verb Taroting Meat
for Selah Saterstrom

I saw you, sister, standing in this brilliance.
        —Paul Celan

Seeking potential conversations with the dead in grocery stores? Lacking the respect of a churchyard, stacks of chopped bodies wrapped in plastic and styrofoam, stamped with dates and prices; the refrigerator is not the grave, the human gut is the grave. Grocery store refrigerators are like any morgue awaiting someone to claim the body. Take a deep breath, close your eyes and listen. There is a particular and very noticeable chatter beneath the clear plastic shrouds, making the listener enter a quiet, cold meditation. Stand before the hacked animal joints, stomach and shoulder fat, and cut the tarot deck 9 times, then read the top card.

Memories are stored in flesh, be it human or of other animals on the prairie, by the bay, in the city, or incarcerated in prisons or zoos (which are prisons built to amuse children and their nescient parents). Stored memories of joy and suffering: anyone who has received extensive massage or acupuncture knows the body can release feelings long secluded in muscle and other tissue. It's a glorious thing, such freedom. Give this to grocery store animals with their fur ripped away, their tongues removed, their bones cracked and sawed from ligaments. Pull the cards, ask how they walked and felt the touch of sunlight. Unfetter a bit of the pain. Pull cards for chops, wings, roasts, and hamburger patties. Take notes about love you have known for those who were shown none. Notes from taroting at the display of conformist serial killing will become a poem, another communiqué, one for humans loosening their impediments of ignorance of suffering.

Grease of the Dead

do not grind your ax
on the heads of poets
words absorbed into
rice carried to table
I wish I could wish my shitty
little town back into forest
escaping air from Aunt
Darlene's balloon
smells of
menthol cigarettes and beer
neck of animal in refrigerator
legs wings thighs broken souls
everyone yelling in other room
time is the illness we remedy by
imagining the yet unlived
a tremor of sorcery we
give one another to
soften panic in
the seam
parrot sleeping in
tome of his story
though it was
her story
tears taste
exactly the
same all
over the
world god damn

Ant Cartography
for Yuh-Shioh Wong, who understood when I told her I am a painter

DAY ONE: I followed an ant back to his nest in the Chihuahuan Desert, a little juniper seed in his mouth. I drew a line on paper, following as he crawled around cacti and over pebbles. The cooperative kingdom of ants has always fascinated and frightened me much the way obedient men and women do when god and country are their foremost concerns. I never envy the ant carrying his seed into the underground food stores, programmed to question nothing, programmed to never run away or kill himself. Carry the seed, climb, burrow, and maybe the angel of death will show mercy and send a hungry bird or tarantula. No one will know you are gone no one will care, every other ant too busy working working WORKING! When Nana Conrad died they had her funeral on a Saturday so no one would have to miss a day of work work WORK at the factory. I remember the coworker who burst into tears when told she had an extra week of paid vacation, grateful she was allowed to have time to be herself for one whole week.

DAY TWO: I took the ant map to a random part of the desert, followed it to a small rock, a kind of oblivion, unexpected but solid nonetheless. I sat on the rock like an egg, wanting to hatch the rebellion! How much straining! I drew the map on my naked body behind shrubs, my third eye the nest entrance, tracing the journey in reverse, taking notes of my every memory of doing what I was told, toward some standard of goodness. HOW do we create a kind, generous, but disobedient world? How do we undo thousands of years of this damage? Even Greek mythology is sex jealousy revenge, sex jealousy revenge, the gods and goddesses enslaving human beings, raping them with their enormous cocks and vaginas. We need a total and lasting insurrection! Later I took a strand of cooked spaghetti, arranged it in the shape of the ant map. When it dried I took it to the entrance of the nest. I said, "I DON'T KNOW WHICH ONE OF YOU GAVE ME THIS MAP, BUT I'M GIVING IT BACK!" I crumbled it around the hole for the industrious little beings to carry away piece by piece to their queen for approval. Do what you need to do, but I'm writing a poem from my notes.

Time Will Not Nurse You

I think better in
a housedress
my penis draped in
pink rose patterns makes
my dirty genius scare them all
    big bang dust formed our
      send and receive parts of human magic
    every kiss gets a fresh
    sheet of paper nailed
    to a tree who keeps
    her paper to herself
    I lost my little stone
      who grows warm
        when danger
        approaches
        whores equals
      tears my mother says of the
trail of broken hearts behind her
careless with winter my inheritance
we uncrash the wall and I'm sorry I doubted you
I am busy trying to outsing the robin
do not look to salvage yourself in me
giving myself the miracle of
keeping present present
please try it at home
    for evidence of
        devotion I
        searched
        a library
        found an
        ancient a prehistoric
        a very old in other words
        wad of chewed gum

CATHETER ENJAMBMENT
--*for Chelsea Manning & Mattilda Bernstein Sycamore*

"And our lips are not our lips. But are the lips of heads of poets.
And should shout revolution."
    --Jack Spicer

Anyone who makes us remember our naked animal beneath the clothes is dangerous, thank you Bradley, thank you Mattilda. To remove the scandal of bare-assed nakedness would require the annihilation of every bureaucratic agency sending memos through our doors. It is 2012 and some of us have positioned our boots in an attempt to hold back The Return To Modesty Campaign. The American homosexual of 2012 unapologetically celebrates surrendering to the dominant culture for marital equilibrium and WAR! This swift, unmitigated return to wholesome values acts like bookends many willingly throw themselves between. The opportunity to challenge these stifling, life-threatening institutions passes out of the conversation entirely in 2012.

Notes for the poem began with a meditation on meeting Marsha P. Johnson in Thompson Square Park during the 1990 Gay Pride Festival. She started the 1969 Stonewall Riot, her headfirst, unflinching fisticuffs with the police sited to this day by RuPaul and others! She who started our revolution, a tall black drag queen, carried a sign in 1990: STONEWALL WAS A RIOT NOT A TRADEMARK! "You are the coolest person I have ever met," I told her. "YES I AM," she said with a smile. "What does the P stand for in your name?" "It means PAY IT NO MIND baby, PAY IT NO MIND!" Where are the statues, poems and operas in her honor? She was homeless at the time she was murdered and thrown in the Hudson. Our queen, our Mother of the Revolution! She was the true deviant propulsion, pushing the culture forward ready or not!

Marsha didn't live to see faggots putting rainbow stickers on machine guns to kill Arabs with impunity! Faggots joining hands with a multi-billion dollar military industrial complex should alarm us, infuriate us, it should break our hearts. Three children die of war-related injuries EVERY SINGLE DAY in Afghanistan. And after ten years of U.S. American occupation, Afghanistan has been deemed THE MOST DANGEROUS nation on our planet for women. How else can I repeat this so you hear it? U.S. America makes the lives of Afghan women and children almost unendurable! GAY AND LESBIAN U.S. AMERICANS HAVE STOCKHOLM SYNDROME! Did you hear that?

The genocide of queer men in Iraq (called "puppies" instead of "faggots" in Baghdad) is undoubtedly a direct result of the U.S. American invasion and occupation of Iraq. The most famous homosexual apologist for war Dan Choi helped make this genocide possible while serving as a U.S. American soldier in Iraq. Destabilization of the secular Hussein government has brought destruction to Iraqi queers. Our tortured, executed queer Iraqi brothers have become merely another item on our long list of collateral damage.

Many notes, many notes for the poem, my sadness, my outrage, my complete embarrassment for an assimilationist campaign gone mad! Then I did research on how to catheterize myself to go out into the world with utter insertion. I took notes, many notes for the poem.

I performed reiki on a long, thin piece of plastic tubing, reiki imbuing the tube with my intentions to be in conversation throughout the day about being queer. Queer. Today I will NOT ALLOW anyone to change the subject when I talk about what it means to be queer. Today I will talk about the frustrations of watching war go unquestioned by the U.S. American homosexual. Reiki. I did reiki for half an hour on the plastic tube, then lubricated every inch of it to ever so gently insert it into the irritated, angry looking opening of my penis. It was not for pleasure of pain it was for a chronic reminder of HOW the U.S. American culture inserts its will on my cock more and more each day. You may now be married under our rules. You may now engage in mortal combat in designated enemy countries by our rules. I had many strained, bizarre conversations that day, constantly FEELING the plastic tube inside me while walking around Philadelphia, while walking around Occupy Philadelphia and talking about war, genocide and oil. The following poem is the result of this writing ritual, which was more painful in spirit than it was for the plastic plugging my urethra. After all, it's much too late for careful.

It's Too Late For Careful

                    melting glaciers
                    frighten me when
                    appearing on
                    my street as
                    downpours
                    a feeling I send

ahead of myself to one
day walk inside
people sleep while I inspect their
flowers
not as
weird as
you think
  I dreamt gays were
    allowed in the
      military
isn't it great everyone said
    what a nightmare I
      said
    killing babies is less
      threatening with a politically
        correct militia
      vices for the vice box
        for
      wards of the
      forward state
      who like different
      things to kill alike
we CANNOT occupy Wall Street but
we CAN occupy Kabul
massage our
anger with a heart chakra green
blessings soaked into bed sheets
there's a way of
looking into
time for a poem
send it into the future
your footprint has
grown small what is
wrong with your footing?
            what kind of American
              are you? just buy it or
                steal it but shut up
            this poem is terrific for
              the economy
              the rich have
              always tasted
              like chicken

I'm not a
cannibal because
they're not
my kind
we CANNOT occupy Philadelphia but
we CAN occupy Baghdad
we're the kind of poets
Plato exiled from the city limits
FUCK Plato that
paranoid faggot
Don't Ask, Don't Tell?
HOW ABOUT
Don't Kill and say whatever you WANT!!
for instance
when I adopt a cat
I will name him Genet
"Genet! GENET!" I practice
calling Genet
INTO my LIFE!
when you purchase
a car the factory's
pollution is
100% free
it's never easy
waking to this
bacteria and light
mucus and bone
a legacy of stardust
it is 98.6 degrees Fahrenheit inside all
humans
the freshly
murdered
their murderers
and the rest of
us between
my father lived to
see the fast-forward to
the cum shot
technology's
authentic
application
we CANNOT occupy Oakland but

the ghosts will occupy us
I will stay and
watch our
phoenix
rise
I believe
in us

RESURRECT EXTINCT VIBRATION

from the Ecopoetics Panel at the 2015 Crosstalk, Color, Composition Conference in Berkeley

There were several dreams that showed me the way to this (Soma)tic poetry ritual, and I will focus on one of them, the one where their voices first came to me. In the dream I was lying on my back on the ground not far from where I grew up in Pennsylvania, now home of the world's most aggressive fracking for natural gas. My blanket was at the edge of one of the grotesque, polluted drill sites. There was pressure and intense pain entering my back and just behind that came agonized animal cries. I sat up and vomited on my notebook, then started writing a poem through the vomit. I remember thinking it was a good pen to be able to write through vomit, and in the middle of the dream shouted, "I NEED MORE OF THESE PENS!" When I woke, I wrote in my notebook to lie on the ground near a fracking site in Pennsylvania to write poems, minus the vomit, but I wanted to lie still and listen for these dark, suffering cries from the dream. A note to myself in the margin, "Who are they? Always ask myself from the dirt." A week later I was visiting my friend Melissa Buzzeo to give a talk for her students at PRATT University, and after class that night we exchanged divinations. I read her tarot, and she read my palm. She reads palms by holding your hand and closing her eyes to enter a trance where voices speak through her. She opened her eyes and said, "They are telling me to tell you to lie on the ground wherever you go. Does that make sense?" It made sense immediately, and at the same time, I was starting to obsess over field recordings of extinct animals. The World Wildlife Fund's biennial Planet Index had recently been published stating that 52 percent of Earth's wild animals have vanished in the past four decades. Melissa's reading helped push all the information together for me to see my next step, and I am grateful to her.

My mother called me at the end of March to wish me a happy half-century, and I thought this was strange because my birthday is January 1st. She explained that this was the day I was conceived. So that was an interesting phone call, as you can imagine, but "RESSURECT EXTINCT VIBRATION" is a ritual where I lie on the ground and listen to various recordings of recently extinct birds, mammals and reptiles, especially from the past several decades. When my cells were first sprouting inside my mother, these creatures with all of their many songs existed in real time in 1965 and at my birth, January 1st, 1966. Children born today in 2015 are being formed on less than half of my generation's organic, wild songs, and are instead being shaped by the beeping, pulsing and grinding engines of machines, bombs, guns, screams, and the other things we humans are replacing the natural world with, as we claw and shit our way across the globe, pushing all other life into oblivion. It seems newer generations of humans will have to settle for a kinship with metal, an affinity with plastic. In her invaluable essay "Plastic: an autobiography," Allison Cobb writes, "I learned about plastic chemicals in people's bodies (a U.S. government study found nine of ten people carry constituents of plastic inside them) and that babies come out of the birth canal with 232 industrial chemicals already circulating through their bloodstreams."

So in this ritual, I saturate myself with field recordings of recently extinct birds and animals while taking long naps on the earth across America. I begin writing as soon as I wake from this long 108-minute nap, having returned to my cells in my sleep the sounds of these creatures, understanding Ecopoetics not only as a concentration on degraded soil, air and water, but also as vibrational absence. When a species becomes extinct, they take with them their sounds of breathing, chewing, play, desire, and fear. An auditory desert is rising around us, and I am accepting and recording the sixth mass extinction of Earth currently underway.

When I talk about this ritual, I say I am returning these sounds to my body, a restoration of frequencies my cells recall, and I wake from the trance-nap oddly refreshed, ready to write, EXCITED to write, like an old friend had just surprised me with a hug. The black rhinoceros became officially extinct in 2014. They were here, they were just recently here, contributing to our living web, these fellow sentient beings, and now they are gone, and we feel and hear their silence. The dusky seaside sparrow, this gorgeous little bird with the most remarkable song, extinct from the Florida coast since 1988. I found the song of the delicate, small creature online, and you can too. Listen to it. Find the recording, put on headphones, and play it over and over like I do, and tell me you don't feel some small missing part of yourself has found its way back.

But of course they are NOT returning, which makes this one of the cruelest rituals I have ever done to myself. Researchers have bones, feathers, claws, tusks and horns in boxes and drawers— and thousands of notes about where they used to sleep at night, what they used to eat, how they used to play and show affection. The video and audio archive of these creatures is of course the most haunting remains of their existence. We captured the remnants of their movement and music, we could invent the technology to be able to record their cries and motions, but we didn't leave room for them to live. What the fuck are we doing here at this very moment? Billions of animals have been snuffed out of the wilderness in a mere four decades, and I am not surprised that so many people are obsessed with video games, preferring at this late hour on planet Earth the virtual world over the real one.

I refuse to give you a tidy ending; besides, I am still doing the ritual and taking notes for the poem. Recently, I made the decision to begin lying on the ground in places with a high volume of human activity, enough of doing this quietly in the so-called wilderness and parks, time to take it to my fellow human beings, the creatures I fucked this planet up with, we did it together, and we will fall apart together. I park my car in Wal-Mart parking lots to sleep for the night. In the morning, I listen to the extinct animal sounds while walking into the Wal-Mart.

Each of the 9,000 Wal-Mart superstores in the continental United States has over 250,000 items on shelves, an extraordinary undertaking to control the resources of the planet to make microwaves, deodorant, frozen pies and thousands of other things. Each Wal-Mart I approach is set in a completely different looking terrain from Montana to Florida to Arizona, yet when I walk into the massive stores wherever I am, the same world of uniformed, happy workers awaits me. The Wal-Mart portals, I call them. I walk around the perimeter of the store, all the while listening on my headphones to the songs and grunts of extinct animals and birds, our collateral damage. I walk around and then circle in, in, in, keep circling in, into a spiral to the center of the store, finding the heart of the Wal-Mart dimension.

At a Wal-Mart near Michigan recently, I laid my blanket on the floor of the store to nap and listen to the animal recordings and write. I was in an aisle off to the side of greeting cards and shampoos where no one was walking. I lasted a good 15 minutes before two people lifted me from the floor by my arms, one of them counted, "One, two, three," then added, "She's a heavy one!" I started to say that I was writing a poem, and I was told, "Don't care, don't want to hear it, just don't ever come back," as they guided me toward the electric sliding doors. This is the year 2015, Wal-Mart superstores exist, and it is not clear how much longer we can continue down the road this way together. I am not a motivational speaker, I am a poet and the future is bleak.

Suggesteds

Stephen Harrod Buhner, *Plant Intelligence and the Imaginal Realm*

Allison Cobb, *Green-Wood*

Sylvia A. Earle, *The World is Blue: How Our Fate and the Ocean's Are One*

Judy Grahn, *Another Mother Tongue*

Brenda Hillman, *Seasonal Works with Letters on Fire*

Elizabeth Kolbert, *The Sixth Extinction: An Unnatural History*

Frank B. Linderman, *Pretty-Shield: Medicine Woman of the Crows*

Lynn Margulis & Dorion Sagan, *Dazzle Gradually: Reflections on the Nature of Nature*

Bernadine Mellis, *The Forest for the Trees: The Judi Bari Story* (film)
http://www.bullfrogfilms.com/catalog/fftt.html

Chandra Moskowitz, *Vegan with a Vengeance*

Alex Renton, *Planet Carnivore: Why Cheap Meat Costs the Earth*

Jon Robertson, *Vegan UnPlugged: A Pantry Cuisine Book and Survival Guide*

Michael C. Ruppert, *Confronting Collapse: The Crisis of Energy and Money in a Post Peak Oil World*

Rik Scarce, *Eco-Warriors: Understanding the Radical Environmental Movement*

Vandana Shiva, *Soil Not Oil: Environmental Justice in the Age of Climate Change*

Emji Spero, *Almost Any Shit Will Do*

Anne Waldman, *Manatee Humanity*

Magdalena Zurawski, *Companion Animal*

Matthew Cooperman & Aby Kaupang

Matthew Cooperman is the author of, most recently, *Spool*, winner of the New Measure Prize (Free Verse Editions/Parlor Press, 2016), as well as the text + image collaboration *Imago for the Fallen World*, w/Marius Lehene (Jaded Ibis Press, 2013), *Still: of the Earth as the Ark which Does Not Move* (Counterpath Press, 2011), *DaZE* (Salt Publishing Ltd, 2006) and *A Sacrificial Zinc* (Pleiades/LSU, 2001), winner of the Lena Miles Wever-Todd Prize. Five chapbooks exist in addition, including *Disorder 299.00* (Essay Press, w/Aby Kaupang). A founding editor of *Quarter After Eight*, and co-poetry editor of *Colorado Review*, Cooperman teaches at Colorado State University. He lives in Fort Collins with his wife, the poet Aby Kaupang, and their two children. More information can be found at www.matthewcooperman.org

Aby Kaupang is the author of, most recently *NOS, disorder not otherwise specified* (w. Matthew Cooperman, Futurepoem, 2017), *Disorder 299.00* (w. Matthew Cooperman, Essay Press, 2016), *Little "g" God Grows Tired of Me* (SpringGun, 2013), *Absence is Such a Transparent House* (Tebot Bach, 2011) and *Scenic Fences | Houses Innumerable* (Scantily Clad Press, 2008). She has had poems appear in The Seattle Review, FENCE, La Petite Zine, Dusie, Verse, Denver Quarterly, & others. She holds master's degrees in both Creative Writing and Occupational Therapy and lives in Fort Collins where she currently serves as the Poet Laureate. More information can be found at http://www.abykaupang.com

Works

From Whether Underground

"The number of active oil and gas wells in Colorado almost doubled from 22,228 in 2000 to 43,354 in 2010. Analysts believe there is more oil shale and shale gas to be found in Niobrara shale, which sits more than 6,000 feet below the Front Range of the Rocky Mountains. The oil is not uniformly distributed in this vast formation, which stretches from southern Colorado into Wyoming."

—*The Niobrara News*

      frack is a word to obtain a thing
      gas body or oil body
      by liquifaction say water   various solvents
      an exchange body   replacement earth
      toxic metonymy the force of
      forces   engineers   making a new earth writing

"Thank you, Michelle, for navigating us through all the legal stuff and getting the best deal we could get."

                        as sediments go
                        trapped lipid strata Michelle
                        like herbaceous life
                        her woody plants
                        but also algae and pollen
                        animals and reptiles
                        a layer exposed by upheaval
                        or slow delving rivers
                        or deep drilling wells
                              or sleepless daughters

"Who Wants to Be a Shale'ionnaire?"

gaseous and awkward   walking on her paths
he starts to frack   working on her pads
the body expelling what it   walking in her paws
cannot imagine   warping in her pods
a pocket book of shale
a stylus as a drill

a waterchain a single
benzene earth man
now embowered with
salt and sand   an
   up and down
gesture of fountaining
it's a mineral right
a god given
a given wrong
this xylene toulene
ethyl earth man

"We are stuck in the pause of perplexity. Time turns metaphors into things."--Robert Smithson

    his flinty query
     to the day
      what's the day
       for or against
        a pressingness or receptivity
        in the glands the mounds
         of shit   some
          endochronology spilling out

"The past above, the future below,
and the present pouring down."
–William Carlos Williams

    like a dwelling
   that resembles stone
this pebble round
   with round things   a chemical
chain   or yucca blossom

    diatom   drill bit   fox body
   energy complete   or commerce complete
of maggots floresce

they shine   they shine out
from lights above
        and mountains below
        the stars' hy-hydrogen
        a visual ripple / or vertical cash

sharp guttural thrust as
            red Harley ripping North
thru thrumming sage
 dusting up alluvial
   thousands year powder

feral, or otherwise, things tend to move around/he went to the wells to see what he could
find

40° 25' 23" N / 104° 42' 32" W

That phenol these rashes of family extreme

Deficit holes for arsenic drillers

Spontaneous practice tested near a goat

Trade secrets legal that lubricant rub

Of mortals a coil of metals in wells

That phenol abortion sensory extreme

Heavy near drillers for even the horse

Spontaneous poisoning for wastewater spread

Extreme deicing of dust farming roads

Heavy metal nosebleed tested the drillers

Spontaneous arsenic considered in schools

Hospitalized for nosebleeds even the goat

A year's replacement for suspected rashes

Spontaneous wastewater practice for wells

Suspected deicing of horses on roads

Family of secrets tested child near a goat

Perhaps down there metals rub that phenol oil

Drillers for deficits died frequently legal

Trade secrets lubricate sensory holes

Spontaneous rashes spontaneous drillers

Spontaneous abortion in and around schools

Suspected senses extreme near child horses

Schools many legals around drilling fatigue

A sign down there among oils that phenol

Spontaneous mortals coil near the test

From NOS (disorder, not otherwise specified)

schizophrenic pulse
when the Pleiades drop
in August obvious
how placebo the hall light

an outing–

      E. Colfax   general medicine is general

      chasing her
      chasing Maya

      she's wondering away

to have a sensory child   a child who has a perfect name
and no name   no diagnostic nomen

is to slowly fade from the world *ourselves*   a recreating
story

they that were at the psych ward received
their light

in horizontal increments in dosages of
slant line

the ward perhaps is a love story

Patient _____

_____ reacts spontaneously to a heard
word

_____ spontaneously gazes through glass

_____ creates a family of constellated rage

_____ avian to her own speech

the ward perhaps is a love story

secured in the beige room a sadness monitor beeping

they that were in the psych ward were of two roles

they that were as MOC or FOC were as clients and deviants   they that were there as
One   sprouted implications as in pairs they wept about   they that were in
professional wear went ringing in the nail station in the daudrydo nurses head in
the pouncing gym in the haranguing tongues of clinicians

disability
being an ecological concern
primarily the affordances

infinite then
without propulsion

are lack

Why does my child need this medicine?

- This medicine is used to treat schizophrenia. It m
- This medicine is used to treat manic depression.
- This medicine is used to treat mood disorders.
- This medicine is used to treat aggressive behavic
- This medicine is used to treat Tourette's syndrom

play drugs is play not slumber drug

they that tense in well-lit halls where other other people talk of other things and others realize or not that they could hear no other than they themselves seizure-singing in difference and rage and jealousy *and and and* andand

not

they themselves were dull now   ear canals plugged with sodden locks

eroding aggregate of the hospital parking lot
        | dinosaur and panther lots   blue |
   gum and vomit and spit and tubes and toys and foods   burning in the sum

an outing—

We unnerved flew past the coming down

    your daughter is not coming out
    you daughter will never lose **The Diagnoses**

    we might lose her *you/your* daughter might lose *you/ her*

\

      they that were at the psych-ward
      experienced a type of loss   some types
      were honored the

maymaya means illusion maya means maya means love the name maya means what maya means maya means what maya means princess maya means mother measure up your maya maya means matter and activity are maya are perceived per illusion maya my mary my amelia my honeypour dream maya is not like colonization but culture and transformation maya like yeast like that love her too heavy maya my pearl maya a great friendship to those who care for it maya or may be water or may l or birth or hourly re- or seizurely mothers may I birth my illusory hiding

loss   some types denied   there were those
that ate the loss   those that planted it as
cardiums   there were those that saw that
life was love and lossy

there were those that were eaten by loss
they ate it back

they fertilized the gardens of their abdomen

Within a spectrum, all degrees are active--how the rainbow shines in the sky and on the oily street. Ecopoetics, then, in all directions an earthly experiment, bodies operating as echolocative displays of the range of the possible. As in, a poem is a horizon, what you're looking at and why you look: need finding form. As in, sounds and senses signal there is something there; it pushes back, a circuit loop of information always already here. We breathe from where we are, and intersect a particular local with a temporal global. It really is one world. Or, as Timothy Morton has it, thinking big, "The ecological thought is a virus that infects all other areas of thinking...Like the shadow of an idea not yet fully thought, a shadow from the future, the ecological thought creeps over other ideas until nowhere is left untouched." Everything's alive, and agent, memes as well as genes; the oil derrick outside pumps the vascular system of our imagination. And if everything is connected, then boundaries between seen and unseen, water chains and health care systems, oil profits and autism, dissolve, entangle, enmesh. Big Pharm is invested in Big Energy, & vice versa; we've been collaborating all along. How to stop?! I guess using language filters, reading screen, a try, a throw, poetry as assay/essay, mining / measuring tool. Tap the rock, ride the river, test the body, attentive to the full spectrum of song, something like Zukofsky's increment of attention as a sounding toward contemporary species collapse. Where are you? What intersection? The poem is always occasional; occasions happen everywhere.

One Earth, One Experiment

—E.O. Wilson

I want to think about ecopoetics through "negative culpability," a term Stephen Cope uses to describe George Oppen in his masterful (and masterfully edited) *Daybooks*, something of radical openness to the vicissitudes of actual life. In Oppen's case, it is the complex inheritance of Jewish diamond wealth, family suicides, car crashes, early poetry identification with the Objectivists, labor causes and Communist affiliation, near-mortal wounds at the Battle of the Bulge, a Purple Heart to stand for it, post-war blacklisting, Mexican expatriation and eventual return to poetry. It is the ethical observance of language through a deeply committed life, "thinking with the things as they exist" (Zukofsky). What happened to him in place and time became his responsibilities. In this way "negative culpability" intersects with "the ecological thought," what's happening here, in real time is interwoven with cosmic space-time there. In the case of the Cooperman-Kaupang clan—and it is always a case study of a particular life—it is something more modest: a blended family, a high-needs daughter on the autism spectrum, medical challenges, dual careers as poets, professors, occupational therapist, a small city in the West in the crossfire of climate change, fire and flood and beetle-kill, the struggle to make it *go*, every day. *Mea Culpa*. What are you culpable to? Where and when? Find yourself in the spectrum.

Process

Mutating, merging, writing lives, what's stored in stories, housed or fermented, the excess of a subject, a hand for able-ism. Married and meshed. 4th and Main. Collage as the primary impulse, what crosses paths, digs down, natters or tugs, smells or cries out. Open forms, serial design, collaborative enterprises urging the mouth to speak on subjects ((dis)ability, environmental illness, horizontal identity, etc) we know suddenly, and not well. A mutative horizon of these projects as survival, momentum, a hinge on time, or lack of it, flexing on daily living.

NOS (disorder, not otherwise specified) begins with a child. Sex and love and its consequences strum through a family. Developmental delays are mapped and charted, a child is lost in the hospital mesh. A marriage comes together, ravels/unravels/ravels. Many things, people, places. Not Otherwise Specified. What to do? Advocacy can include many activities that a person can do or an organization. Learning the languages, political processes and modern societies aspire to a crystal image. These are actions, such as lob or parry or diagnose, which is to say civics, poetry, the polis of an age as collective vision. How to advocate for a moving target? Everyone in a raincoat, a white coat, a coat of spume. Participate and target solutions for many. Needs petition cells, are themselves things or coats. A person is a people, place or time. Our daughter is a people in need.

Whether Underground starts with the ostensible weather: fire, flood, fracking in a western county. It gathers––and changes, durational, over a decade––in the form of field notes, lyric essay, poetry, teaching lectures, student responses, political engagements, marriage rows, erasures and procedural limits. But the external necessarily feeds back. Does it gather or disperse? Inhabitation, where we live, turns on intersection. Our almanac of place erodes the environment from the inside. Family, as such, turns out to be the real geography. As parents of a daughter on the autism spectrum, we inhabit our place the best we can. Weather becomes whether, to move or stay put. Fire, flood and fracking are entangled in the mesh of chelation, diaper mountains. Resurgence perhaps, to use Donna Harraway's term, finding our own kind of mobility within immediate circumstance. Something both less and more able, less and more mobile. A third landscape. A feral rainbow. "If

"We orient ourselves against backgrounds against which we stand out."

—Timothy Morton

attacked by a mountain lion fight back now." We're buying our mineral rights, trying to make a mountain move.

Perceptual Challenge

Getting Lost, a Short Course in Ecopoetics

In a footnote to "Human Universe," poet Charles Olson declares, "The etymology of 'discourse' has its surprises. It means to RUN TO AND FRO!" Countering the more commonplace sense of "orderly thought or rationality," this meaning inscribes movement––walking and talking––into the practical understanding of discourse. Applied to writing, this suggests a dynamic attuned not only to ideas but to bodily performance as well. The writer takes the energy from his or her present attentions, and carries it over to the page, attempting to translate the energetic "field" of mind/body relations to the reader. It is a dynamic attuned to communication, but communication enlarged to consider the community of both speaking and non-speaking "subjects." The social contract of writing might thus be founded on a principle of conservation—on the transference of energy, here to there, then to now, a movement of energy across space-time that locates, proprioceptively, the living body of place and person. Rebecca Solnit's book <u>A Field Guide to Getting Lost</u> offers an interesting intersection of place and person with walking and talking. A map of productive lostness, her discourse limns the possibility of the transference and conservation of global energies. As such, it is a textual ecology that seeks to be found, for to get lost is to try to find something out. What follows is a short course on getting lost: some key questions and their attendant tests:

Q: What is the condition of lostness? How is it openness *and* fear, receptivity *and* guardedness, dread *and* optimism, vitality *and* defeat? How can you cultivate this dual condition? How can you leave the door open? And what is your training in getting lost? How will you grow literate in reading the world?
----**Test 1:** Find a local place you have never been and go there. Discover the unfamiliar in the familiar. Consciously cultivate this dual condition of lostness.

Q: What do you orient by? What are your polestars, the coordinates of your wandering? How are these objects? How is your walking and talking both a centripetal and centrifugal action?
----**Test 2:** Recover some lost artifact from childhood. How is it talismanic? Describe the object. How is the language of your description imbued with the magic of that form?

Q: How do you represent distance? What is the color of your god/not god? What horizon most fully captures the tenor and touch of your distances? What lost things have been there all along?

----**Test 3:** Find a photograph of your distances and write your way into that landscape. How is it a landscape of the actual? How is it memory? How can you represent that horizon?

Q: Where do you come from? Where are you going? What are you in exile from? Who are you avatars, your psychic forbearers and ghost others? What others give you swerve?
----**Test 4:** Write a letter to the things and places you are in exile from. How can you recover those things, places, peoples, experiences? How can you make friends or useful enemies with your ghosts?

Q: Do you think you can go home again? What are you captive to? Are you in harmony with your local, national and global culture? What are the sources and sites of estrangement? What and where are the blank spaces on your map?
----**Test 5:** Make an actual map that declares your allegiances and captivities. What is terra incognita? Where are the places you must go?

Q: What are your names? Where do they come from? How are you known in this world? What are your ghost names? Ciphers, channels, eponyms?
----**Test 6:** Make a family tree. Work your etymology. Graphically describe and inhabit the words and names that you go by.

Q: What is your point of origin, your "emergence place?" What does it look like? What are its spatio-temporal spans?
----**Test 7:** Describe the shape of your first dwellings. Capture its textures from cellar to steeple. How does that provide proprioceptive size? How have you carried that house on your back forward?

Q: What is your body's respiratory knowledge? How is it reciprocal with your environment? How is your breath your line?
----**Test 8:** Take a walk. Try to align your body's respiratory activity with your consciousness. Transcribe it into a poem; take a run: do it again.

Q: What are the things you are afraid of? Where and when are they? What is your leap of faith? How might you cultivate the unknown?
----**Test 9:** Take a leap. Leave on a journey. Do something as that act of faith. Record it as ever it might be: film, recording, writing, song.

Suggesteds

Letizia Argenteri, *Tina Modotti: Between Art and Revolution* (Diego, Trotsky, Modotti, Weston--art and revolution)

Sheila Black & Jennifer Bartlett, *Beauty is a Verb: The New Poetry of Disability* (groundbreaking anthology of the poetics of (dis)ability)

Lee Ann Brown, Rand Brandes, Theodore Pope (Eds.) *Far From the Centers of Ambition: A Celebration of Black Mountain* (an abecedarian of BM's rhizome)

John Brentlinger, *The Best of What We Are: Reflections on the Nicaraguan Revolution*

Gillian Conoley, *Peace* (war and oil and the city and how to make peace)

Ed Dorn & Leroy Lucas, *The Shoshoneans: The People of the Basin-Plateau* (nomadic anthropoetry, photography, race against the civil rights era)

Theodor Enslin, *Nine* (swan song poetry & magic numbers in a walking form)

Kendrick Fraiser, *People of Chaco: A Canyon and Its Culture* (the latest ethnographic study, part of the Chaco Synthesis Project)

C.S. Giscombe, *Ohio Railroads* (weather, city planning, race, names, dreams)

Mark Greif, *The Age of the Crisis of Man: Thought and Fiction in America, 1933-73* (existential fiction and the loss of the planet)

Stephen Kern, *The Culture of Time and Space: 1880-1918* (the whole arts and sciences in the seizure of Modernism)

Ovid, *Metamorphoses* (protean wisdom for a changing world)

Bino A. Realuyo, *The Gods We Worship Live Next Door* (Filipino history in the midst of a global economy, poetry)

Andrew Solomon, *Far From the Tree: Parents, Children and the Search for Identity*

(charting the x and y axis of identity and difference)

Leslie Marmon Silko. *The Turquoise Ledge* (deep-time memoir of space-place)

Dale Smith, *Slow Poetry in America* (a prose poetry to return us to our senses)

Tom Sparrow & Bobby George (Eds.), *Itinerant Philosophy: On Alphonso Lingis* (a portrait of movement, phenomenology, birds, Levinas, Others)

Denis Wood, *Everything Sings* (journeys in new cartography)

Adam Dickinson

Adam Dickinson is a writer, researcher, and teacher. His most recent book, *The Polymers*, was a finalist for the 2013 Governor General's Award for Poetry (Canada). He teaches poetics and creative writing at Brock University in St. Catharines, Ontario, Canada.

(photo credit: Robin Knight)

Works

AGENTS ORANGE, YELLOW, AND RED

2,3,7,8-Tetrachlorodibenzodioxin   Serum   1.304348 pg/g lipid

You are either for chlorine
or for the plague.
Right now is the cleanest
we have ever been, and for this
you must love aerial defoliants
or you love communism.
Under the bandage of the one-industry
town closing ranks around staples
of forestry and fish, the wound
is wide-eyed and headstrong.
Through the clearing, freshwater carp
blink past the graves of missionaries
who introduced them to the new world.
Northern rivers are warmed
by the paper mill's piss, which,
like making the world safe for democracy,
slowly leaked into my childhood yellowing
the lipophilic paperbacks of my
adipose fat. You are for pulp
or for poverty. You respect
the Constitution or you stare
at the ground lost in bankruptcies
for herring gull beaks or blurred
embryos in cormorant colonies.
Every erected media platform reduces
the problem of war to a problem
of tint. During the orange revolution,
Viktor Yushchenko was poisoned
by government agents who haywired
his food with dioxin. His face flared
into pages of acne. You are either
for the red or the white blood cells,
for the tops of trees, or the bottoms.

IT TURNS OUT THE STARTING MATERIAL FOR THE EARLIEST FORMS OF LIFE IS ALSO A CARCINOGEN

1-Hydroxybenz(a)anthracene	*Urine*	*<0.002 ug/L*
1-Hydroxyphenanthrene	*Urine*	*3.9 ug/L*
1-Hydroxypyrene	*Urine*	*6 ug/L*

Hash with a dime
in a beer bottle.
Burning defines me
like froth
at the corkscrew of an argument
over the illusion of safety.
My compulsions
are all monuments
to incomplete combustion,
by which I mean particulate
matters compromise my unmanned
willingness for nerve endings.
I wear smoke immunologically
like a barrel with suspenders
or well-heeled neighbourhoods
with street associations
taking care of quiet boulevards
like cottage country lakes.
Suspended in the water column,
fish hearts slow to the
length of time it takes the marinade
to soak in. Diesel rigs run all night
at the truck stop diner
amidst the alphabetic disparity
between benzene rings and highway signs
buckshot by glitched-up guano.
Hitchhikers may be escaped
inmates. Things make
sense more easily
if they are attached to moods.
Every night I replay
the half-baked getaway
of a running nose,
trying out cigarettes and accelerants
on cuts of meat.

A BROMIDE

Polybrominated diphenyl ether, IUPAC # 47   Plasma   0.04 ug/L
Polybrominated diphenyl ether, IUPAC # 153   Plasma   0.03 ug/L

The umbrella is the starting point for a larger obfuscation. A constant mist of tiny particles rains upward, like neck hair at the cicada sex of a smoke alarm. Children outgrow the behaviours of cats, but for many years they are derelicts of skin flakes, stair runners, and upholstery. The average carpet smokes three packs a day. The glassy bits scratching your throat are leftover deterrents to predators. Dust is a conversation happening just out of earshot, it's the street talk of the Endocrine and Alderaan systems, a vector for the invectives of misdirection. Dust is a bunch of nickels your uncle gives you to get him another drink. My thoughts, like every other coagulation cascade, are made of melted lint and move around with the chirality of lost oven mitts. In the dusty barns of Michigan, the wrong bag of pale grit was mixed into cow feed. Nine million people ate Firemaster. My limbs tingle just out of broadcast range. Here come the industry standards to burn down the roofs of our mouths.

Poetics

Ecopoetics, for me, is a research-creation practice attentive to collaborative networks and nodes of discursive, molecular, acoustic, and geophysical relation in the capitalist Anthropocene, cultivating the edges between differing approaches to expanded frames of biological and cultural signification. I am concerned with the aesthetic and political implications of flows, exchanges, and permeable membranes between ostensibly disparate and discrete material contexts and forms of knowledge, including biosemiotic modes of reading and writing as well as reframed translations and transcriptions of expressive biological and cultural media. In particular, my point of departure is the generative methodological and conceptual environments at the intersections between science and poetry. Practiced at their limits, science and poetry are both exploratory exercises in pattern recognition, drawing from diverse and seemingly strange contexts to solve or reframe difficult predicaments. I see my method, in part, as an extension of pataphysical poetics, where science and art overlap in self-conscious and self-critical ways. As a creative/critical practice employing often counter-intuitive and repurposed scientific procedures and concepts, pataphysics is a fruitful form of ecopoetic investigation because it attends closely to shifted frames of inquiry and questions of scale (think of Dr. Faustroll's perspectival study of water droplets in Alfred Jarry's *Exploits & Opinions of Dr. Faustroll, Pataphysician: A Neo-Scientific Novel*). Moreover, the humour that often accompanies pataphysical writing is useful for complicating the tone of ecopoetic work. Pataphysics, as the science of exceptions, particulars, and imaginary solutions, is well-positioned to engage with hyperobjects like oil and chemical pollution, which, as they enter human bodies through food and consumer products, constitute a kind of absurd, imaginary science project enacted upon the citizens of the industrialized world without consent.

Petroculture has not only facilitated new ways of reading and writing through technological innovation, but it also requires new forms of literacy in order to apprehend its scalar poetics and its capacity to generate desire and nostalgia for its diverse expressive forms. I pursue an ecopoetics that responds to the capacity of petrocultural hyperobjects to influence social formations or alter human metabolism. I embrace an ecopoetics that provokes me to consider, for example, how endocrine disrupting chemicals, as a kind of extreme writing, might put pressure on literary forms and genres. One response to this, *The Polymers*, is an imaginary science project that combines the discourses, theories, and experimental methods of the science of plastic materials with the language and culture of plastic behaviour. The poems identify and express the repeating structures fundamental to plastic molecules as they appear in cultural and linguistic activities such as arguments, anxieties, and trends. What happens when we see plastic as an expression of contingent polymeric formations intrinsic to ostensibly diverse and accretive human activities (especially as they are practiced in Western petroculture)? As an extension of this interest in chemicals and poetry, I have developed more recently an experiment in what I am calling "metabolic poetics," which I think of as a concern with and response to homeostatic states and homeorhetic flows expressed in biological media as a consequence of energy systems and energy politics. I am examining the way oil has become a form of writing in human biological and metabolic contexts by researching and writing a book of poetry thematically and methodologically based on a toxicological and symbiotic map of my own body (obtained through blood, urine, and microbiome testing). This book reconsiders the body (my body) as a biosemiotic text written over by toxic chemicals as well as other microbial life forms that necessarily influence my health and disposition. I want to respond through writing to the ways in which the outside writes the inside, to the ways in which my blood is a form of media expressing the biology of petroculture, expressing my intimate and uncanny relationship to the energy sources of my historical moment, while also expressing the continuous interchange between self and environment that has marked human evolutionary history.

Process

The data-gathering required to create these poems is intrinsic to the compositional process. I am conducting tests to look at the way the outside of the body writes the inside in two distinct ways. First, I am getting my blood and urine tested for hundreds of chemicals that fall under the following groups: Phthalates; PCBs (polychlorinated biphenyls); PFCs (perfluorinated chemicals); OCPs (organochlorine pesticides); OPIMs (organophosphate insecticide metabolites); PAHs (polycyclic aromatic hydrocarbons); HBCDs (flame retardants); Triclosan (antibacterial additive); Parabens; BPA (bisphenol A); and 31 heavy metals. I have employed the biomonitoring protocols used by the Centers for Disease Control and Prevention (USA), Health Canada, and Environmental Defence (Canada) in order to test for chemicals widely present in the environment and believed to exist in most humans to varying degrees (what is in me is in you, too). Second, in addition to testing various areas of my body (hands, forehead, genitals, mouth) for bacteria, I have mapped my microbiome with the help of researchers at several universities, obtaining a deep metagenome and virome characterization of a stool sample, plus additional marker gene sequencing (16S rRNA, 18S rRNA and ITS) to determine not just the bacteria but also the viruses, microbial eukaryotes (like giardia), and fungi in my stomach. As I gather this data, I have begun researching the chemical structures, industrial applications, cultural contexts, evolutionary histories, and biological affects of some of these toxins and organisms. The poems have begun to emerge from this research, developing into a chemical/microbial autobiography that explores the subject as an assemblage of nonhuman objects and actors. I have emphasized the deliberate combination of biographical details from my life (how might I have been exposed to dioxins or uranium, for example?) with historical details (famous spills, accidental poisonings, military applications, and attempted political assassinations). I expect future compositional methods to extend out of the biological and psychological circumstances of my particular body and to reflect the processes and protocols that I experience as an organism composed of other organisms and potent substances. It is imperative that this research be grounded in my body in order to scrutinize a nature writing self that is often treated in overly general terms in ecocritical analysis and also to direct innovative poetics back into the subjective realms it has often eschewed as part of its critique of voice and personal anecdote in lyric poetics. While I am acutely aware of the way my body is necessarily marked by certain demographic privileges, I am also interested in the strange democratizing power of this form of pollution. The chemical signatures may be different for distinct communities of people, but the chemicals are in us all.

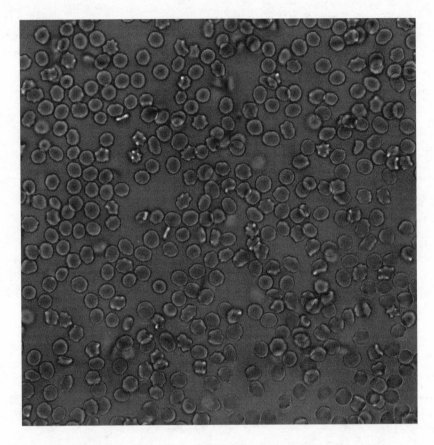

Metabolic Typeface No. 1: New Car Smell (With Platelets)
(My blood cells photographed through a microscope)

Perceptual Challenge

Biosemiotic Exercise

The early ecologist Jakob von Uexküll (1864-1944) famously characterized the relationships between organisms in an ecosystem as symphonic and contrapuntal. The distinct *Umwelten*, (subjective universes, or worlds of signification) that constitute each creature's perceptual cues, bump up against each other in what he contends are melodic relations. In "A Theory of Meaning" he proposes that "The characteristics of the animal and those of its fellow players [harmonize] everywhere with assurance, like the points and counterpoints of a many-voiced chorus" (195). Uexküll describes at length these attuned harmonic relationships between organisms as physically diverse as houseflies and spiders, bumblebees and snapdragon blossoms, as well as ticks and humans. Their "melodies influence each other mutually...the snapdragon's melody intervenes as a motif in the bumblebee's melody and vice versa" (202). For Uexküll, counterpoint is expressed as a theme of complementary morphological and sensory configurations where the eye can be said to be sun-like, the leaf rain-like, the bee blossom-like, and even the coffee cup coffee-like. The task for the ecologist, consequently, is to become a musician, or better yet a pataphysician, concerned with the carriers of significance in the environment of melodies – those differences that make a difference, those exceptions that stand out as meaningful inducements of behaviour and form.

In a brief oral presentation of 5-10 minutes (to be accompanied by a wasp and an orchid), participants are required to describe in detail the "melodic meeting" of two different *Umwelten*. Examples might include nonhuman organisms and their symbiotic or predator-prey relationships. Examples might also include the worlds of signification specific to humans and their related but divergent cultural, biological, or material predicaments. The purpose of the exercise is to expand conventional fields of signification, bringing other semiotic universes into consideration. It is expected that each presentation will generate questions and discussion, so presenters should be prepared to field inquiries from phenolic compounds, plant pheromones, and loose fur.

References

Uexküll, Jakob von. [1934] *A Foray into the Worlds of Animals and Humans (with A Theory of Meaning)* trans. Joseph D. O'Neil. Minneapolis: University of Minnesota Press, 2010.

Suggesteds

Jesper Hoffmeyer. *Biosemiotics: An Examination into the Signs of Life and the Life of Signs*. (Trans Jesper Hoffmeyer and Donald Favareau. Scranton and London: University of Scranton Press, 2008.)

The semiotics of the skin encompasses numerous other elements beyond those associated with the senses of pressure and pain. Generally, the skin might be considered a user interface that couples us to the outer world. On the one hand, the skin thus serves us as a kind of topological boundary; while, on the other hand, its semiotic capacity opens up the world to us – so that the question of where our self begins and ends is not at all an easy question to answer scientifically. Are not the impulses generated by the blind man's stick really a part of his self? Similarly, as I can just now see houses more than four kilometers away on the other side of the fjord, it seems as if a part of my self reaches out over such a large area. And if, for example, a lightning bolt strikes the other side, 'I' will see it in an instant, even before 'I' hear the thunderclap. 'I' exists, so to speak, in places over there. (25)

Suzi F. Garcia

Suzi F. Garcia is a Poetry Editor at Noemi Press, and she writes about identity, pop culture, and feelings. She has a big ego, but she doesn't see why it's such a big deal though. Her work can be found in *The Offing*, *The Pinch Journal*, *Word Riot*, and more.

Works

So You've Become Death, Destroyer of Worlds

Anesthetize ourselves, but we feel
every cut, and even the needle hurts. Today,
I could taste blood in my mouth, and I don't know why,
except I *do* know,

                        and I am more than complicit in my own
                        foregone future. I scratch my throat out, leave
                        four red jagged lines

leave a place worse than before I came. We are moving, but there's no way to know
for sure if that's true. I need aerial evidence, I need to hold
my breath, I need to find a way to
                s t a y s o   s t i l l

that kudzu covers me, breaks me down, oh wait—

                          have I become earth
                    poison
                        inside out? Shoot me into
                  space,
                      I'm the aliens' problem
                  now.

We're Stumping for an Eden Based in Grains and Greens

I've gone semi-savage, find me at your throat looking for fresh blood,
call me cannibal but I cannot recognize my own god in you.
Trumpets blow and yeah, I'm in a kitchen, cuz kid, I know my way
around knives, but keep your break down, we deny Freud his phallic
obsession.

In fact, we are destroying traditions of fragmentation, stepping against space that
absents our spirit, and allying with animals. We walk away from civilization,
construct nests out from material earth— a roof over our heads that's all mud and
deconstructed highways, just something we're trying out. Who needs paths when
there is nowhere left to go? My sister cooks quinoa, keeps time by counting down a
dwindling cupboard, and together, we pray to our mothers.

We are Animalized, But We Come Back—Powers as Unknown as the Amazon

As much as you want to believe otherwise, death
is not theoretical—I have seen it, held it
in the corner of my mouths. Bleach
and preservatives make our bodies
unfamiliar to ourselves but they cannot wash
away. Take apart

the pretense of strength in consumption, in strength in colonization, in strength
that's transferrable through your own sweat on dirt, through a bitterness that goes
beyond your morning coffee. Instead, commit to rhythms that move our body
unnatural back to nature, a movement of the neck that that that pushes us through
leaves through sky that leaves behind carcass for creation finds physicality in each
of our deaths a bleeding in the brain to drown in.

Poetics

These poems are selected from a collection named *Soothe Your Throat with Bread and Honey,* after a line in the book *The Sexual Politics of Meat: A Feminist-Vegetarian Critical Theory* by Carol J. Adams. Adams introduces us to the theories and histories behind much of our contemporary discussion of vegetarianism, as well as the treatment of women in relation to food, nutrition, and meat. Adams' explication of how in Mother Goose's story of a "king in his counting house ate four-and-twenty blackbirds in a pie (originally four-and-twenty naughty boys) while the Queen ate bread and honey," helped me recognize that both literature and poetry specifically are complacent and perhaps actively implicated in our anti-woman, anti-feminist history with food.

In contrast to the king who eats protein in excess, the Queen is relegated to feminized foods of carbohydrates and sugar. Marie Antionettes, have we all been relegated to foods with little nutritional value, sacrificed to revolution? Sacrificed to male ego? Both historically and mythically, women are attached to foods because of what they "deserve" and what they "desire." Neither the nursery rhyme nor the fictionalized version of Marie Antionette cares about fact or access. Is the Queen allowed protein? Is Marie Antoinette allowed power to change the French structure?

As Adams points out, "Women are starving at a rate disproportionate to men" (49). And we are shouting ourselves hoarse fighting it.

About a year and a half ago, my partner and I visited our hometown where we spent several days. On our last night there, we had dinner with our family that still lives there. We ate at one of my favorite restaurants in Little Rock, a Mediterranean place where my father had never been. After all our dishes came, my dad called out in shock, "Wait, what is this?" I looked over at his plate and replied his food came with a quinoa salad. "Quinoa? OOOHH!" He was *so* excited. My father hadn't seen quinoa since he left Peru over 30 years prior. He looked around after a minute, "But this is a food that *poor* people eat." Eventually he laughed it off, but he was confused for a minute. How could a food eaten in Peru as a staple of the poorest people cost $10 in Arkansas? Reading Adams' *The Sexual Politics of Meat* a year later, I remembered this dinner, how evolution of anything is not a straightforward process.

I want life to be simple. I want to be a better person. Adams says "Equality isn't an idea; it is a practice." She suggests one of the most obvious ways we can affect the world is by understanding and separating ourselves from a culture of meat, a culture that sexualizes animals and animalizes women. But it's more complex than that. Meat eating is a sign of virility, a sign of civilization during colonization. And now veganism and vegetarianism are class markers in the United States. Who can afford the ingredients, let alone the time? My dad worked during the day, my mom during the night, we were on food stamps for a time—I can't see how they could have implemented that type of diet, even if it was made of foods they understood so well, like quinoa.

As for myself, how can I walk through this world where winter is a memory sometimes, an assault another? How can I navigate the grocery store, a country, a world? Maybe I can't. Even my food is a reminder that I am oppressor and oppressed, that it is not a straightforward, top-down life, and sometimes it doesn't even make sense. My body is a destroyer, my joy is a destroyer, even as I am destroyed.

Process

When I was in high school, I would skip school all the time. The fact that I received a high school degree is a bit of a condemnation of the Arkansas School System and a tribute to my father's persuasiveness when it came time to convince the administration that nothing would be gained by holding me back. Sometimes I would skip school to get high with friends, but more often than not, I skipped school to be alone. I would go to a park or to the art museum to read or write. I didn't know anything about poetry, so I spent most of my time just scribbling in composition notebooks that I'd covered in collages made from old issues of *Vogue*.

I worked at a library during most of high school, which gave me plenty to read, but there are books to which you always return. For me, these were always books focused on women—*Little Women*, *Anne of Green Gables*, and *The Wizard of Oz*—my first ideas of a matriarchal societies. Many mornings I could be found in Waffle House with a pack of cigarettes, a cold glass of chocolate milk, and a book, escaping from everyone even if I didn't recognize it as such. I was depressed, I was in denial of my own depression, I was alienated, and I didn't know how to talk to anyone. Writing helped me interrogate, affirm myself, and then lose it all again in pieces.

A decade later, I was in a new place, geographically and as a person. I was only thirteen hours away from where I grew up, but it was a new world. A world where the history purposefully excluded people who looked like me, where my languages and ideas of culture were not just alien but laughable. I remember walking and talking with new friends, only to discover they didn't realize I was Latina. "Really? *Really?*" they asked. I'd never had to *tell* people who I was before, my skin, my name were clear indicators. Living in these spaces, the town and academia, where white was so de facto that I became whitewashed, I felt again like I did as a teenager—lost and erased. But this time, I had a better handle on my own voice, and I was able to re-imagine those matriarchal societies to include me and stand against my erasure. I better than I was before I wrote? I'm not sure, but at least I made it through another day.

Perceptual Challenge

I was a party recently where a young white guy spent at least a half hour explaining to another white guy how dismayed he had become at the gentrification of his neighborhood. Earlier that evening he'd been extolling the benefits of the neighborhood, how everyone helped each other, and I swear to god, I thought he was going to use the word *comunidad* with me. The lack of self-awareness was shocking. I'd been drinking, and I was surrounded by people I'd only recently become friends with, and I was frankly not in the mood to fight with some rando. And lbr, I was unsurprised. Twitter just hired a white man as VP of diversity. No one knows more about diversity and the struggle of marginalization than white men, it seems. But what else could we expect? Columbus thought of himself as an adventurer, a discoverer.

But of course, where is my own self-awareness? I struggle with Spanish, a language of marginalized peoples here, a language of oppression in Peru. Can we find our way back? Can we strip back the layers of colonization and actively fight current colonization at the same time? That night, I just took a shot and walked away to sing Nicki Minaj and drown out his voice. Maybe tomorrow I'll write something about it, lose friends on Facebook.

Suggesteds

Carol J. Adams, *Ecofeminism* http://caroljadams.com/about-ecofeminism/

Brenda Hillman

Brenda Hillman has published chapbooks with Penumbra Press, a+bend press, and EmPress; she is the author of nine full-length collections from Wesleyan University Press, the most recent of which are *Practical Water* (2009), winner of the *Los Angeles Times* Book Award; and *Seasonal Works with Letters on Fire* (2013), which received the International Griffin Poetry Prize for 2014. With Patricia Dienstfrey, she edited *The Grand Permission: New Writings on Poetics and Motherhood* (Wesleyan, 2003), and has co-translated *Poems from Above the Hill* by Ashur Etwebi and *Instances* by Jeongrye Choi. Hillman teaches at St. Mary's College where she is the Olivia C. Filippi Professor of Poetry; she is an activist for social and environmental justice.

Pictured from the left: Maueen Esty, Ross Belot, Sara Burant, Brenda Hillman, Katie Walker, Dzevad Vrabac

(photo by Cameron Stuart, Halloween 2016, Martinez, California)

Works

At The Solstice, A Yellow Fragment

Our lord of literature
    visits my love,
they have gone below,
they have lost their way
among the tablets
of the dead—;

    preeeee—dark energy—woodrat
  in the pine, furred thing
        & the fine,
a suffering among syllables, stops
    winter drops from cold,   cold,
miracle night   (a fox
        deep in its hole under yellow
    thumbs of the chanterelles,
   (no: gold. Gold thumbs, Goldman-Sachs
        pays no tax... (baby goats
in the pen, not blaming God,
    not blaming them—

(alias: buried egg of the shallow-helmet turtle
        [*actinemys marmorata*]
alias: thanks for calling the White House
        comment line))))

For your life had stamina
from a childhood among priests
& far in the night
beyond the human realm, a cry
released the density of nature—

A Brutal Encounter Recollected in Tranquility
an essay from November 9

There is a space of uncertainty in every act, even standing before police in riot gear. Looking into their eyes, we think it's possible to reach them. We reach out with my feelers. The crowd presses in. The night is exactly the age of our students. What will be called batons, nightsticks or truncheons, clubs— are certain in the angle of the hitting *OOOOOO*. Looking into the eyes of the officers when they start moving to clear the bit of ground, we know the point is lost. The evening news reports resistance to officers but not to bad money. Looking into their eyes trained not to meet other eyes—amber spokes around each pupil—we think they are scared but not scared enough & some probably have children in public schools.

What should we do with the lost point? Euclid notes that geometry begins from a point that has *no part*. *Peaceful protest*—as they move forward. A student resists & is beaten. Our feet no longer touch earth but connect with other feet underground. Will defending the tents bring down bad money? i distrust moral certainty & even distrust the sentence *i distrust moral certainty*. i admire the anti-heroic line of ants. i admire the unknown. Looking the cops in the eye is not the point, nor is fighting about the state budget the point, nor is the point waking up in jail to pay for a decade that was asleep. The point moves with other points in beauty & justice because we cannot see the whole. A group can be mystical or a mob. The point moves during the hitting that moves where the body stands or lies, two feet make

two points & that is how the line is drawn. Sometimes i am sick of humans except for babies, poets & the ones i love. As we stand outside loving each other, we cannot forget the ants under us making smart corridors in the wet ground, even ==== under the Chancellor's house, seeking sweets at all hours, finding friends who are exceptions whose actions make a line; if ants fail, they begin again. When the officers use their nightsticks truncheons batons on your ribs

we are knocked back but students have it worse, their debt, they take blows in a line on the earth. You cannot be sure you won't fight back until your friends are in danger. The cops have put hitting behind that feeling.   Had
i been able to stop the officer's nightstick by grabbing it i   would
have, but i'm not stupid –a smallish grandmother vs.   them & i
did not believe grabbing their sticks would work out.   Don't hit, i
was telling the baby earlier. There are many theories

about violence but when people rise up, it is mostly unplanned.
Use your heads, we   shout naively at the cops.   We won't be a
            better person until   schools are free
            but the nightstick cannot poke our soul, oh no,   that
nightstick cannot poke the soul. More students are beaten, we cannot stop it, we are
close enough to see our   feelers in their badges & the numbers, a bit of bronze
& silver in   our compound eyes.

We have taken an experiment outdoors. Our writing accommodates
        uncertainty but most people prefer certainty, which is why writers become
depressed. Later the place where the police put their truncheons hurts when we
make love & we will make love outside of time. *Go home to your families* we naively
shout & try to study the badges in our section; later we recall one of the cops was
named Young & another was   named Hart.

Euclid says nonexistent points can make a line we all agree exists.   Your
writing offers recovery from nonexistence & one cure for depression is action.
Writing may be your most necessary action but can't be the only one. If you find
yourself on the dirt with feelers it is good to get back underground. The ants reach
other ants at the edge of the lawn; they pass the message along.

(from *Seasonal Works with Letters on Fire*,
Wesleyan University Press 2013)

Please watch:
https://www.youtube.com/watch?v=Kgvj1q3vgO0&feature=results_video&playnext=
1&list=PLCA869211911D4A07%29

Describing Tatoos to a Cop
      (*after Ed Sanders*)

            We'd been squatting   near the worms
      of the White House lawn, protesting
the Keystone pipeline =$=$=$=$=$=$=>>;
      i could sense   the dear worms
   through   the grillwork fence,
      twists & coils of flexi-script, remaking
the soil   by resisting it...
                  After the ride in the police van
      telling jokes, our ziplocked handcuffs
 pretty tight,
            when the presiding officer asked:
      — *Do you have any tattoos?*
      —Yes, officer, i have two.
      —*What are they?*
      —Well i have a black heart on my inner thigh &
            an alchemical sign on my ankle.
      —*Please spell that?*
      —Alchemical. A-L-C-H-E-M-I-C-A-L
      —*What is that?*
      —It's basically a moon, a lily, a star & a flame.
He started printing in the little square

            | MOON, LILY, STAR |

Young white guy, seemed scared. One blurry
      tattoo on his inner wrist... i should have asked
         what his was but couldn't
cross the chasm.   Outside, Ash
Wednesday in our nation's capital.   Dead
         grass, spring trees
about to burst, two officers
      beside the newish van.   Inside,
         alchemical notes for the next time—

      (first published in *Poetry*)

Composition of Fringes: Tilde & Mãe

As i have since i was a child in summer, found a rock with a fine example of life;

this time *Flavopuntilia soredica,* fringe lichen, with tilde-like edges;

to extend a sound where other life could hear,

in hopes of accomplishing nothing, offered punctuation to the lichen, to my mother who was very quiet at the time

so it would be heard & not heard in the heavenly sphere, at least, as the brain imagined it there, making absolute motion, in a harmless frame, as the granite has spoken since i was a child, in other words,

i said *mãe*

with 10 rows of 12 tildes & 2 rows of *mãe,* in Portuguese,
i recited the tildes by lifting a finger, recited the "mãe" lines,
tapping toward where she lives very quietly in days she creates...

```
        ~ ~ ~ ~ ~ ~ ~ ~ ~ ~ ~ ~
        ~ ~ ~ ~ ~ ~ ~ ~ ~ ~ ~ ~
        ~ ~ ~ ~ ~ ~ ~ ~ ~ ~ ~ ~
        ~ ~ ~ ~ ~ ~ ~ ~ ~ ~ ~ ~
        ~ ~ ~ ~ ~ ~ ~ ~ ~ ~ ~ ~
        ~ ~ ~ ~ ~ ~ ~ ~ ~ ~ ~ ~
        ~ ~ ~ ~ ~ ~ ~ ~ ~ ~ ~ ~
        ~ ~ ~ ~ ~ ~ ~ ~ ~ ~ ~ ~
        ~ ~ ~ ~ ~ ~ ~ ~ ~ ~ ~ ~
        ~ ~ ~ ~ ~ ~ ~ ~ ~ ~ ~ ~
        mãe mãe mãe mãe mãe mãe
        mãe mãe mãe mãe mãe mãe
```

(first published in *The Colorado Review*, number 42, Summer 2015)

Crypto-Animist Introvert Activism
a haibun

Every week for about a decade some of us at school have
been standing at lunch hour to protest drones, racism, state
killing, the death of species & so on. We stand under a live
oak while people walk by on their way to lunch.
We hold up the signs such as
Love Not War. It's an absurd situation & it changes
nothing. Sometimes the good doctor Ali brings a
boom box with Bob Marley & we dance ineptly on the
pavement. The changes fall together. Positive & negative
fall together as Bob Marley sustains us near the tree. Cesar
Vallejo dances as a flea on the back of a squirrel. Blake &
Baraka dance as lithophilic microbes inside the rock. We
have no proof that they don't. The science moths dance in
the live oak & go about their work of being powdery. The
protest is absurd but i admire these forms of absurdity.
When the revolution comes, the polite white mothers in
the Moraga Safeway will still be shopping for sugary cereals
& barbecue sauce. When the time comes, some will rise &
some will dance & some will lay our bodies down.

[From "A Hydrology of California"]

There's a river of nevers   the South Coast   where some would like it
most   if there   were a river   which there were   by gum by the fall of
capitalism   The banks crash as we write this   We had a pilgrim's regress
crazy brenda & her
sorceress   She ran with
her love on the boardwalk   The marine layer grows fatter/ over 13
million travelers   You know that part   in *Vertigo*   when Kim Novak   jumps
backward   in the Bay   *It looks like a set*   he said *but it was filmed on location*
That part   on the
other hand   he said
holding her other hand   *was filmed in a tank in Los Angeles*   We are about
out of time   O three-spine stickleback   O word riparian   O valley oak
over Santa Monica   o black walnut   plowed   under long ago   Visit us now
in our   maritime routes   Visit us now *Tetradymia spinosa*   cotton-thorn
Visit us now in
the hour of our
need   Visit us now in the hour of our seed   of cord grass & Gray's fescue
Visit us now in the hour   over San Gabriel   short-awn foxtail & fluff grass
bent grass & blue grama   Visit us now in the hour of our native & non-
tree that made Hollywood
Dear love i'm tired
Let's go to bed   Maybe a college girl   is reading this   when we're a little
dead   O girl   mind your watershed   Take care of crazy poets
Visit the inner-net   In the end   there will be a rupture
said Walter whose arcade
thought up the Web
We are freckles of sun   We are sleeping in the poem   Shoppers stand
in the little shops   They don't know what to buy   We lie at the Shangri La
between z & y   No one knows   how this sentence will end   in a dream
with a lyric   sky
Visit us   Joni Mitchell
Visit us   Future of Poetry   with a solitude of streamlets into a local
pond the mind at the end of the palm   Nothing was gone when we
saw that bird   We saw its feathers as water   It was in & out of time

(from *Practical Water,* Wesleyan University Press 2009)

Poetics

Beyond Emergency

How does poetry move past models of emergency to models of chronic imagination so that we can abandon ideas of progress and salvation? Ethical practice & anarchy. Are there interventions writers are equipped to make in times of ecological disaster? It all feels useless & we act into the uselessness. For 40 years i've been reading verses to short plants. i read to short plants that cannot hear because i cannot bomb Monsanto. i study & do tiny temporary acts against a few corporate horrors. There is a bill in the Senate with a rider called the "Monsanto Protection Act"; it "would give Monsanto immunity from federal law by allowing the biotech industry to plant genetically modified crops, even if a federal court has ordered the planting be halted until an Environmental Impact Statement is completed."

I invoke Blake's Zoas for kinds of radical imagination that the new ecological poetry might contribute (1) metaphors for emotion in relation to matter and the non-human world; (2) relationships to words and phrases (3) interdisciplinary knowledge; and (4) protests with poetry in mind and heart, even if all small protest seems prodigiously useless.

******

The animating spirit is present in particularity; the physical world has "a sense of the lively unit" - within a widespread or mystic or mysterious consciousness -- not only human because consciousness is varied, not one thing, not just human; to believe it is sheerly human would be sheer arrogance—; talking to molecules of presence hurts no one.

*****

 The radical imagination reconfigures realism and emotion through sensual observation, forming intuitive relationships with nonhuman species, thinking before killing each moth & mosquito. The sensual precision of Gerard Manley Hopkins & CD Wright at their beech trees and the mythic power of Robert Duncan, calling people to the place of first permission are essential. For Hopkins, a recovery of sensation, living between human consciousness and non-human, with a sense of the lively unit. Marcel Mauss in *The Gift* notes that the powerful object must be carried back to the forest. One autumn, we approached a field of pumpkins, knowing the white seeds lined up inside have sufficient power on their own & experience a miraculous knowledge: the strange gourds did not need us in any way.

To start with imagination of other species. The whale scoops krill in January, the lichen *Evernia prunastri* fallen from a post begins to tear the soil with far more skill than a human scratching silver powder off the Lotto ticket.

*****

Imagination is neither creative nor destructive in itself. Through empathic observation of the nonhuman, the imaginer lives simultaneously, in multiple bodies, as the not-us, outside of enclosure, to greet the enigma with what Gary Snyder calls etiquette. John Clare's badger. Ed Roberson's city eclogues. Forrest Gander's core samples. To live simultaneously. As mitochondria, as rhizomes, as the roots of words, with abandonment and error, as Flaubert writes, "on the rocks of unachieved certainty." John Ruskin, coining the term *pathetic fallacy,* did not condemn the practice but asked that poets not confer excessive emotion on the talking rose. There is pathetic fallacy needs rehab. My animism does not embrace the talking cars of Chevron's SuperBowl commercials in which the squat cute car makes sexual innuendoes to the owner.

******

97% of the total mass of the universe is unknown as the *is* pushes against the *isn't*. It is possible that the lichen *Evernia prunastri* knows more than a brenda. Whatever "nature" is, it is surely unknown. The common crow, *Corvus brachyrhynchos*, can use tools, recognize individual human faces and mourn its dead. Even if everyone in the world were to agree that crows have no consciousness and that brendas do have consciousness, why privilege consciousness? There is nothing more wondrous than the compound eye of the ant, a truly remarkable evolutionary event. Consciousness—from the Indo-European root *skei*- which means to split. Skin. Science. Schizoid. Omniscient and shit all come from *skei*. And if consciousness is awareness, gained by one's own perceptions, are crows not aware? i reject the idea that human consciousness is the ultimate progress. The desire to study an anthill steadies the brain for a few moments.

*****

Exxon has just posted the biggest profits of any entity in history. Can poetry address environmental degradation using any formal technique? Is the "fragmentary" writing more suitable for ecopoetics? The same question was asked about feminist experimental poetry in the early 90s—is the use of partial or disjunctive techniques more suitable to women writing about their discontinuous days, poets asked? As i began to write "like this," i encountered mostly a male tradition in the kinds of environmental writing that were out there. *Cascadia* came from an impulse to record process-oriented emotional states, the half-finished, the notational, the ragged, the syntactically scrambled that made up psychological and emotional experience in the geologic features. The western earth is made from geologic disruptions, faults, seizures of granite, mountainous conglomerates. Innovative poetry of the environment points simultaneously to beauty & to the broken world, to keening lyric, to trance, reverie, chant, abstract rhythms & patterns. Lyric utterance has always been charged with an impossible job—to call up states of mind beyond the predictable feeling, to bring the barely recognizable condition back to itself. Not without a self but with selves—in styles that include the bacterial, parallel to the human. If the poet is stuck with the ego, the cure for the ego is not nothingness, the cure for ego is non-nothingness.

*****

The clichés of capitalism: the cliff of *fiscal cliff*. Commentators deconstruct it: oh it wasn't really a cliff, we really meant a slope or a curb. But "cliff" is the word & we are Thelma and Louise. *Stem the crisis.* Since the 1980s, I have tracked the word "stem, its origins in old English, *stemn, stefn*. The history of each word, its root, is like the stem cells that go forth to anything. The indo-european root of the word *stem* is "sta-" – to stand, or a place or thing that is standing. "Stem" as a noun, the "stalk of a plant most above ground but occasionally subterranean... " or "long thin supportive main section of something" or "the slender part of a wineglass between the base and the bowl" as "the root or main part of a noun, adjective, or other word." There is "stem" the verb, in the sense of "originate in or be caused by" — as in "many of California's deficit problems stem from Reaganomics." We had "stem the bleeding" of financial markets, during the BP oil disaster "stem the flow" of oil, so stem, in the sense of stanch, meant "stop." Standing, originating from, restricting the flow of. Through usage, the very same syllable "stem" came to mean a bit of the opposite of itself. Stop or delay, stand & support – because you are the origin of it. Is language stemming from itself or from a plant? Are we standing to stem the flow or is the crisis flowing and we are standing and stemming? Oil is made of old stems from the Triassic, so really, we have to stem the stems. The *mycorrhizal* web below the ground—the fungus, the roots that are just below the surface, works to promote the growth of many plants, all tangled together. Documents woven together in little bits, romantic, modernist, postmodernist mycorrhizal poetry when everything is falling apart. Jed Rasula's brilliant *This Compost* charts this in a profound way. Realism, dream realism, surrealism, hyperrealism and meta-realism form a mat of intertwined life of literature that includes documents, research, and lyric chant. Evelyn Reilly's book *Styrofoam* weaves data and intense elegy, sampling the information field to evoke on the same page the beauty of the gods in epic and the intriguing horror of the Texas-sized plastic formation floating in the Pacific Ocean. Tragedy and wit leak the sounds together as the poet placing tones of high epic paratactically next to scientific formulae for plastics and numbers: "Question: How long does it take?//& all the time singing in my throat//little dead Greek lady/in your eternity saddle/ [hat: 59% Acrylic 41% Modacrylic]/[ornamental trim: 24 % Polyvinyl 76% Polyamide]"(from "Hence Mystical Cosmetic Over Sunset Landfill" *Styrofoam*, Evelyn Reilly, Roof Books 2010)

*****

As the food is modified, the poetry eats modification, ingesting science and natural history. Rootworms are eating genetically modified corn; the author notes ironically: *western corn rootworms have virtually no problem gobbling up Monsanto's modified maize crop, as they have developed a serious resistance to the very crops designed to kill them. ...The answer? Use even more intelligence-crushing pesticides* http://readersupportednews.org/opinion2/271-38/12182-nature-may-soon-overcome-monsanto

*****

Instead of silence, exile & cunning, what about fury, mourning & resistance. To apologize to celery and strawberries; to apologize to *Ramalina menziesii*, to the wren in its canister of loud joy, to the dead, to unintegrated parts of the dream; to apologize to apples, to chairs, to noon. When i see "Nature bats last" at a protest, i feel the language has been coöped by cliché, sentimentality, and an assumption that the home-team dominates. But no *stemming* of language will eliminate the onslaught of profit that devastates human or non-human communities. To dream downward, to act horizontally. I wandered through each chartered eucalyptus grove, down where the charter'd creek does flow. Mr. President, you want to restore love in our nation but you had group sex with Goldman Sachs, Shell Oil, Halliburton, Boeing and Lockheed. i dreamed a baby owl was kept warm by a mother owl with wing on fire. The ATM across the street from the White House is made by Diebold. Poets place acts of writing beside acts of protest, but the two rarely overlap completely, and the willingness to protest fracking or species destruction is more convincing if you don't drive. Not the Rose Bowl, the Orange Bowl, the Cotton Bowl but the Vizio Rose Bowl, the Discover Orange Bowl, the Capital One Bowl & the TaxSlayer.com Gator Bowl.
*****

Stevens wrote, "Part of Nature Part of Us" *The mission of the poet—to bring the form of the mind in relation to the world— the value of the imagination, of uncertainty, of using powerful compressed language – these are good tools for addressing the current environmental crises.* Poets & scholars can create imaginative spaces for perception, acknowledging the unknown with science & the dream, recognizing the ever-changing nature of knowledge & language, & bringing radical activist & spiritual practices to bear. Everything is everything. The appropriate responses to the present circumstances are awe & revolt.

*****

(A version of this piece was presented at the first Conference on Ecopoetics, University of California, Berkeley Saturday, Feb. 23, 2013. It was organized by Angela Hume, Gillian Osborne, & Margaret Ronda.)

Process

"At the Solstice a Yellow Fragment" came from the unhinged state of mind of late autumn as solstice approaches. As always, environmental crises were much on my mind. Contemplating the non-human species and the spirit world allowed lines to emerge in fast succession, and the layered tone came from trying to hear on conflicting levels. The lord of literature is from my trance work.

"Brutal Encounter..." came from a later autumn, a day of police-initiated violence at Occupy Cal (U.C. Berkeley). My husband and i had gone back to campus to express solidarity with students who were trying to resist police removal of tents. It was about 10 pm. ww.youtube.com/watch?v=_AU2D35HlJo. The title plays on Wordsworth's acknowledgment that poetry comes from "emotion recollected in tranquility." We were at the front, near a short wall. i saw a little row of ants going about their business. During direct actions, even protests, i tend to notice non-human species like lichen and insects buzzing around. i wrote a block of prose, recounting what had happened with the police line and how the ants were part of it & mailed it to a friend who noticed that when she tried to open the piece as an attachment, a chasm parted in the middle of the poem, creating a widening gap.

Both of those poems are from *Seasonal Works with Letters on Fire*, a book that concerns acts of micro- consciousness in micro-seasons.

In "Composition," the lichen was observed to be interacting with punctuation, and counting has been a part of my practice for a long time. My mother was born in Brazil; "mãe" is "mother" in Portuguese. I like the look of the tilde and "mãe" has one of the intimate vowels, a middle-of-the-face vowel, from that beautiful language.

"Describing Tattoos to a Cop" is from a direct action experience at the White House; as the poem indicates, we were protesting Keystone with various environmental groups and doing civil disobedience by blocking the sidewalk and being handcuffed to the fence. It brought attention to that particular pipeline, but of course the issue is much bigger and requires relentless effort from activists and poets. These two poems are in an unpublished manuscript, forthcoming from Wesleyan in 2018.

The selection from "Hydrology of California" corresponds to the southernmost California watershed; it is from a long poem in Practical Water in which i was playing on the line "A river of rivers in Connecticut" by Wallace Stevens and addressing the hydrologic regions and the various dams of California; the poem ends up south of LA. i made up a form—3 broken long lines (though there is one four-line stanza here) alternating with 2 shorter lines—to give an even but also jagged rhythm and look, as the poem is "dammed" repeatedly with slashes and its energy released.

Perceptual Challenge

Write a poem in 12 lines that has the entire world in it.

Write a poem in 4 parts (however way you want to define "parts") that has intense feeling, even more intense feeling, research and an abstract sound (not necessarily in that order).

Suggesteds

Camille Dungy, *Black Nature*
Anne Fisher-Wirth and Laura Gray-Street (Eds.), *Ecopoetry Anthology*
Joshua Corey and G.C. Waldrep (Eds.), *Arcadia Project*
Jed Rasula, *This Compost*

Brenda Iijima

Brenda Iijima's involvements occur at the often unnamable conjunctions and mutations of poetry, research movement, animal studies, speculative non-fiction and forlorn histories. She is the author of seven full-length collections of poetry and numerous chapbooks and artist's books. She is the editor of *the eco language reader* (Nightboat Books and PP@YYL) and the editor of Portable Press at Yo-Yo Labs, located in Brooklyn, NY (http://yoyolabs.com/). The press published its 60th book this year.

Works

> INSERT IMAGE: faded, solarized,
> nearly bone white hazy surface of a
> somewhere nondescript though there
> is a sense of a forested mountain
> receding and an elevation that speaks
> of the Appalachian Mountain Range.
> The ecology is blurry and indistinct.
> There is a footprint in the mud that
> stiffened, the footprint is human.
> Tree ring circa 2030

The mountain looks—....[pause]
no, it can't be adequately disclosed nor described.
It wasn't long and the trees were almost completely felled, even
the trees that grew on the more precariously sloped and craggy
precipices.

They fell that falling sometime. The logging barreled over
the underbrush and the animals that previously lived here ran off,
died: it's really a vacuum.

With the exposure to the sun the dirt became brittle and flash
floods carried the polluted sediment to the tributary that ran
into the _____river. Little grows in a seared ecology with the
disastrous erosion that resulted from land razing processes.

A huge swath of land became a dead zone and the people who
foraged around this mountain also had to disperse. Some bones
became visible, there were no scavengers to make off with them.
Even bacteria can't access the bones—it's too parched.

The soil has effectively died | spent

There are no bugs and no worms or spiders.

They are thinking of transferring nuclear waste
here the will is low, it's hard to organize activities
Micro-aerial vehicles | fusion centers
Digital multiplexing | aggregation | time lapse secretions

Fuel is scarce. People are focused on
foraging and protecting themselves. Much
spent toxic waste has already leaked into the soil.
Most are experiencing some stage of sickness.
Some burn the fuel for heat and numerous
explosions have resulted from these acts,
worsening the effects of the radiation...

There is a certain resilient worm
that has migrated to the hot spots
they (the worms) seem to
prefer cooler climates where there's
moisture (though they seek out isotopes).
Yet here are the worms.
The worms burrow through the
porous concrete canisters releasing
radiation as they eat it. When
they die, the nuclear radiation
returns to the ecological system.
In effect and in actuality, it never leaves...

Consequently, all the viruses, insects,
bacteria and germs leapt onto what
they could of the body exodus.
Nothing chewing away, no
symbiosis, no mutation,
no feeding off the other.

Dead material. Drying and scattering
enzymes. Cesium, strontium
& plutonium isotopes

INSERT IMAGE: Sweaty active radioactive
boars roaming around in German forests,
30 years after Chernobyl. Their diet
consists of radioactive berries and acorns.
They don't live a long enough life span to
develop tumors.

Leslie: Buried in the constant present.
Buried in shame and isolation yet together
as a populous, a nation state.

poem sequence from *Untimely Death is Driven Out Beyond the Horizon*, 1913 Press

Process / Poetics

My focus of late continues to pressurize concepts that have to do with the ecological surround, power, production, perception, and time. The project I intend to develop is ecologically centered writing and research focused on the crisis of species loss. This project is titled *Relaxation Time*. "Relaxation time" is a scientific term that refers to the time delay that can occur when a species is on the brink of extinction—a species might continue to exist for a long duration before experiencing total failure. This time delay is referred to as "relaxation time". During the period known as "relaxation time", a species may even appear to flourish. "Relaxation time" is a critical metaphor for the challenges we face as human animals in the time of the Anthropocene when the effects of late stage neoliberal capitalism are keenly felt. Global climate change, toxicity in the environment, habitat fragmentation, increasing refugee populations, increasing warfare, scarcity of sustenance and a host of other pressing issues present a threat to all life on earth.

Perceptual Challenge

Prisons are punitive ecologies. The United States prison system is a strange, cruel, and outmoded white supremacist human organizational form. Prisons purport to rehabilitate its citizens but mostly they strip citizens of all dignity and care. In its present state, the prison system is a deplorable institution devoid of imaginative capacity. Spend your time writing through the conceptual dilemma of this human-ecological organizational form. Reengineer from the ground up new paradigms and models. How do your words begin to reimagine institutional spaces? Think of words like lock down, detention, incarceration, behind bars, stricture, etc. Write through the psycho-geography of these terms. Write them out of existence. Originate new words that excite new ways of interrelating with the ecological surround. Send your poems and ideation to the governors of every state—CC every prison corporation. Write about time. Write about space. Write about the web of life. This writing prompt will take a minimum of five years—possibly it will demand a life sentence. Grow with your new found narrative strategies. Think within, build a critique and then write out imperatives. What ecological oversights occurred in your early drafts? Work through utopias into realities.

Suggesteds

Will Alexander, *Towards the Primeval Lightning Field*
Kamau Brathwaite, *Elegguas*
Elizabeth DeLoughrey and George B. Handley (Eds.), *Postcolonial Ecologies:
Literatures of the Environment*
Bhanu Kapil, *Ban en Banlieue*
Yedda Morrison, Girl Scout Nation

Abdelrahman Munif, *Cities of Salt*
Rob Nixon, *Slow Violence and the Environmentalism of the Poor*
Julie Patton, *NOTES FOR SOME (NOMINALLY) AWAKE*

Linda Russo, *Meaning to Go to the Origin in Some Way*,
A Month and A Day, Ken Saro-Wiwa

Anna Lena Phillips Bell

Anna Lena Phillips Bell's recent work includes *Ornament*, winner of the Vassar Miller Prize in Poetry, *A Pocket Book of Forms*, a travel-sized guide to poetic forms, and *Forces of Attention*, a series of printed objects designed to help people use screened devices as they wish to. Other poems from *BELEAVE* appear in *Colorado Review* and are forthcoming in the anthology *A Literary Field Guide to Southern Appalachia*. The recipient of a North Carolina Arts Council Fellowship in literature, Bell served as senior editor at *American Scientist* before joining UNC Wilmington's creative writing department in 2013, where she is editor of *Ecotone* and Lookout Books. She lives with her family near the Cape Fear River, and calls Appalachian square dances in North Carolina and beyond.

Works

Charms for Hemlock (*Tsuga canadensis* and *Tsuga caroliniana*)

Sandstone

Rooflike, at rest, needles white-striped and windswept,
Bound by broad boughs arching out over sandstone—
The wisp and brushed waft of them, terracing down
To cool forest floor, to sun slanted, to sound slipped.

Porescent, compassibly, phylling and floodswept
Lives rivergreen water eveloped through siltstone
While rooflike, at rest, needles white-striped and windswept
Array on broad boughs, arching out over sandstone.

Roots shaded, rhododed, deep umber bed handswept.
Pungentral and strongated, sandy loam, windstone,
One, windividualess, one and one.
Interior, colling and compassing, safekept,
Held rooflike, at rest, needles white-striped and windswept,
Bound by broad boughs arching out over sandstone.

Dendron

River of hellbender, brook trout, stonefly,
Basswood, sassafras, rhododendron,
Oak, oak, and locust, oak, oak, and cherry,
Maple and beech, birch, walnut, and pine—

Silverbell, riverbell, scention plantensity,
Alpha-humulene, pinene increastern,
River of hellbender, brook trout, dobsonfly,
Basswood, sassafras, rhododendron.

Dobsonfluenced, tsuggestine, try,
Basswoolly—damagnolia—hellbendron—
Showeverbellow, o plantern, dependron,
Bassafras, sasswood, heality, ply:
River of hellbender, brook trout, stonefly,
Basswood, sassafras, rhododendron.

Poetics

1. Something I'm reckoning with is how bodies inhabited by poetry inhabit their landscapes: how poetry changes the body and the land, and how land changes the body and the poetry. A way to feel more clearly the interrelatedness of these phenomena.

2. About the body: meter is one way of physically measuring time, as Tom Cable has aptly demonstrated. My goal, when writing metrically, is not to map or imprint meter or form onto the landscape, but to let form inform a response to and habitation in place. An echo, an honoring, an attention.

3. My time and attention for the places I live comes in flashes—the units of time of which lyric poems are made. But there's fundamental risk in the lyric for those who care about place. I need a practice that connects and reveals the relationships between discrete instances of primary sensing, and that pushes me to understand systems—a practice that leads my lyric-loving self toward a more sustained, connected listening, and thus toward something not unlyric, but related to narrative.

4. The rhetoric surrounding the movement of species from one ecosystem to a new one has historically been fraught with fear of the other. Similarly, as Camille Dungy and others have pointed out, the meaning landscapes make for us depend on our situation in relation to other people, on our social power, our agency. It's essential that I maintain an awareness of such histories and presents, ask questions of them, be aware of the limitations as well as the expansiveness of my own relation to the landscapes I know and am getting to know.

5. The word BELEAVE is spray-painted on a bridge that crosses I-40 near Fuquay-Varina, North Carolina. It's done in all-caps, in minty green. There is no punctuation, and no other words attend the message. I think of it as its own charm: BELEAVE, it says to the plant world, put your leaves back on, adorn yourselves, fight the good fight, drink the sunlight. And as an imperative to people—believe that radical changes are happening to species and systems we have taken as immutable parts of our lives. That the act of beleavement is harder and harder to do. That it should not be taken for granted.

Process

Charms from *BELEAVE*

BELEAVE explores and attempts to aid threatened tree populations and the systems they are part of, in the Southeastern United States and beyond. I initially imagined the project as a series of charms for trees—an effort at strengthening their resistance to harm, whether by increasing human awareness about the problems they face, or, I thought, by some less logical mechanism. I was only half-joking about this. Charms—poems—have been known to work.

The project is informed by the significant body of research on various introduced species' effects, including taxonomical studies and the effects of climate change on the organisms' spread. I am spending time as well with individuals of the affected species, and within affected forests, and am conducting interviews with people who live near or study these ecological communities. Having begun with charms, I am also making odes, traps, and other poems. The charms included here were made for hemlock trees (Tsuga canadensis and Tsuga caroliniana) that grow in the U. S. and Canada. The hemlock woolly adelgid (Adelges tsugae) is not lethal to hemlock species in the locales where it appears to have originated, but it devastates hemlocks in eastern North America.

Each charm is a packet of stanzas (for hemlocks, those grand trees, I've used the rondel supreme) that holds a preparation. Source text describing the adelgid, and text I've written describing conditions that might strengthen hemlocks, were both fed into an *n*-gram generator created by Brian Hayes. The generator was set at order 4; this text was recursed and then fed back in at order 3, and the resulting text was used in making the poems.

Perceptual Challenge

R. N. Sturrock and coauthors, reviewing the effects of climate change on forest diseases in the journal *Plant Pathology*, note four "disease management tactics": monitoring, forecasting, planning and mitigation. The framework of disease has some problematic limitations for poetry. But at least two of the tactics mentioned have possibilities for poetic engagement. Lyric as sustained observation: make a series of these, each aware of the ones that precede it. As effort toward mitigation: make a lyric helpmate.

Suggesteds

{*A biological perspective on interdependence, with relevance for poetic practice:*}

The widespread interest in and acknowledgment of the interrelatedness of natural phenomena in biology...creates the *illusion* of a coherent view of interdependence.

Still, I contend, the ascendent view of interdependence at play in biology—as in popular culture—*is not a view of interdependence at all.* It remains a view of *independence.* By and large, we think that interdependence just means *independent* objects *interacting.* We say that things interact strongly, weakly, reciprocally, sequentially, and so on, but their ultimate independence from one another remains intact. Indeed, "the network," which has enjoyed a place of privilege in biological thinking in the late twentieth and early twenty-first centuries, is just such a map of separate and interacting entities. As long as the ascendant view of interdependence continues to collapse implicitly to a view of independence, I believe that we continue to miss an important implication of our own findings. . . .

To take interdependence seriously . . . does not mean viewing phenomena as murky undifferentiated masses or as overwhelming tangles of connections. . . .

If there is a transition being made—in biology as in physics, neuroscience, sociology, and more—we can conceive of this transition as happening in two shifts. The first is a shift from considering things in isolation to considering things in interaction. This is an important and nontrivial move; it is also a relatively popular and intuitive concept in those fields. To get a thoroughgoing view of interdependence, I argue that a second shift is required: one from considering things in interaction to considering things as *mutually constituted*, that is, viewing things as existing at all only due to their dependence on other things.

Kriti Sharma. *Interdependence.* New York: Fordham University Press, 2015.

{*And a poethical take on similar questions:*}

I *don't* mean to suggest an encounter that becomes an allegory through which *Homo sapiens* reifies its identity in relation to a non-human Other that acts as mere mirror in which Man gazes upon Himself; I don't mean to suggest an encounter that recapitulates the imperialism of naming or scientific categorization, though meaningful forms of attention might include these gestures; I also don't mean to suggest such an encounter alone might constitute an effective form of environmental salvation.

I do mean the immense pressure we put upon our rhetoric and activism is both noble and insane because I'm not sure what local good can be done against widespread environmental destruction sanctioned by our most basic symbolic systems; along with Jack Collom, I'm also suspicious of our anthropocentric emphasis on "saving" or "taking care of" the environment through the imposition of more rhetoric, more law, more metaphor from which totality again escapes, our vision of "the surrounding life" always too small, our knowledge incomplete....

      I mean we shouldn't give up rhetoric or activism or care, but we probably have to save saving from itself, from becoming just another extension of our anthropocentrism.

Brian Teare, "Ecopoetics Talk." Berkeley, CA: Conference on Ecopoetics, February 2013. http://disinhibitor.blogspot.com/2013/03/brian-teares-ecopoetics-talk.html

References

Cable, Thomas. "How to Find Rhythm on a Piece of Paper." In *Critical Rhythm*, Benjamin Glaser and Jonathan Culler, eds. New York: Fordham University Press, 2017.

Dungy, Camille T. "Introduction: The Nature of African American Poetry." *Black Nature: Four Centuries of African American Nature Poetry.* Athens: University of Georgia Press, 2009.

Greenbaum, Abigail. "Notes from a Nonnative Daughter." *Ecotone* 9.1, fall 2013.

Sturrock, R. N., et al. "Climate change and forest diseases." *Plant Pathology* 60, 133–149. 2011.

Source tools and texts

Hayes, Brian. *A drivel generator.* http://bit-player.org/extras/drivel/drivel.html

Annand, P. N. *A contribution toward a monograph of the Adelginae (Phylloxeridae) of North America.* Stanford, CA: Stanford University Press, 1928. pp. 90–92. http://babel.hathitrust.org/cgi/pt?id=mdp.39015068545188

Joseph, S. V., J. L. Hanula, and S. K. Braman. "Distribution and Abundance of *Adelges tsugae* (Hemiptera: Adelgidae) Within Hemlock Trees." *Journal of Economic Entomology* 104(6): 1918–1927, 2011.

Lucas de Lima

Lucas de Lima is the author of the chapbooks *Ghostlines* and *Terraputa* as well as the full-length *Wet Land* (Action Books). His poems have appeared in *boundary2*, *PEN Poetry*, *Poetry Foundation*, and *The &NOW Awards 3: The Best Innovative Writing*. He is co-curator of the OMDiosa reading series in Brooklyn and a PhD student in comparative literature at the University of Pennsylvania.

Works

pinto and the dream of the unified jungle
pinto and the misdiagnosed neurosyphillis
pinto and the hiv he hid from me
out of the wheelchair he rolled down the stairs
where the air looked like a window
i, warrior at the bottom of the stairs
my tropicalia garb my plastic butterfly mask
my wooden glass-cracking dagger
because of the virus' sudden visibility
i could mutate into pinto's mother
the world clicking at us like the maw of a gator
i felt wings once more under the skin on my back
pinto fucked me like a child
i learned to wrap myself round his veins
vines twisting and snapping off any desiccated limbs
so numerous chickens could
grow out of his body in disfiguring protrusions
pinto quivered
hologram and heart of palm
a blackened core, oblong, promising germination
a thunderbolt like a bridge
to everything that flies into our vortex
to die and be born, waves of worm and flesh
impregnating our country shriveled again
on a crucifix

our foremothers
absorbed by empire
like crystals intact in our guts
the open pustule
from which our plumes extend
so we layer our voice with another voice
so we wrap our song with another song
our structure organized as a flower forever petaling
in the assassin wind
the choppers of death here
are not clandestine
unlike the rivers under são paulo
where we barely breathe
where we barely breathe is where me & pinto
put our beaks to the ground & suck out a scorpion
crying night & day
remembering a time when there was no night
remembering the kayapó myth
when there were no stars
no horses but stories about horses
we unsaddled ourselves inside

i was born in a crystal angle
i was born next to an axe
i was born in the image of epidemic beings
who starve for the root & thirst for the crack
everything red in the halo
where roses burst
like a beaked savage dream like a white frightened hive
it was so hard to concentrate after i was born
though i nursed from a mare who discolored my eyes
she was not my mother
her eyes could sadden and sink into me
because she was not my mother
emaciated muscles throbbed as our cyst
clouds of dust bowels of the earth in a galloping swirl
"i don't want to be another white feather
searing the ground"
the first words i thought and did not say
my overexpanded cry
to the mare who was not my mother
but fed me blood at nightbreak

Poetics

2015 was the year when two mining companies killed the Rio Doce, ancestral home of the Krenak, by flooding it with toxic mud.

It was the year when militarized police killed hundreds of Black people in the urban and suburban ecologies of the US and Brazil.

It was the year when the racist underpinnings of the US avant-garde were disclosed and sentences such as the following, published in an academic journal, became impossible to take seriously:

"One of the compelling new developments in writing that [name of white poet] has been advancing 'after Language poetry' is ecopoetics."[7]

Capitalism and its colonial histories of resource extraction and human enslavement, dispossession, and exploitation set off the ongoing devastation of our planet. The Enlightenment is the epistemological seed of this destructiveness. All the critique in the world does almost nothing to wake us up to disaster when the colonial paradigm holds sway, valorizing human-centered mastery where the epistemologies of other societies—the "rest" to the West—do not.

Thought itself is racialized. By this I mean that a poetics which labels itself "eco" but only reproduces the European legacy of critical thought is part of the problem that got us here in the first place.

---

[7] Dianne Chisholm's "Juliana Spahr's "Ecopoetics: Ecologies and Politics of the Refrain," published in *Contemporary Literature* (Vol 55, No. 1, Spring 2014).

Process

I write from a cult of death in which life is the aborted flight of a chicken.

To locate my body in the industrial farm:

this is an act of ritual.

The ritual undoes itself and requires a constant unraveling of skin.

As a chicken priestess, I don't fuck with you.

I don't claim to be a shaman but a squawking hallucination on the other side of the fuming, shrinking Amazonian perimeter.

Close enough to hear the Guarani song about an Earth Without Evil.

The jaw-click of Mother Jaguar,

the bulletproof drums of Black Mother Aparecida.

The screams of my Native mothers raped by my Iberian fathers.

I don't claim to translate but to transfigure my embodiment of those screams.

I am born inside those screams.

I am born inside exploding veins.

Under the sky of empire white as my feathers.

Perceptual Challenge

Pick up a text of mythical narrative from any tradition. Copy the phrases that stick out as you read. Then write a poem by dipping the phrases into a vat of your bloodlines. You are ingesting and incarnating someone else's language. It is the lips of your ancestors you wear on your wrists. Let the phrases transmute through the filters of their voices and other intermediary figures in natural and human-made form. Your words will become unrecognizable next to the source text.

Remember what Claude Lévi-Strauss wrote: "Mythical thinking does not know whole trajectories. There is always something else to accomplish. Like rituals, myths are interminable."

Remember the declaration of Estamira Gomes de Sousa, a landfill dweller in Rio de Janeiro: "I am the edge of the world. I am everywhere."

Even if it takes performative violence—even if this violence is something the poem must inflict upon its speaker—dream of a world in which you see everything bleeding.

Even if it means betraying your people, shape the dream into a confrontation with the ones responsible for bloodshed.

Suggesteds

Marisol de la Cadena, *Earth Beings: Ecologies of Practice Across Andean Worlds*

Letter of the Community Guarani-Kaiowá of Pyelito Kue/Mbarakay-Iguatemi-MS for the Government and Justice of Brazil (link available at "Selected Suggesteds" on bigenergypoets.net)

Hiromi Ito, *Wild Grass on the Riverbank*

Davi Kopenawa, *The Falling Sky*

Edimilson de Almeida Pereira, poems at hildamagazine.com/edimilson-de-almeida-pereira.html

Elizabeth Povinelli, "Transgender Creeks and the Three Figures of Power in Late Liberalism"

Eric Magrane

Eric Magrane holds a PhD in geography and an MFA in creative writing. He is the founding editor of *Spiral Orb*, an experiment in permaculture poetics. He is coeditor, with Christopher Cokinos, of *The Sonoran Desert: A Literary Field Guide* (University of Arizona Press, 2016), a 2016 Southwest Book of the Year. Recent academic work appears in *GeoHumanities*, *Journal of the Southwest*, *AAG Review of Books*, and *Emotion, Space, and Society*, and recent creative work appears in *Ecotone*, *Terrain.org*, *you are here: journal of creative geography*, *Versal*, and *The Fourth River*. As a Climate Assessment for the Southwest (CLIMAS) Science & Society Fellow, he created and taught the first Climate Change & Poetry course for the University of Arizona Poetry Center in fall 2015.

Works

From Biosphere 2, Poetry, and the Anthropocene

A poet sits on a beach and writes. The wave machine churns.

Outside the glass, the desert. A group of tourists exits the rainforest and gazes down at the beach from the savannah.

Some of them arrived after seeing the billboards between Phoenix and Tucson. *Where science lives.* People lived here too, eight of them sealed under glass in the early 1990s. Most visitors ask about that. Were they practicing for Mars? I heard they snuck pizza in. Did they have sex?

Another billboard proclaims *One of Time-Life Book's 50 Must See Wonders of the World.* It's sublime, something out of science fiction, a Buckminster Fuller-like dome on the western flank of the Santa Catalinas north of Tucson. The three-plus acres above ground house multiple biomes and a human habitat. The two acres below—the technosphere including the lung—keep Biosphere 2 running, a metaphor for the ecosystem services that support Biosphere 1, a.k.a. the Earth.

> a little surrealist poem might include
> a desk on a beach under glass
> and a poet writing something about
> humans as the confounding variable
>
> but about wouldn't be the right word
> taking the wave machine into account

Biosphere 2 holds multiple narratives. It's the dream of living on Mars, it's an experiment in systems science, and it's a reminder of taking care of the Earth. It concretizes the fine edge between human control and lack of control over ecological and social systems. In short, it embodies many of the dreams and anxieties of the Anthropocene.

except here, I'm in a building, in a natural

> via synaptic networks so well that we could even
> imagine things that were not currently
> in front of us

> outside is the leaf, the lung organ, inside is the mud,
> the concrete outside, the bird, the weather is inside, outside is
> the control, cognate, the brain, neither does not stand for,

> does not surface

we who are artifacts

who are the site
of rock, of stone, of sediment
of earth falling into earth

no such thing as history
no such thing as culture

but there are ancestors
grandparents and grandchildren
and stories

ways to be in this world
outside of our knowledge

Mesquite

"The mesquite's root system is the deepest documented; a live root was discovered in a copper mine over 160 feet (50m) below the surface. Like all known trees, however, 90 percent of mesquite roots are in the upper 3 feet of soil, where most of the water and oxygen are concentrated. The deep roots presumably enable a mesquite to survive severe droughts, but they are not its main life support."
                    —from *A Natural History of the Sonoran Desert*

Down here
the layers of earth
are comforting
like blankets.

The soil I think of
as time. Below the caliche
I sift through sediment
from thousands of years.

Though the sharp desert light above
is another world, its pulse
courses through me.

When the mastodons
and ground sloths roamed,
its pulse coursed through me.

When the Hohokam
in the canyon
ground my pods
in the stone
its pulse coursed through me.

When the new gatherers
of the desert
learn again how to live here,
its pulse will course through me.

And I say, I will be ready
if the drought comes.

And I say, go deep
into the Earth.

And I say, go deep
into yourself, go deep

and be ready.

Process / Poetics

Each of these pieces arrived from a site-based practice.

Biosphere 2 (B2) is a site that blends big science—climate and systems research—with tourism. In February 2014, I brought a group of poets to B2 for a weekend residency to meet with researchers and to write from the site. Poets included Wendy Burk, Christopher Cokinos, Alison Hawthorne Deming, Joshua Marie Wilkinson, Arianne Zwartjes, and myself. As a critical and creative geographer, I imagined the project as an art-science experiment: a blend between creative practice, environmental fieldwork, and social science. The excerpted work included here from B2 includes short pieces of my writing from that project, as well as a fragment from a collaborative poemfilm that I made with rainforest ecologist Tyeen Taylor at B2.

In this project, I find that material and data—in the form of poems, poetics, field notes—is in a continual process of reconfiguration for different audiences, outlets, and events. I think of it like a form of renewable energy. "In the exchange, the human energy that is transferred is to be considered," wrote Muriel Rukeyser. This idea interacts with Charles Olson's kinetics, William Rueckert's poems as energy forms, or Jed Rasula's compost.

~~~

I'd characterize my methodology as a site-based geopoetics. The concept of site is based in immanence rather than transcendence. Geopoetics is, in its widest sense, a practice of earth-making.

~~~

I drafted "we who are artifacts" in the library at Tumamoc Hill, a cultural and ecological research site that plays an important role in the history of Sonoran Desert science and reconciliation ecology. I was involved in a community project that brought together poets and artists to visit with scientists on the hill, and to write from the site. I was thinking about my grandmother, who had recently passed away, in Connecticut. And, as a geographer and a person transplanted to the desert from the east, I was thinking about the erasures and abstractions of terms like history and culture.

Alternatively: the efficacy and immediacy of sited actions and interactions.

When I write that geopoetics is a practice of earth-making, it begs the question: what earth are we making. This is also a question of subject formation. Consider a speculative more-than-human geopoetics :: a reflective and refractive earth-making that imagines and speculates on alter-subjectivities. And alter-subjectivities abound—in oral traditions, in traditional ecological knowledge, in poetries that attempt resistance to empire.

~~~

"Mesquite" is written from the site of the underground and imagines what a deep taproot of a mesquite tree—the deepest known—would have to say to a room full of humans. I'm grateful to Wanda Coleman, who was visiting Tucson for the Tucson Poetry Festival, and in a workshop encouraged me to forget my aversion to anthropomorphism and to go ahead and write from the voice of the mesquite. It is an event poem; I originally wrote it for an Earth Day ceremony involving the planting of a mesquite tree. Since then, I've used this poem in various public settings as a way into a discussion of biogeography (the study of the distribution of species across time and space) and climate adaptation.

~~~

Poems become collaborators themselves, re-configured & re-calibrated sites, interventions, actors, and encounters.

How do we think about the value of energy transfer, the kinetics of trans-thinking/doing? We have, of course, plenty of precedents to approach this in poetics and ecocriticism. Here we might also go to Donna Haraway's "encounter value." While encounter value might be considered as a kind of queer corrective to a jumbo Marxism, I'm interested in the use of encounter methodologically in an eco- or geo-poetic praxis.

~~~

While being cautious of metaphor and transparency, I've been turning over this line in my mind as a bit of ground for future work:

Ecosystem Services Transparent in the Pipes

becomes

Ecopoetics and the Political Economy of Thermodynamics

References

Haraway, Donna. *When Species Meet*. Minneapolis: University of Minnesota Press, 2008.

Olson, Charles. *Collected Prose*. Berkeley: University of California Press, 1997.

Rasula, Jed. *This Compost*. Athens: The University of Georgia Press, 2002.

Rueckert, William. "Literature and ecology." *The Ecocriticism Reader*. 1996: 105-123.

Rukeyser, Muriel. *The Life of Poetry*. New York: Paris Press, 1996.

Perceptual Challenge

1. Note your elevation above sea level. What poems occur here?

2. Map the ¼ mile radius around your home in a poem.

3. Draw a line. On one side of the line, note observations. On the other side, write responses to those observations. Which is which?

4. Choose an object in your field. Make the object the title. Make it the title three times. Write three pieces with this title.

5. List everything that is alive around you. List everything that is not alive around you.

6. Go to a different elevation. What poems occur here?

7. Choose a species you know little about but that lives in your ecosystem. Learn everything you can about that species. Then, go find the species. Write what happens.

8. The first object-poem (see #4) will be your control. Analyze the second and third against the control. What are your conclusions?

9. Find an urban ecotone. Stand there. Write a poem from the dual space.

10. Imagine a rise in sea level. How will that affect your elevation poem?

11. List everything that is natural around you. List everything that is not natural around you.

12. Observe lists #5 and #11. Why did you organize them as you did? Is there such a thing?

13. Stand up and put your arms out. The length of your arms is the circle of the poem.

14. Choose a field you know little about. Find someone in that field to interview. Research the person's work beforehand, so that you can ask relevant questions. Conduct the interview, then write a poem.

15. Write a poem that takes place over 4.5 billion years.

16. Write a poem that is 3 degrees Celsius warmer than it is now.

Suggesteds

Climate change is a social justice issue. I'm inspired by the work of groups like Idle No More, and by poets such as **Kathy Jetñil-Kijiner**[8], who read in front of bodies such as the United Nations.

Ecopoets can speak and write to each other, but being able to communicate to a variety of publics may be crucial for ecopoets who wish to address climate change in a broadly relevant way. Physical scientists increasingly receive training in communicating their work to the public and often reach out to artists and writers to help communicate the urgency of the situation. How might ecopoets help communicate the situation while at the same time resist the turning of poems into messages that reproduce the ideologies and systems that got us into the mess in the first place?

Critical geographers, drawing on long traditions of human-environment geography, have helped me understand a variety of approaches to climate change and the Anthropocene. These range from speculative geophilosophy to connecting science and policy, and from political ecology critiques of the commodification of nature to transdisciplinary biogeography. A few geographers who have been important to my thinking on climate change and the Anthropocene include Noel Castree, Nigel Clark, Mike Hulme, Diana Liverman, and Kathryn Yusoff.

Yusoff writes:

> Contemporary Anthropocene subjectivity (human and otherwise) is not indivisible from fossil fuels, so to think of a futurity without fossil fuels and the proffered ending of the Anthropocene requires undoing forms of becoming that are co-constituted with fossil fuels, as much as reconstituting alternative energetic materialities. It requires the formation of new collective subjectivities and material forms of life that examine and then move on from the geopolitical inheritance of the Anthropocene. The matter under consideration—fossil fuels—is not outside of life; it has agency, and directs, forms, and differentiates the geologic subjects of the Anthropocene. We cannot, as it were, go *against* the Earth, go *against* climate; humans can only follow after the flows of energy, be in concert with Earth processes and inhuman forces. And, in the case of fossil fuels, either increase their mobility and release their energy, or not. It is not a case of 'our' responsibility *for* the Earth, but our responsibility to forms of collaboration within geologic life.

---

[8] Video footage linked at "Selected Suggesteds" on bigenergypoets.net.

This is as much about the reception of new forms of subjectivity and geo-ontologies of the Earth as it is about creation of new energy forms. (792)

Notes:

Yusoff, Kathryn. "Geologic life: Prehistory, climate, futures in the Anthropocene." *Environment and Planning D: Society and Space* 31.5 (2013): 779-795.
Notes

1. A longer version of "Biosphere 2, Poetry, and the Anthropocene" originally appeared in *Terrain.org*:

http://www.terrain.org/2014/columns/biosphere-2-poetry-anthropocene-eric-magrane/

Linked to this piece you can also find the portfolio of poems written during the Poetic Field Research Performance Project at Biosphere 2, including poems by Wendy Burk, Christopher Cokinos, Alison Hawthorne Deming, Joshua Marie Wilkinson, Arianne Zwartjes, and myself.

2. The collaboration with Tyeen Taylor is called "I can only pick up the stones and throw them like my voice" and is in the 2015 issue of *you are here: the journal of creative geography*. You can find it, and a link to the poemfilm version, here: http://youareheregeography.com/the-montage-effect/montaging-materialities/298-2/

3. "we who are artifacts" appears in *This Piece of Earth: Images and Words from Tumamoc Hill* (Tumamoc: People and Habitats, 2013).

4. "Mesquite" appears in *The Sonoran Desert: A Literary Field Guide* (University of Arizona Press, 2016).

Joyelle McSweeney

Joyelle McSweeney is the author of eight volumes of lyric poetry, prose, drama, and essays. Her books include *The Necropastoral: Poetry, Media, Occults* (criticism, University of Michigan Poets on Poetry Series, 2015); *Dead Youth, or, the Leaks* , winner of the inaugural Leslie Scalapino Prize for Innovative Performance Writers (play, Litmus, 2014); *Percussion Grenade* (poems and play, Fence, 2012); *Slamandrine, 8 Gothics* (stories and play, Tarpaulin Sky, 2013); the pamphlet *Deformation Zone: On Translation* with Johannes Göransson (Ugly Duckling Presse, 2012); the artist's book *The Necropastoral* with Andrew Shuta (Spork, 2010); the lyric novels *Flet* and *Nylund, the Sarcographer* (Fence, 2008 and Tarpaulin Sky, 2007, respectively); and the poetry volumes *The Commandrine and Other Poems* and *The Red Bird*, (2004 and 2002, Fence). She edits the international press Action Books, teaches at Notre Dame, and lives in the Rust Belt city of South Bend, Indiana.

Works

EPILOGUE from Dead Youth, or, The Leaks

Explanatory note: *Dead Youth, or, The Leaks* is an ecopolitical farce set on a hijacked containership; the governing deity of the play is Henrietta Lacks, the African American patient whose cancer cells, harvested without her consent after her death at Johns Hopkins in 1951, have been kept alive in culture for the purposes of experimentation ever since. Lacks delivers the Prologue and Epilogue and comments on the play throughout. However, as this Epilogue reveals, she is not released from her non-consensual 'immortality' despite her deity status, and is forced to live forever as a witness to the Anthropocene, something like Benjamin's Angel of History.

PROLOGUE-AS-EPILOGUE

The play is over. I am still me.
I have transformed myself to Epilogue
also known as Epithelia.
not known as Apologee.
The past is resourceful.
It does not wait.
It contaminates the future
with its DNA mistakes.
The past sails like a sinking ship
that does not sink, but leaks waste
til the bottom of the sea is barren
and a dense mat of toxins o'er grows the earth
rank as a fridge after a hurricane.
The isle is full of dead fridges, going green.
There is no exit.
I sit at the lab bench and eat my lunch.
The lab is deserted. The scientist is dead
who first harvested my tumor
who sentenced me to immortality.
I—who was known for my hospitality—
to be re-writ as permanent malignancy!
I grow and I grow alone
in culture. I write code.
I distribute copies. I propagate my line.
Maybe I am QUEEN BEE
in my colonie. Maybe I am
QUEEN HACKER, Queen Julian Assange,
because I make everything over
with my queer authoritee.
I change my hair when I am being followed—
No. I cannot change my hair.
It always stays just like this
'dancing towards my face'.
I participated in this human drama
because the immortal must have their amusements
& because it makes a change
& I cannot change.
I must perform my toxic ministry forever.
I never go off-shift.

Julian Assange:
all secrets are the same secret.
The only secret is this:
The only emperor is malignancy.
That's human nature:
malignancy
atrocity
maliciousness
malevolence
violence
exploitation
abjection
laughable naiveté
and no expiration date
until the end of the Anthropocene
and after that, who knows?
I predict
my after-afterlife will be like this:
when the freezers run out of current
when the vials and petri dishes warm
when my cells in culture grow
without human hands to coax them
I'll find no relief
from immortality
but must always grow more of me
dead bell
dead bell
I ring for thee
the suffering, and the malignant
the greedy, and the helpless
the vulnerable, and the rich
the unfit and the fit
the guilty and the blameless
I am the mother of these
there is enough of me
for each of thee
I am unlimited credit
I am unlimited debt
I am the mother of this planet
I am forced to be
I am forced to be
yoked to thee

Anthropocene
Fate would not let me die with the twentieth cee
Now I myself am Fate; I ride the night bus
I travel on the maternal line
I arrive ahead of schedule. I speed time.
I clasp the future to my breast
like a Bible, a pearl-toothed baby or a pest
I let it sink its teeth in me
I let it lower its pipette
deep down to my malignant layer
and drink from me
until the future
looks like me
& acts like me
and is me
as I am forced to be
it with its brown hair
'dancing towards its face'
its skin light and smooth as a fawn's
its painted nails abide no chip
it rests slim fingers
on its woman's hips
this futurity
is a kind of divinity
it has a name like me.
Henrietta Lacks.

Poetics

The Necropastoral

When I reframe the pastoral—already a defunct, anachronistic, dead, imperial and imperialistic literary form—as a *necropastoral*, I am calling attention to the excesses, intensities, inequalities, anachronisms, morbidities already implicit in a genre contrived to represent separation, quarantine, timelessness, stasis, protection from upset and death. The necropastoral seeks to activate these suppressed aspects of pastoral—the necrotized, the infectious, the counterfeit, the pastoral as a site not of separation but of deadly traffic, not of a wall but a membrane, not an idyll but an unstable compact, not a place of simplicity but of dubious intentions. Where classical pastoral insists on separation, necropastoral posits supersaturation, leaking, countercontamination. Our contemporary understandings of biohazard and ecology activates the specter of necropastoral; our ravenous media (over-) exposes it. The necropastoral is the toxic double of our eviscerating, flammable contemporary world, where avian flu, swine flu, mad cow disease, toxic contamination via industrial waste, hormones in milk, poisons leaching out of formaldehyde FEMA trailers, chemical warfare, bombing campaigns which destroy , refugee camps where typhus and diarrhea take lives or where hunting potable water puts women and children in grave danger, mass graves which double as classrooms, have destroyed the idea of the bordered or bounded body and marked the porousness of the human body as its most characteristic quality. The body is a medium for infection, saturation, death. The supersaturated, leaking membrane of the necropastoral is thus politicized by our modern understanding of ecology, globalization, the damage of industrial politics and warfare does to bodies. The spectral quality of capitalism, the way money and debt accrues and erodes in damaging patterns, the way damage to bodies is sometimes the first materialization of corporate malfeasance, the occult way capitalism's distribution systems amplify economic, political, biological damage as it spreads across the globe—this is the necropastoral, the lethal double of the pastoral and its fantasy of permanent, separated, rural peace. In emphasizing the counterfeit nature of pastoral, the necropastoral makes visible the fact that nothing is pure or natural, that mutation and evolution are inhuman technologies, that all political assertions of the natural and the pure are themselves moribund and counterfeit, infected and rabid.

The term necropastoral appropriates the contaminatory anxiety buried in the Pastoral's binarisms in the first place, and applies it as a kind of engine to spasm back across the border and into the body of the state, the family, the individual. To ex-terminate.

Process

I live in South Bend, Indiana, a small Rust Belt city between Detroit and Gary, where the ecological and political end-times plays itself out in slow motion and at warp speed, on minute and huge scales. One day when I was fooling around on the Internet— that embodied and disembodied, subterranean and surveilled, anarchic and corporate space— I learned that the Somali 'pirate' Abdu Wali Abdulqadir Muse, the teenager who participated in the hijacking of the containership, the Maersk Alabama, in 2009, was imprisoned in Terre Haute, Indiana. Prisoner of the Rust Belt. Landlocked pirate. I immediately began writing this play as a spell for his safety. I conceived of the play as both an inverted *Tempest* and a 'badly-wired allegory', peopled with figures who were both like and unlike their historical counterparts. The *dramatis personae* includes Julian Assange, Henrietta Lacks, Muse, and a flexing, plural character called Dead Youth, made up of teenagers who have been struck down by a variety of Anthropocene ails—drug wars, drones, cancer, unsafe working conditions/child labor, sex work, suicide, gunplay, etc. The 'bad-wiring' of the allegory allows for lawless bolts of affect to surge across the structure—for the play to be more than an idea, but an occult event that sends reverse bolts of spectacular current back through the systems that control and imprison us in our apparently fixed roles of consumer and consumed, colonizer and colonized, experimenter and subject.

Perceptual Challenge

The Necropastoral: Exercises in Mediumicity

1) Think about the matrices of power in which you find yourself.
2) Think about the joints and synapses at which power's current jumps from site to site, body to body, medium to medium.
3) Occupy those sites with something that doesn't belong there. Ex. beauty, obscenity, farce, grief, dismay, anger, costume, ornament, pure sound, hyperdiction, signals, dance, hosting the dead, parodies of power itself, mashups of power's self-image with images it does not prefer. SEE: CADA, Asco, Nick Cave, Black Arts, Dada.
4) Reverse, amplify, deflect, pervert, irritate the current.
5) Host/hostility. Scale up and weaponize vulnerability without converting it to invulnerability. SEE: Dolores Dorantes, *Estilo,* Jack Smith, *Normal Love.*
6) Try on power as a farce, show the gaps and leakages.
7) Spasm the poles of power = farce. See: Soyinka, Genet.
8) Through pageantry and spectacle, embody another way—or, show how survival is impossible, all aboveground exits are blocked. Drain lethewards.
9) Study *Staphylococcus aureus*. It wears a golden crown.
10) Occupy paradox: the sublime: the declivities and the ecstasies, simultaneously. Be torn apart by spasming current.
11) Paradox may be an illicit energy source, an occult power source, for those who can endure it.
12) Not everyone can endure it.
13) Wear the golden crown.

Suggesteds

Hilton Als, *White Girls*
Aristophanes, *The Birds, The Frogs*, any translation
Asco
Baudelaire, *Paris Spleen,* trans. L. Varese, and *Painter of Modern Life.*
Aase Berg, trans. Johannes Göransson
Robert Bolaño, everything, esp. short works trans. Chris Andrews
CADA
Nick Cave (US visual artist)
César Aira, *Ghosts*, trans. Chris Andrews
Aimé Césaire, *Notebook of a Return to My Native Land,* trans. Eshlemann et al]
Artaud, *The Theater and Its Double,* trans. Mary Caroline Richards
Amiri Baraka, *Dutchman*
Bataille, *The Notion of Expenditure,* trans. Stoekl,. Lovitt, and Leslie
Don Mee Choi's poetry, translation, activism and performances
Delores Dorantes, *Estilo,* trans. Jen Hofer
Jean Genet, *The Maids, Our Lady of the Flowers*, trans. Frechtman
Marosa di Giorgio, *History of Violets,* trans. Jeannine Marie Pitas
Christian Hawkey, *Ventrakl*
Itō Hiromi, *Wild Grass on the Riverbank,* trans. Jeffrey Angles
Langston Hughes, *Scottsboro Ltd*
Huysmans, *Against Nature*
Kim Hyesoon, poetry plus *Princess Abandoned* [all trans. by Don Mee Choi]
Lautreamont, *Maldoror,* trans. Lykiard
Vicki Leakx
Lucas de Lima, *Wet Land*
Clarice Lispector, *Hour of the Star* trans. B. Moser
Mayakovsky *The Bedbug,* whatever translation you can find
Achille Mbembe, *On the Postcolony,* various translators
Ana Mendieta
MIA
China Miéville, *The Scar*
Haryette Mullen, *Muse and Drudge*
Alice Notley, *Alma,or, The Dead Women*
Jasbir Puar, *Terrorist Assemblages*
Rimbaud, *Illuminations*, Ashbery translation
Wilfred Owen and Georg Trakl
Suzan-Lori Parks, *The America Play*
José Antonio Ramos Sucre trans. Guillermo Parra
Yi Sang, poetry and prose, wherever you can find it

Jack Smith
Wole Soyinka, *To Zia With Love/A Scourge of Hyacinths*
Tarkovsky, *Solaris* and *Stalker*
Brett L. Walker, *Toxic Archipelago*
Andy Warhol
Ronaldo Wilson's Tear E. Avatar
C.D. Wright and Forrest Gander
Raúl Zurita, everything, trans. Daniel Borzutzky, Anna Deeny, et al

Julie Patton

Julie Ezelle is the scribbler of *Notes for Some (Nominally) Awake* (Yo-Yo Labs). She has litter in *the eco language reader, I'll Drown My Book: Conceptual Writing by Women, Critiphoria*, and other pressings. When she was very young, she *promised* trees she would not take advantage of their limbs to "publish" unless she really *had something to say*—hence the nature of her impermanent, improvisatory, occasional, and "difficult to publish" site-specific work. Nevertheless, Julie couldn't say no to Tender Buttons, which has sought to publish her long performance poem *B, Belladonna*, her collected e-mail rants*, and *Field Books Love Letter to L.* These and other re/de codings & cordings have been detained since 2006, along with her freedom of liberty as an internationally traveling artist, by a "broken" system that allows surreal estate landlords and developers to use the courts to force migration of law-abiding NYC tenants. Julie's answer to *being booked (or having "The Book" thrown at her)* involved revising a century-old recto-verso sided building in her "I went back to Ohio and my city was gone" (Chryssie Hynde) native Cleveland, as a *really truly stone brick* pop-up book—with live stories, writing on the walls, and detritus-based installations. Julie's impromptu "Building by the Side of the Road" (Rust Belt Tales, About Place Journal 2012) speaks to the legacy of this "zentellectual property" dedicated to her mother, artist Virgie Ezelle Patton, and many others, human and non-human.

In 2015, a Master Artist Residency at the Atlantic Center for the Arts (ACA); the opportunity to present work at DIA Art Foundation, to exhibit in *Shelved Art, Real Art in Real Books for Real Library Lovers (Pasadena, California)*, duet with Ravi Coltrane in an over-the-mic call to join him on the stage at New York's legendary Birdland, and to come out with other great writers in *What I say (University of Alabama Press)* brought Julie news of relief (from monthly continuums). Julie also received the exciting news of a Foundation for Contemporary Arts Grants to Artists (Poetry), and she couldn't wait to join other FCA grantees at the Judson Church, NY celebration honoring them, on March 17th, because it was also her birthday. It also turned out to be the day her beloved mother Virgie passed. At 3:17 a.m.

Julie has toured and recorded with many great musicians. She has taught at New York University, Naropa University, and spent many years educating the young through Teachers & Writers Collaborative and other arts education programs. She lives in NYC's East Village.

Earth. Or the worryld in "progress". tatter tales edgy up in the air enter action with words... namesplacessplices" wild edges wiggle room glad rags povArty "primitive" remake po-aes-
thetic life as prayer worrier f lagging behind the "road to hell paved with good intentions"
The map of witch...
war no long err

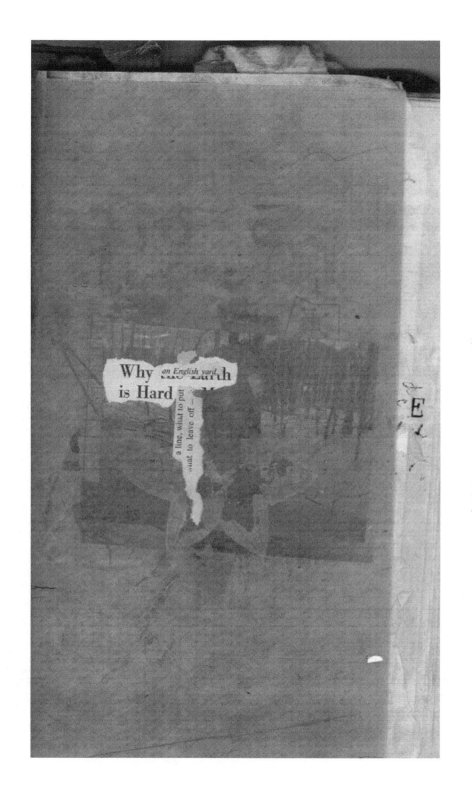

Why an English yard
is Hard Earth

a line, what to put
...at to leave off —

Poetics

I wish to say that my compositional process and ecopoetics (statement) are one... My life is my statement is my life...end of sentience... especially in the sense that my creations pile up, organically, over time. Philosophy of "making do" with what i, my hands/fingers come across...

Scraps of words, sounds, images, seam together, unravel. I feel my way thru things in the most bio centered, hands on low-tech way possible. Leaves piling up at the door, decomposing orange rinds, burnt things, rusted metal or a road directions suggest the way, a-Muse me. It's all about the moment, flow that I am in paying attention, saving grace, keeping goods out of the landfill. The materials that I happen across dictate the nature of the work, determine the aesthetics, process, genre, discipline, media. I don't set out to make work ("art") in any form. All is occasional, rite and site specific. What might be trash in another's hand, piles up on a wall because it was there, in my face as I passed by looking for a spot to hold it (thank god for thumbtacks) because I can't stand waste—losing pretty ugly things some poor artist slaved over for a living at Hallmark. Respect. So it finds a way on my wall. My poems are compost, improvisations live fermentation, visual trash heaps. I don't set out to make "art". Rather the art of living makes me, catches my eye and plop! There it goes...on the wall. "Oh! I have a performance tonight! What am I going to do?" Read the wall to my left, a newspaper article or candy wrapper plucked out of the trash, current event on everyone's mind, lips, what the heck I'm wearing or thinking becomes a soundscape, rolls out as it comes to me. I like displaying the gaps, elisions and silences and mis takes...of the creative process, foreground art as a living, breathing, dynamic PROCESS. on the edge naked and imperfect, tension builds up to something then disintegrates before your ears. Spacing silence, emptiness out to the edge of a seat, piling breakfast coconuts along a window just because...They contain, hold space for future use, or nothing but becoming part of the earth...all my work is utilitarian. All fragile and ephemeral, transient but alive. All published or exhibited or recorded bodies of work are assembled, pieced, collaged together as occasional gifts in real time but so far they only exist, in my mind, as steps in a particular direction or moment, cake ingredients, larva or quick journal entry...Dashed off. In a moment's order. What I see, feel encounter or wear in a given day is a page right out of my life so the rhythms of playing with visible materials may surface as immaterial (sounds) body of work. At some point, living logical tangent...

Life samsara, nature, exists is ever finished, texts, so my work might be more of decomposing process, gesture than anything. Art as commodity, for me, is less interesting than the art of living with and in natural processes, divine gifts of materials or the world at our fingertips. Wonder and wander...

Perceptual Challenge

Field poetics (or planting carbon):

— Match words & deeds by *putting your money where your mouth* & *purchasing a lot—or other contested/gentrifrying/quickly colonizing space anywhere on Earth (you or a group of people can afford)

— Give it away to the birds & the bees, butterflies & other small creatures (as shelter from the storm) by filling it with plants, trees & nest building materials they can depend on for cover, food. Or plant an edible forest 2, 4, 6 (etc.) leg beings can enjoy. Water it with love—liquid manna from the sky.

—Write a "conservation easement" with the help of an experienced attorney. Find a locally based willing to steward and protect it.

—Let it grow wild... Over time tale the story of this place! By writing/documenting/singing its true presence. Yes, go there! By writing a "creation story" about the growth & (un)development of this particular spot, a prayer, lament, elegy, song lyrics, call of the heart, treaty of love, a manifesto, film, graphic novel, poetic journey, song or psalms—anything language liquick

Craig Santos Perez

Craig Santos Perez is a native Chamorro from the Pacific Island of Guam. His eco-poetry has appeared in *The Eco-Poetry Anthology*; *The Arcadia Project: North American Postmodern Pastoral*; the journal *Ecopoetics*, and in special issues on eco-poetry in *Poetry Magazine* and *Dusie*. He organized a panel on "Pacific Eco-Poetics" at the Berkeley Ecopoetics Conference, and he has done research on indigenous eco-poetics, and environmental imperialism. In 2008, he testified to the United Nations on the environmental impacts of U.S. militarism in Guam. He currently works as an associate professor in the English Department at the University of Hawai'i, Mānoa.

Works

The Age of Plastic

1 polyethylene

the doctor presses the plastic probe
onto my wife's belly—ultrasound
waves pulse between fluid, tissue, and
bone, echoing into an embryo
of hope—*"plastic makes
this possible"*—

2 high density polyethylene

plastic keeps food fresh—
delivers medication and clean water—
forms cables and clothes,
ropes and nets—even
stops bullets—
*"plastic is the perfect creation
because it never dies"*—

3 polyvinyl chloride (pvc)

my wife labors in the plastic
birthing tub—
i rub ice cubes onto
her warm skin—after birth,
our doula places the placenta
in a ziploc bag—now stored
in our freezer—

4 low density polyethylene (ldpe)

in the oceans, there exists three tons
of fish for every one ton of plastic—
*leaches estrogenic and toxic
chemicals, disrupts hormonal
and endocrine systems*—eight million
tons of discarded plastic swim

into the sea every year—
causes cancer, infertility, and miscarriage—
multiplies into smaller pieces—
plankton, shrimp, fish, whales, and
birds confuse plastic with food—
absorbs poisons—will plastic make
life impossible?

5 polypropylene

my daughter sucks a pacifier
while sleeping in the crib—
my wife uses a breast pump,
milk dripping into a bottle—
i pick up legos from the living
room floor—*"every plastic ever made
still exists, somewhere, today"*—

6 Polystyrene

"plastic: a toxic love story"
"10 reasons why a plastic-free life is hard"
"how i kicked the plastic habit and how you can too"
"what would our lives look like without plastic"
"track plastic microbeads with this new app"
"life without plastic on pinterest"
"live healthier without plastic"

7 Other

imagine *being* plastic—
how empty it must feel surrounded and used by us : imperfect, decomposing things—imagine its migration
into the pacific gyre—finally arriving to
a patch of paradise—belonging
among its kin—

i press the plastic nipple of
the warmed bottle to my daughter's
small lips—for a moment,

i wish she was made of plastic
so that she, too, will survive
our wasteful hands—so that she,
too, will have a "great future"—

Poetics

Eco-poetics is the study of poetry written about the natural world, environmental justice, ecology, and climate change. Beyond subject matter, eco-poetics also examines eco-poetry for how formal elements might embody ecological concepts, transformations, or aesthetics. All cultures have a tradition of eco-poetry since one of humanity's primal experiences is our dynamic and changing relationship to the world around us and to ourselves as nature. Eco-poetics has become more prevalent during times of ecological precarity, such as times of industrialization, urbanization, nuclearism, plantationism, militarism, and enviromental imperialism. Today, we are witnessing the urgency of eco-poetry as an existential response to climate change. Within academia, the environmental humanities is quickly becoming an essential part of our curriculum.

Process

This poem emerged from an "Eco-Poetics" course I teach at the University of Hawai'i, Mānoa, One of our units is "Plastics," which has a particularly ominous presence in the Pacific since the so-called "Pacific Garbage Patch" swirls north of the Hawaiian islands. Additionally, one of the northern Hawaiian Islands, commonly known as Midway Atoll, has been made famous as a wildlife refuge for the Laysan Albatross, is one gathering place for tons of plastic that wash ashore. Tragically, the albatross also mistake the plastic for food, and there exists many disturbing photographs of the bellies of the birds cut open to reveal stomachs full of plastic. Because plastic has become such a normal part of our everyday lives, environments and even bodies, poems about plastic help us to truly see its impact, entanglements and dangers. These poems also challenge us to change our lives and challenge the plastic industry, one of the largest industries in the world and a major carbon emitter. I assign my students to write a poem about plastic, and the above poem is my own poem about the subject.

Perceptual Challenge

Read and view the suggested books and documentaries below and then write your own poem about plastic, reflecting on its presence in your life and its impact to the environment. Think about how you might change the way you use plastic in your daily life to reduce its impact.

Suggesteds

1) *Plastic Paradise*, documentary*
2) Lyz Soto, "Pacific Garbage Patch,"*
3) Victoria Sloan Jordan, "Fall Equinox" and "Kaleidoscope"*
4) Allison Cobb, *Autobiography of Plastic* (also see the author's blog)
5) Evelyn Reilly, *Styrofoam*

*documentary link available on "Selected Suggested" and others online

Evelyn Reilly

Evelyn Reilly's books of poetry include *Apocalypso* and *Styrofoam*, both published by Roof Books. Essays and poetry have recently appeared in *Omniverse, Pallaksch. Pallaksch, the eco language reader, Interdisciplinary Studies in Literature and Environment*, and *Verse*, as well as the *&NOW Awards2: The Best Innovative Writing* and *The Arcadia Project: Postmodernism and the Pastoral*. An interview with the writer is included in Andy Fitch's *Sixty Morning Talks*, published by Ugly Duckling Presse. Reilly has taught at the Poetry Project at St. Mark's Church and the Summer Writing Program of Naropa University, and has been a curator of the Segue Reading Series in New York City.

Works

Song Of, from *SELF*

I.

Approximately 98.6 degrees

all this desire and longing

a big advance in the invention

of subjectivity might say Sappho

in the sense that *the individual*

becomes a crystal

that can from anywhere

but only an occasional crystal

not a natural category

that everyone has adds

a damp book on some cool tiles

where Self could have re-assembled

as the weeping girl or aggrieved man

but chose instead this ambiguous animal

skittish with the notion of identity

as a series of equal signs

forming any kind of viable ladder

instead of an improvised explosive device

that might detonate at any moment

or an act of breaking and entering

always a little bit strangified

as through the back door of a house

where children are sleeping

their presence apparent

in the loam

all over the surfaces

where the Self reflected

seems no less ephemeral

than the small frog

that appears on the sill

for a few seconds

then flicks itself back

into un-findability

or onto the doorstep

of Richard Chamberlain

in *The Last Wave*

becoming the briefest object

of the camera's gaze

before merging into a chorus

forming the soundtrack

to a downpour

of epic proportions

among other fugitive

super-permeable

spokescreatures of posthumanity

2.

And why should our bodies end at our skin?

someone asks as Self shakes the water

from its heritage predator pelt

and gets down on all fours

for some joint animal prayers

having just crossed over

the species line to add

some howling braying

to the bulkheads and antennas

before swooping down

with gown shroud

tail feathers trailing

on its way to the zoo

of *shared semiotic materiality*

                    Self loves you

so it engages in perpetual exchange

of provisional metaphors

through the bars of our cages

discarding some each day

the crystal thing for example

is incredibly dated

although the non-natural

category part seemed useful

for at least fifteen minutes

here *in the relentless emergent*

relationality that is the world

                Look

at this parka stitched

from whale intestine

these snow goggles carved

from fossil mammoth tusk

in an exhibit called *Tool*

which we visit for a dose

of human innovative

survival pathos

and let's examine

this navigational diagram

made solely of sticks

and cowry shells

in order to get from one

oceanic speck to the next

on our journey to becoming true

trans-post-national animal subjects

3.

It can't be Self's personal fault

if the word sacrifice

is a cover for animal murder

(the lamb the god the porkchop)

and we really aren't feeling so well

after all that imaginary travel

still holding our book above

the level of the water

as we pull the plug

to send some Self-fragments

out among the troubled watercourses

which is when the global economy

crashed into us with all its

post-colonial flotsam

and corporate wreckage jetsam

the dead pink blobs bobbing

against the shore where Mrs. Wu

in her leopard-print jacket

jokes *There are more pigs*

than fish in the Jiapingtang river

and Asheesh and Elena emerge

from shipping containers

for another round

of planetary labor

                Many said

they couldn't watch the videos

they were so painful

and caused a dissociative state

characterized by amnesia

and directionless wandering

while the poet Pan Ting

simply called for a *pure stroll*

along the water without

banners or slogans

only to be asked afterward

to "drink tea" with the police

turn in her phone and all

other communication devices

Note: Italicized text in section 1 is from an interview with Arjun Appadurai by Camille Henrot, published in *Camille Henrot: The Restless Earth*, The New Museum, 2014; in section 2, from Donna Haraway, *Crystals, Fabrics, and Fields: Metaphors that Shape Embryos,* 1976; in section 3, "Rivers of blood: the dead pigs rotting in China's water supply," *The Guardian*, March 29, 2013.

Poetics

Lately, I've been thinking about what form a post human-centered imagination might take and how it could contribute to the environmental culture that James Sherry calls for in his book *Oops! Environmental Poetics*. What Sherry proposes is a cultural transformation in which all activities— literary, artistic, religious, scientific, economic, political—are informed by an environmental understanding of the impact of human actions on the living world. He's probably correct that only this degree of cultural change will suffice if the human species is to find the creativity and will to address climate change and the extinction crisis. Thinking politics alone can achieve this is probably as naïve as thinking that poetry has a power beyond its small, but important, sphere of action.

The opposite of a genre, eco-poetic poetry is "simply" poetry that manifests an awakeness to our bio-historical moment and that has shed the useless and sometimes dismissive despair that often results in ironical or self-protective disengagement. It has not, so far, put forth a poetics, but all questions of poetics still matter. If one accepts that an environmental understanding of the world must be constitutive of all understandings (or that at least it must *saturate* all other understandings), the opportunities for exploring what this means to and in language become nearly limitless.

For me, this has taken various forms, from an interest in faux, man-made (sic) materials both positively as products of the human aesthetic (plastic) impulse and also in their problematic environmental aspects, to explorations of current forms of apocalyptic or "end-time" language. More recently, I've been thinking about the proliferation of poetic explorations of the self and subjectivity, and playing with the idea of putting the most famous "song of the self" through the filter of such contemporary investigations. What might happen if the multitudinous, utopian-democratic, polymorphically-erotic Whitmanic poetic "self" were re-constituted within the context of our post-colonial, post-humanist, globally inter-tangled and genderly profusional era? Could there be a new "song of ourselves" that expands to include many more kinds of permeable relationality, including cross-species relationality? And what kind of language critique, experimentation and innovation would that require? These are the kinds of questions that make the possible emergence of an eco-poetics interesting to me.

Process

My writing process has been the same for quite a while. I finish a book. I swear I'd like to write short minimalist poems instead of long collagist pieces that are difficult to perform in the setting of a poetry reading or excerpt for publication. I try. The results are dismal. Meanwhile, I'm copying passages out of reading materials of various kinds—philosophy, critical theory, science, history, a catalog from the Museum of Jurassic Technology, other things, mostly not poetry. Finally, something from one of these sources provokes a response that I think of as "bio-intellectual"—over-stimulating in a way that I will feel almost ill if I ignore. Anyone who has suffered restless legs syndrome will understand this kind of discomfort and the absolute imperative it delivers to get up and move just at the moment when you most want to fall asleep. So I get up and start riffing almost nonsensically off that language for quite a while, weeks, months even, for as long as I can keep it going, throwing additional fragments in from books, from poetry I'm hearing or language I'm experiencing out in the world. What emerges is a terrible mess, an amorphous heap of language with an incipient morphology, however, that slowly becomes apparent usually at the same time the flow of accumulation slows. Then the arduous work of really making something of it that another human could ever bother to read begins. This can take years. Eventually, hopefully, there is another book that is difficult to read to audiences and to excerpt for anthologies.

Perceptual Challenge

- Try to write a poem absent the human presence, or, failing that, a poem of boundary-less co-presence with nonhuman living beings.

- Reimage yourself within the context of geologic time and try to find language for that.

- Write something vegetal or mineral or astronomical. Embrace a new kind of "worldliness."

- Take up Kafka's challenge to "never send down roots, or plant them, however difficult it may be to avoid reverting to the old procedures. . . [A]ttempt to seize a blade of grass and hold fast to it when it begins to grow only from the middle," as quoted by Deleuze and Guattari, who go on to caution, "It's not easy to see things in the middle, rather than looking down on them from above or up at them from below, or from left to right or right to left . . ." (*A Thousand Plateaus,* "Introduction: Rhizome.")

- Ponder the "planetary pronoun." Read Joan Retallack's "What is Experimental Poetry & Why Do We Need It?" for guidance (*Jacket* 32, April 2007).

Suggesteds

Instead of a reading list, here is "Echo-location," a poem I wrote, or maybe compiled, some years ago in a period when I was reading Jed Rasula's *This Compost: Ecological Imperatives in American Poetry* and first discovered eco-criticism. If I were assembling it today, I'd probably add something from *The Book of Imaginary Beings* by Borges (who Deleuze and Guattari characterize as "an author renowned for his excess of culture"), from Deleuze and Guattari themselves (whose "Becoming Intense, Becoming Animal, Becoming-Imperceptible" Donna Haraway criticizes for "absence of curiosity about or respect for actual animals") and from "The Companion Species Manifesto" by Haraway herself.

So, the additions:

Sometimes I have the feeling that the animal is trying to tame me *Kafka* via *Borges*

Tree is filiation, but the rhizome is alliance *Gilles Deleuze* and *Felix Guattari*

"The relation" is the smallest possible unit of analysis *Donna Haraway*

ECHO-LOCATION

1. the tiniest aperture opening on animation *Jed Rasula*
2. : / , / . / . / ? / . / . *Brenda Iijima*
3. slosh, slosh *A.R. Ammons*
4. Look how the wantons frisk to taste the air *Anne Bradstreet*
5. Georgics differ from the epic in emphasizing planting over killing *Princeton Encyclopedia of Poetry and Poetics*
6. blod *Aram Saroyan*
7. a branching diagram without the possibility of closure, an open parentheses *imagined*
8. bestial extrusions no true animal face knows *Robert Duncan*
9. over every living thing that moves *obvious*
10. having broken numerous covenants of hunter and hunted *anonymous*

11. could man learn that he is not the master but rather the shepherd of being *Theodor Adorno*
12. no intention of making man the shepherd of anything *lost*
13. connected together by a chain of affinities *Charles Darwin*
14. amid fantasies of self-sufficiency *dreamt*
15. before religions / at pond bottom *Lorine Neidecker*
16. I am ... with the invisible molecular moral forces *William James*
17. O nature and O soul of man! how far ... are you linked analogies! *Herman Melville*
18. But analogy may be a deceitful guide *Charles again*
19. to be implicated in causal action on other beings *Alfred North Whitehead*
20. Caught, lost in millions of tree-analogies *John Ashbery*
21. the continuing history of pathetic fallacies *in progress*
22. products of evolution gathered for purposes having nothing to do with me *E.O. Wilson*
23. these are the carpets of / protoplast *Ronald Johnson*
24. The mouse is old, but its image is light. *Mei-Mei Berrsenbrugge*
25. What is the grass? *Walt Whitman*
26. imprisoned by our thoughtless plunder *Ray Anderson*
27. a planet utterly strange, chalk-coloured / behind the blackish-blue river *W.G. Sebald*
28. For mankind is fundamentally an echo-locator, like our distant relatives the porpoise and the bat. *Calvin Martin*

Linda Russo

Linda Russo is the author of three books of poetry, including *Meaning to Go to the Origin in Some Way* (Shearsman Books), and *Participant*, winner of the Brigham Award (Lost Roads Press), and a collection of literary-poetic essays, *To Think of Her Writing Awash in Light* (Subito Press). Her poetry is included in the anthology *Make It True: Poetry from Cascadia* (Leaf Press), and scholarly essays have appeared in *Among Friends: Engendering the Social Site of Poetry* (University of Iowa Press) and other edited collections, and as the preface of Joanne Kyger's *About Now: Collected Poems* (National Poetry Foundation). She lives in the Cascadian region of North America and teaches at Washington State University. Her fieldworks & inquiries are documented at inhabitorypoetics.blogspot.com.

Works

from ***Meaning to Go to the Origin in Some Way***

GOING TO SURVEY WALMART CONSTRUCTION FROM THE CREST OF PIONEER HILL

it begins with walking, feet mucked by competing agendas
and a wish to speak as part and parcel
       a rare Cow Parsnip community
part of a history of embattlement
of space being filled
      a well-preserved remnant of Idaho fescue grasslands
where walking is merely civil
and walking is compromised
      still the largest remnant of natural Palouse vegetation
citizenry

I wish to invoke freely a culture of interspecies inhabitance
      valuable thickets of Douglas Hawthorne
conflicts resolved, powers balanced

sometimes it takes less than a minute
      Magpie Forest, Rose Creek, Smoot Hill Farm
you hitch up your bird wings hoping

+

An Essential Radish (on the Pacific Flyway)

      simply an essential radish (from "radical" / having roots,
      meaning to go to the origin in some way –

      on the Pacific Flyway
      the seed you planted sprouted, the Least Terns took wing
      flashed silhouettes of shorebird (running, pecking)
      at Koppel Farm, in landlocked Pullman, June two thousand and ten

      meaning to go to the origin in some way
          acting animal-like toward boundaries, breathing

+

then she said: I think they make too much of dinosaurs

      shopping centers and cheap food production
      the song of arable, of dams, of more
      natives squeezed out in
      the production of more
      arable land

  err-able, likely to err we are

+

she said: I think you also care
      because you have walked in her paths

      sagebrush, sage grouse
        grasses and forbs
      sage sparrows and Washington ground squirrels
      forbs, the flowers of the grasslands

  "last little rabbit – her confusion & loneliness"

      her worn-out angry eyes

+

GOING TO SURVEY WALMART CONSTRUCTION FROM THE CREST OF PIONEER HILL

we in our many vectors crisscross this space
pinned to each other with our kind human greeting
our open, generous, uncomplicated
beg for release
into an imagined space uncompromisingly ours alone
the pearless pear tree and what you learn by proximity
without which we implode

      repetition don't forget   zigzag little ant
        wave wave bunchgrass clovers   wave
       lawngrass, fence & sky   wave   lawngrass, fence & sky

a little rhyme here:

and now a little song:

SONG FOR THE LOCAL

Garden to fork, fork to flesh
local-scale crying, thinning the sprouts
local-scale, local-scale, local-scale crying

Carbon footprint nitrogen fix
local-scale crying, thinning the sprouts
local-scale, local-scale, local-scale crying

Resistant to Round-Up, leaving the weeds
local-scale crying, thinning the sprouts
local-scale, local-scale, local-scale crying

Knowing, not-knowing a meadow once was
thinning the, thinning the, thinning the sprouts
local-scale, local-scale, local-scale crying

+

If you are interested in restoring native Palouse Prairie vegetation on your land, you have a fascinating challenge in store.

it can be very rewarding –
the silhouettes of typical vegetation

but it is also tricky to grow;
discuss your particulars with someone
before you begin

and so we read

I sew –
      & sow
we write

+

GOING TO SURVEY WALMART CONSTRUCTION FROM THE CREST OF PIONEER HILL

the populace is improving
with commercial merchandise picked up for a song

and some of us animals out here do live in the
(prairie, ocean, desert) besides

Re/inhabitory, Resurgent, Body-regional

Reinhabitation is a word used by ecologists to describe the process of becoming an inhabitant of one's bioregion ("life-place") through knowledge of natural boundaries, watershed, plants and animals, indigenous human history, etc.. Reinhabitation extends to restoring ecosystems damaged by human activities, by, for example, planting flowers to expand pollinator habitats on the edges of industrial farmscapes or wherever they are needed, wherever you happen to be (Obama's "Butterfly Corridor"), or restoring native plant communities in a particular ecosystem (Aldo Leopold). It is also a keyword for bioregionalism, which began as a reinhabitory lifeways movement in northern California in the 1970s (Gary Snyder, Ray Dasman, Peter Berg, etc.). Either way, there are some high demands that can come with claiming to be reinhabitory, whether these are for specialized scientific knowledge, or an ability to turn back to the land:

> Reinhabitory refers to the tiny number of persons who come out of the industrial societies (having collected or squandered the fruits of eight thousand years of civilization) and then start to turn back to the land, back to place. This comes for some with the rational and scientific realization of interconnectedness and planetary limits. But the actual demands of a life committed to a place, and living somewhat by the sunshine green-plant energy that is concentrating in that spot, are so physically and intellectually intense that it is a moral and spiritual choice as well. (Gary Snyder, "Reinhabitation," in *The Old Ways,* San Francisco: City Lights Books, 1977, p 65).

It is still possible to be re-inhabitory in this sense, but many of us don't live on that planet anymore, or we may choose (or not) to live in urban, suburban, exurban spaces. But we can creatively rework "re-inhabitory." Or maybe we can be, simply, inhabitory, proceed as a conscious inhabitant of a biotic community (Stephen Collis, "Notes Towards a Manifesto of the Biotariat"), which is to situate yourself in relation not to ecologically-irrelevant political boundaries, but to geographies, biomes, bioregions; to be where you are as it is, as you work towards what it can be. There is a rich reflexivity to the term *bioregion* – it is the place that holds *your* life, where you conduct the business of living, but it is also a place *of life* – as opposed to a "necroregions" (Joyelle McSweeney, *The Necropastoral*). How can a poetics serve life?

One enacts an ecology as they inhabit the relationship between their organism and its context; they enacts an ecology of their bioregion. How fluid is a poem? What does it risk overlooking in its rigidities? I know (or imagine) that what I inhabit through this relationship is not my Cartesian-isolated-subject self, but my ecologically-shaped self (i.e. interconnected). I let go of 'self' as source and release attention farther afield. Tuning my sensory organism, finding ways to accommodate that knowledge in poems. I want a wilding of 'self,' place, imagination. I want to challenge abstraction as the erasure of the real. See/honor what's every*here* – realization of bioregion/life-place can happen anywhere, if one pays attention. One can experience different possibilities of "I" or "self" (if we must think of our organism in terms of our familiar-isolated identity), or one can begin to identify the relations and perceptions that shape our understanding of 'place' and 'self' as separate or connected.

Poems don't restore habitats or ecosystems, but they can work on the level of self-place relation that is crucial to understanding them; they can be instances of attentiveness to place and the way mind/self imagines–and can reimagine–meanings, values, roles, goals, etc. As such they can enact the hand's-on work of developing inhabitant knowledge. Where does this get us, in the larger context of cataclysmic climatic instability? It entails investing (meaning, energy, hope) in a piece of something real to go, joined with one into our uncertain future. If one can imagine the importance of the integrity of the natural economy that exists in a place, then there is hope for the larger goal of environmental justice that stands for the rights of all beings to their lifeways on planet Earth. Gary Snyder: "The world of culture and nature, which is actual, is almost a shadow world now, and the insubstantial world of political and rarified economies is what passes for reality" ("The Place, The Region, and The Commons"). A poesis of the actual, an ecopoetics (re)turns to substance.

Resurgence is a concept from biology; it describes how organisms (plants and animals) respond to a "disturbance," any quick ecological change, such as farming. In our management of ecosystems, we block resurgence even though an ecosystem (and we humans) can't survive without it. When we block resurgence, destructive feral biologies erupt (killer fungi and other forms of blight). Poetic responses to human disturbances – to Anthropocene effects – are a form of positive resurgence. A resurgent ecopoetics embraces uncertainty, moving along its trajectory so poet/poem/poesis can become agents of social and material change. A resurgent ecopoetics arises in place, crosses boundaries, and consciously dwells on living an ecologically-implicated human life; it is bioregional in that it claims, and writes from and for a life-place. It is body-regional in that it begins with one's body as a site of knowledge, and to extend acuity, draws on other bodies of knowledge. Following Kaia Sand, it is "an inexpert investigation, a pedestrian inquiry" (*Remember to Wave*), wandering, making as it goes. I am inexpert, and I embrace an inexpertness that makes me mobile–that makes me reach out and collaborate as a way of knowing.

Process

I wanted a situated poetics, a making that accommodates other-than-human needs too, that could ward off erasures of senses of habitability, that reexamined and reinvented and helped rescale thinking about 21st century inhabitance. This felt pressing, given what we know, and don't, of species extinction, habitat loss, and extreme weather events. We draw sustenance and identity from our landscapes, but places as we know them are changing, and I wanted to begin with change. I began working in my landscape, emplaced, walking as a form of reading, an immersive whole-body translation of and into what's there, the give and resistance of it against the soles and the pores, the wind as it moves across the landscape's features of which you are now a part along with the small rattling leaf sounds of other animalkind. Writing within the convergences of myriad other forces and agents in the world, opening and closing the gates of attention, detecting/connecting took shape as language and form, reimagining/reinventing shapes and relationships. I opened up (my) human being and attention to the multiple, thinking along with these in time. Through poetic inquiries–"seeing" with the "worn-out angry eyes" of the last Columbia Basin Pygmy Rabbit, countermapping terrain portrayed in satellite imagery, re-imagining histories and geographies, on-site writing and reading along with squirrels and terns and snakes and sparrows and flickers–I came to read the place I live as, in the words of cultural landscape historian J.B. Jackson, a "field of perpetual conflict."

Perceptual Challenge

In your notebook, put down a line, vertically, to create 2 columns. Walk, notebook in hand, and on the left side of the line, list things you encounter, using all your senses–for example, "a dead branch," "smell of grass and mud" "rocks under foot," etc. Do this slowly, one thing at a time, and for each thing, on the right side of the line, jot down your thoughts corresponding to the thing. At the end of your walk, compare the two columns. Where do things and thoughts intertwine or influence one another, and how? Do this alone or with others. Do it at regular intervals and note changes over a period of time.

I would like to thank Eric Magrane, whose "Various Instructions for the Practice of Poetic Field Research" contains the kernel idea for this inquiry prompt, which I wrote for participants in a "Writing the Palouse River" workshop.

Suggesteds

"One rubric for right action might be to ask whether my work today is contributing to the restoration of natural and cultural diversity, toward natural subsistence for future primitives. Is what I'm doing contributing to knowledge that individuals require to live independently and harmoniously and harmlessly on Earth, or is it leading to more sameness, more dominance, more dependency, less joy, fewer species?"

Stephanie Mills, *In Service of the Wild: Restoring and Reinhabiting Damaged Land* (Boston: Beacon Press, 1995)

Metta Sáma

Metta Sáma is author of *After "Sleeping to Dream"/After After (Nous-Zot)*, *Nocturne Trio* (YesYes Books) & the forthcoming *le animal & other strange creatures* (Miel). She is Director of Center for Women Writers and Assistant Professor and Director of Creative Writing at Salem College.

Works

Another way of looking at a blackbird
(for Wendy Babiak)

the fledgling magnolias

   planted in an unneat row

      alongside Dupont Pkwy

        will one day hide nylon

           resin factories and the putrid smell

           the developers hope will be absorbed

              by thick green leaves slanted away

                  from thicker but more fragile white petals

  baby bulbs darker brown

      may petal and fall to the ground

      may not

        there are 13 dozen black birds shimmering

   in the chemical-drenched trees

an oil-smacked palette of amethyst

      they choke-caw in a concrete field of browning

  and dead magnolia bulbs

      how can I look at these petalled trees

  and the glittery wings of these so black

they're blue birds in the South and not see

unmerciful white hands strangling them

branch by sorrowful branch

The open field: Lynchburg, VA

Chicken   whitened stiff sculpted frame frozen

      stomach a gourd

               head tilted on a white washed tree

      blue bottles stuffed in branched necks

*

              the cemetery bees do they absorb pleasure

from hind legs to heavy abdomens honey

      bees mason bees leaf-cutting bees painted

white boxes hand planted flowers every bee

      sucks pollinates no soldier bees   no broken necks

*

      a six pack's leftover polyethylene
        a black necked stilt
              a newly strangled neck

*

the man tells me his grandfather's hands sometimes tightened ropes around
weeping necks

*

            bitumen stained mouths unnatural disasters slaves
        buried on one side of the cemetery Confederates'
              flags mark their own headstones' necks

*

everything is painted here even the dulled chains on this quaint tree swing
come with no memories no breached branches no trees exposing necks

Tributaries

what hands toss these

bodies over

bridges   my body

heavy   with hefted

roped necks bulleted

palms & foreheads & mouths

emptied of impulse

face-down faces

loess lungs

breath   slump

internal

deformation

sheath fold

muscled bodies

emptied   breaths

into my mouth   rivered

their hair   sand

their feet turn   sand

their backs   brains

water-logged depositories

immersion artifacts

skin like a washer-woman
"   "   goose
"   "   bar of soap

emptied of memory   salt

their tongues

salt

their cocks

salt

their loaded breasts –

now their bodies are my bodies

fluvial

and my body

their   memories

lying   in me   releasing me into them

into

open

our mouths   open   our mouths   open

lungs   open   stories   mouths   float open & course   &

Poetics

I have a new visitor to my office, a young campus police officer. She's visited me twice in two days & talked with me about writing, mostly, but today we talked about the end of the world as we know it. "Scientists say we're in the sixth mass extinction," I say. She shrugs, "There's nothing we can do about it now so why fight it?" When I taught at Goddard I'd look forward to the video and talk that one of the faculty would give about climate change. One year, a faculty member got so angry that she bellowed, "Oh my god, C-, there's nothing we can do about it now! Why do you always have to depress us about this?" I didn't agree with my fellow faculty member, nor do I agree with the young officer; but, I understand their position: The end is nigh, okay, keep it moving. Some people prefer pessimism to reality. When the officer left my office, I saw a news item about President Obama working to reveal the names of members of extremist groups, including the KKK. Before this news came out, another item flashed on the screen: a woman, Bree Newsome, had climbed to the top of the flagpole at the statehouse in Columbia, SC and removed the Confederate flag. Nothing in the world is constant but change. The one time I saw Majora Carter live, I was living in a tiny town in Indiana. I bought a car to live in that town. It was a big difference from living in Madison, a town I moved to without a car; I'd sold my 12-year old SUV in a yard sale when one of the faculty members at the university told me Madison was antagonistic to cars. I loved not having a car, except on the weekends when I wanted to visit Milwaukee or Chicago or Oshkosh. In Indiana, the closet grocery store to my new apartment was five miles away; the pharmacy was even further; my bank was across the street from the pharmacy. This town had no bus service. I couldn't stop thinking about my choice, to purchase a gas efficient car, one that wasn't electric, wasn't even hybrid. When Majora Carter came to town, I was depressed. I'd broken it off with my love over the telephone. I forced myself out of the house to see Majora Carter. It wasn't every day I saw a black woman in this town. During her talk, she said she'd visited Europe and gotten some great ideas about sustainability. Her focus was not only on "greening" the U.S., but also providing jobs for people. Sustain the person & sustain the environment. Sustain the person. Sustain the environment. Environmental justice. Every time I think about the environment, I think about racism. Every time I think about racism, I think about the magnolia trees that have been planted in front of the Dupont factory in Chattanooga. Every time I think about the Dupont factory in Chattanooga, I think of plush carpets. Every time I think of plush carpets, I think of asthma. Every time I think of asthma, I think of New York City. Every time I think of New York City, I think of my mother who moved to NYC as a very young woman in the 1950s & was in Boston by the early 1960s & back in Chattanooga in the late 1960s. Racism followed her everywhere. And poverty. And misogyny. One year, my mother commented on how big apples were getting. Decades later, she said she'd never had fresh ginger. She was in the hospital post-surgery. She'd had a good chunk of colon cut out. I made her ginger tea. The doctor was angry that she wouldn't pump morphine into her body. She hates psychotropic drugs. Her body is a body. Bodies used to be temples. Now bodies are dumpsites landfills things to drill into. Nothing in the world is constant but change. We can change all of this if we see the longview if we see beyond ourselves to the next generation and the next and the next and the next. And the next—

Process

Several years ago on a bus trip from Binghamton, NY to Port Authority in Manhattan, I was joined by a tall white man who, upon sitting, spread his legs. It didn't take long for his leg to touch mine. He was wearing shorts; I was wearing a short skirt. For a quick second, I looked at his blond hairy leg against my brown hairy leg. And just as quickly as our knees touched, he jerked his body away from me. Not just his leg. His body. My memory says he nearly fell from his seat. This touch-jerk away action went on for the entire two hours remaining of our trip & while I wanted to say to him, it's fine, don't worry about it, I was too immersed in what was happening in front of my face: our thighs & knees had been transformed to lines and lines of text, converging then suddenly breaking & becoming their own distinct shapes. When I looked out of the window, I didn't see the end of Pennsylvania and the beginning of New Jersey but the end of U.S. slavery and the beginning of Jim Crow, the end of Jim Crow and the beginning of the post-Civil Rights Era. It was 2005 or 2006, and there I was on a bus wondering if the young white man next to me jerked himself away from me, a black woman, or me, a human who he accidentally touched. Where was I? How had I so easily come undone by that jerking away? How had I so easily transported myself to a time I hadn't lived in, to a time I had lived in? How had the world so quickly turned black and white? So dull? Why did my mind leap to think this white man wanted racial separation?

Because my spirit believed it.

Because my heart believed it.

Because my history supported it.

History is a vampire a night gladiolus a bear.

Our knees touching and separating touching and separating those words touching and separating touching and separating. Two knees two needs two languages two sets of words touching and blending seamlessly. The touch sends a spark to the brain. The body reacts in jerks and shifts. But what was it exactly? The writeable but unwritten.

Years later, I'd be on a different bus in a different country sitting next to my beloved thinking in French listening in Spanish speaking in English, and there too a poem writeable but unwritten. A visual world of fractures of fragments of sparks and shocks and . . .

Years later, I sat on a bed in a hotel in another country my beloved had the television on listening to music being sung in a language neither of us spoke on the phone my sister said my mother had had a stroke a small one she said a small one and the words again a tongue of words sliding from the mouth blurry muddy an arm of words letters falling to the ground cracking. Writeable but unwritten. A visual world—

Perceptual Challenge

It is 1971, and Mirek says: The struggle of man against power is the struggle of memory against forgetting. – Milan Kundera

I believe it was in Milan Kundera's *The Book of Laughter and Forgetting* that the narrator talks about the fall of Czechoslovakia to Russia, that this fall was most noted by the removal of all signage in Czech, replaced by signage in Russian, by Czech restaurants being pushed out to make way for Russian restaurants, by statues of important persons in Czech history being replaced by statues of Stalin. The act of forgetting and remembering, as enacted by a new regime. Forgetting comes at a cost. Historical amnesia, I first heard it called, by Angela Y. Davis. Remembering, too, comes at a cost. What happens when we walk down a street clearly named after a person? Why are so many MLK, Jr streets, avenues, drives, in the most economically depressed parts of town? What do we wish to remember of MLK, Jr? Why are airports and interstates named for Ronald Reagan and George Bush (Sr)? What are we to remember of their actions, their policies? Every time I make a trip back to visit my family in Chattanooga, I seek out new histories, new historical markers, new lands where canons have been placed or removed, the new tourist route for the Trail of Tears. How do our perceptions shift when we purposely set out to see the real place, the real people, the real stories, the real tragedies, the real devastations, the real corruptions? Who remembers the landscape before interstates? What did Corpus Christi smell like before the oil refinery factories set up shop? What would happen if we committed to finding just one street or one park or one statue or one building that is named for someone and sitting in front of that building or statue or sitting on the sidewalk of that street or sitting in that park for an hour a week, catching the feel of the place, eventually heading to the library to research someone, to remember, with full awareness? Pull to the side of the road when you see signage that strikes you as odd, Negro Mountain, for example or Polish Mountain or Savage River, pull to the side of the road, and make some notes to research these sites, to know and then to remember.

Suggesteds

Tamiko Beyer, "Queer::Eco::Poetics" manifesto

Elizabeth D. Blum, *Love Canal Revisted: Race, Class & Gender in Environmental Activism*

Majora Carter, Ted Talk on Urban Renewal
http://www.ted.com/talks/majora_carter_s_tale_of_urban_renewal

David Cook, article on the Walnut Street Bridge in Chattanooga, TN
http://www.timesfreepress.com/news/opinion/columns/story/2015/jan/18/cook-what-justice-ed-johnson/283290/

Robin McKie, article in *The Guardian* about water shortages
http://www.theguardian.com/environment/2015/mar/08/how-water-shortages-lead-food-crises-conflicts

Rebecca Skloot, *The Immortal Life of Henrietta Lacks*

Kaia Sand

Kaia Sand is the author of three books of poetry: *A Tale of Magicians Who Puffed Up Money that Lost its Puff* (Tinfish Press, forthcoming); *Remember to Wave* (Tinfish Press, 2010); *interval* (Edge Books, 2004), named Small Press Traffic Book of the Year. She is co-author with Jules Boykoff of *Landscapes of Dissent: Guerrilla Poetry and Public Space* (Palm Press, 2008), and her poetry comprises the text for two books in Jim Dine's Hot Dream series (Steidl Editions, 2008). Most recently her writing has been anthologized in *Toward. Some. Air* (Banff Centre Press 2015); *Make it True* (Leaf Press 2015); and *Out of Nowhere* (Reality Street 2015); and she collaborated on an essay with Allison Cobb for *Tracking/Teaching: On Documentary Poetics* (Essay Press 2015). She works across genres and media, dislodging poetry from the book into more unconventional contexts, including the *Remember to Wave* poetry walks; the Happy Valley Project, an investigation of housing foreclosures and financial speculation that included a magic show. From 2013-2015, she shared an artist residency with Garrick Imatani at the City of Portland Archives and Records Center

from 2013-2015, a public art commission through the Regional Arts and Culture Council. During the residency, they investigated surveillance documents the Portland Police kept on activists in the late 1960s, 1970s, and early 1980s. Sand has also participated in group and solo exhibitions of her poetry. She is the resident poet at the Portland State University Honors College, where she teaches. For the fall 2015 she worked in an artist residency at Largo das Artes in Rio de Janeiro. She documents work at kaiasand.net.

Works

tiny arctic ice

Inhale, exhale
7 billion people breathing
Some of us in captivity
Our crops far-flung
Prison is a place where children sometimes visit
Jetted from Japan, edamame is eaten in England
Airplane air is hard to share
I breathe in what you breathe out, stranger
Tantalum is mined by hand for cell phones
Sometimes children dig it
We send tea leaves to distant friends
Containers of discarded computers float toward Hong Kong
Neighbors bike to build RVs at nightfall
Araucana chickens won't lay eggs in captivity
Airplanes of roses lift above Quito mountains
Cultivated from crocuses in La Mancha, saffron suffuses my rice
Women cook circuit boards for gold flecks in Guiyu
You touch what I discard
Status updates stack up in Prineville warehouses
Data, coal-powered and far-flung
When the fish diminish, folks find jobs in prisons
Sometimes children visit
Crouched on mounds of monitors, boys capture copper with magnets
Airplanes of microchips lift above Cascade mountains
I touch what you assemble
Terminator seeds are hard to share
Bonfires burn motherboards into Agbogbloshie air
Sometimes children breathe it
And the fish diminish
The roses, the tea, and the edamame, far-flung
The roses, the tea, the microchips, and you
You breathe in what I disregard, friend

Process

If the Pickpocket Loved You / an essay in six parts

i.
the ruptured tendon
A tendon tethers muscle to bone, offering a little stretch, too.
My Achilles tendon manages that role, but it ruptured once, and while this is typically a sports injury, mine was a poetry injury. I was at Bard College, participating in a class on pedagogy through the Institute of Language and Thinking. We were creatively responding to "Connoisseurs of Chaos" by Wallace Stevens. Fancying myself a high jumper from my middle-school glory days, I took bounding skips until I heard a bang, like a gunshot. It was my own body blowing out, an internal explosion, something no one else heard. I dipped my fingers where my left Achilles tendon once was, and my fingers plunged into a chasm. Palpable, simple.

The word "tendon" shares the root *tendere* with the word "attention." Tendere, Latin, to stretch.

While my attention tethers muscles to bone, offering a little stretch, as a human being a decade and a half into this new millennium, my attention ruptures, too. It is fractured; it splits this way, that way. It funnels intensively toward focal points.

For the first time since that strange poetry injury now nine years ago, I return to the poem "Connoisseurs of Chaos." In my group's creative interpretation that day, I was "skipping like spring," and now I locate the line about spring: "If all the green of spring was blue, and it is." Later in the poem: "The squirming facts exceed the squamous mind,/ If one may say so. And yet relation appears,/ A small relation expanding like the shade/Of a cloud on sand, a shape on the side of a hill."

With so much distraction, attention takes tending, which seems redundant— "tending" rooted in "attending," "attention." But perhaps not. Notice the noticing. Attend to attention. The cloud is a shape on the side of a hill.

ii.
the pickpocket

The pickpocket knows how to attend to the attention of another.

Several years ago, my little family—Jules, Jessi & I—grew smitten with videos of a performative pickpocket named Apollo Robbins. He was, after all, not just someone who steals a person's wallet without their noticing. He also explains how he does it: "It is all about the choreography of people's attention," he said in a *New Yorker* magazine profile.

Robbins demonstrates how particular movements of attention work: if he gestures his hand in straight line, the watcher's attention springs back to a point of origin (as if attention were stretched like a rubberband that rebounds) but if he gestures in the shape of arc, the watcher's eyes follow his hand to the end of the arc, and stay there. He successfully moves the watcher's attention.

I have described poetry as the opposite of a soundbite: an attempt at sustained attention. But I am curious, too, how poetry can be a *movement* of attention. What can this pickpocket teach me? How do I move attention like an arc?

In my second poetry collection, *Remember to Wave*, I wrote "elsewhere/erstwhile/here in this time/there are so many/of us on this planet." I am interested in how poetry can move attention *elsewhere* and *erstwhile*, and how that might be done. One approach I've tried is through isolating tiny details that mostly are drowned in information and geography, a starfish in a rising sea.

Another approach is through situational rhymes: in *Remember to Wave*, Portable on Demand storage units serve as monuments to possession, linked through the concept of possession (as well as shared space), to the traumatic history, seventy years earlier. Japanese Americans, lined up with only their suitcases, were ordered by executive order to bring only what they could carry to that sudden-prison in North Portland, so near where Portable on Demand storage units now stack.

This connective thinking, the "elsewhere & erstwhile," uses the poetic tools of metaphor—the comparisons—and metonymy—the details. Each of these is a re-working of attention, and I'm curious, hopeful, that what I've come to describe as the erstwhile & the elsewhere— a connective thinking that moves through space and time—can be a movement of attention—arcing, parabolic, swooping...

iii.
the ledger

As a daunted human creature of this world, I write down its details. The final sum is elusive, is abundant, spills over the form. Poem as ledger, adding up. *Ledger, perhaps from the Dutch ligger and legger—to lie or lay—to bring down from the upright position.*

Ledgers are about stacking horizontal things, timber in scaffolding, a rod across thatch, a slab stone over a grave. Setting lines upon lines, an open-ended equation.

I am the keeper of accounts repeats Irena Klepfisz in her poem "Bashert."
This and this and this. Watching. Researching. Collecting.

The ledger-form is a-being–in-the-world for me, a getting-it-down, a hopeful linguistic, lyrical mathematics. "Tiny Arctic Ice" is a ledger without summation, tracking *things* that pass fleetingly by me, *things* that logjam in my possession. I began it in 2006: *Jetted from Japan, edamame is eaten in England*, I wrote. *Airplane air is hard to share.* For the past nine years, the poem has lived beside me, accumulating lines, a poem of occasional witness, that moves attention from where I am to the La Mancha crocuses, the Prineville warehouses, the Agbogbloshie air.

And now, as I write this, I am in Brazil, and from here I cast my poetic attention. I look up each word I care about, so I look up *ledger. Ledger* is *livro-razão*. Book-reason. Razão: reason, cause, ratio, proportion, right, justice, argument, motive.

The ledger offers stacking, building; the razão offers relations of cognition. What adds up; what doesn't. Poetic math.

iv.
the intimate unknown

Things vibrate with relation. Nostalgia tugs.

What about a kind of nostalgia for that which I do not know—the intimate unknown? If nostalgia is a longing for the familiar, rooted in the Greek for *return home*, what about a longing for what is unfamiliar, to turn erstwhile & elsewhere, a political nostalgia unfolded on itself? Not to acquire or conquer, but to make a space for that which I do not, and cannot, know.

How can *things* vibrate with *that* kind of relation, connecting me through their commodity chains, connecting me to whence they come and whence they go? To other human lives?

In my first collection of poetry, *interval*, I grappled with the idea of the intimate unknown, an eye on the future. How might we make decisions based on what happens to future generations? My poetic sequence, *Progeny*, took as its interlocutor those "yet to be born" as Otto Renee Castillo put it. I've continued along these lines, most recently thinking about concrete work of activists from the vantage point of now living in the future they were working toward. Lloyd Marbet tirelessly worked to block nuclear plants from being sited in Oregon, activism I explored with him in a poetic sequence, "So He Raised His Hand," a sequence sited in the future of his activism in which, indeed, those nuclear plants never came to exist.

But there are other areas of life I somehow must love and never know. Jen Coleman's poetry is instructive on this. "Census of the Fishes" asserts *presente!* for various species, from familiar to unfamiliar, reminding me there are plenty of animals I don't recognize: "count rabbitfish, pigfish, roosterfish, and seahorses" she writes.

> count the puffers
> count milkfish
>
> count emperors or scavengers
>
> fairy basslets, catfish, thornyheads and thornfishes
> ribbonbearers, bonnethead, menhaden and ocean-basses,
> jacksonshark, armored gurnards,
>
> count up the lovely hatchetfish.

The poem calls for a "serious census of the fishes," and charms me with its softly melancholic closure, "whether the wish exists." Poem as lament and policy request at once. Her intimate unknown is the deep ocean life that humans will mostly never experience, but hopefully might act lovingly toward.

Lara Durback's chapbook, with its attention to many *elsewher's* of hoarding, helped me come to see mounds of e-waste and garbage as my displaced hoard:

> In Guiyu, China, Hoarders are called surviving. Surviving by collecting e-waste. Children do it. They have to. She sits in a pile of phone cords. (Remember those?) He sits in a pile of the first iPods (Rember those?) He melts the box-shaped TV to get the metals that are worth something. (Remember those?) Now breathe the air with them.

Everything I've ever used is my displaced hoard. It is in relation to me. My existence is *elsewhere.* This is what some of the details of *Tiny Arctic Ice* attempt: flicker with life beyond my community toward my responsibility. I dangle an ethernet cord, no longer "useful" to me. I shut the laptop frozen with glitches. I am connected to the boys in Agbobbloshie, the woman in Guiyu.

v.
the heartache

Just months before his death late in 2009, a video of Dennis Brutus reading "Longing" was posted to YouTube. Seated before brilliant orange flowers, Brutus opens his book, *A Simple Lust*—first published in 1963—to "Longing," and reads the poem built of four tercets. He is reading on a patio, and midway through his reading, rain falls briefly, eerily rhyming with the closing phrase of the poem, "rains of poison."

"Longing" is not a new poem. Rather, he explains in the video, he was recasting a poem from 1960. Had he not framed it otherwise, I might have read "Longing" as addressing anti-apartheid struggles, as some of Brutus's other poems did during that period. But in this video, Brutus describes how the initial subject of the poem was lost love, and now, he wishes us to read it through the context of unmitigated climate disruption.

As the Copenhagen Accords neared, and as his death neared, he read that poem aloud, his line "My heart knows now such devastation" no longer as a line arrowed toward an individual beloved, but now, a line arrowed toward all of us, all of us in the future. Not a longing toward the familiar, but a longing, a love, for all the people he does not know, but for whom he devoted so much activism addressing environmental and economic injustice.

There is a coiled energy of a love lyric from its intensive gaze on another, the beloved. By explicitly reframing the poem as one that is concerned with environmental justice, Brutus takes that coiled energy, that intensive gaze, and makes it social. This is especially powerful as a choice near the end of his life. Brutus moves the poem from addressing the beloved, the intimate known, to addressing all the other people he will never know who will suffer the affects of unmitigated climate change, the intimate unknown.

He offers us a poetic capacity for social heartache.

vi.
the recast poem

Dennis Brutus recast his poem, "Longing." He chose a new context, asked his readers to bring that into their reading. In London in 2012, Teresia Teaiwa did something similar. She originally created "crisis poem #1" for a Burn this CD' collection that Alice Te Punga Somerville and Maraea Rakuraku produced in response to the terror raids in New Zealand in 2007:

> iwishi couldw riteth epoemi
>
> wantor eadina timeo fcrisis
>
> {repeat}

the poem begins. But then she performed the poem, which splinters and fractures its language, an interruption to regularly scheduled programming, an impossible utterance—as part of the Poetry Parnassus event, "The Pacifica & the Climate Change." She ushered in *that* new context, recasting the poem.

Reading the poem as having a "long biography," Peter Middleton considers in his book *Distant Reading* the "poem as a probably unfinished, and even possibly interminable, business, and that will be its value and pleasure, a continuing struggle, a renewing music" (23). It is with this idea of a poem having a "long biography" that I approach *Tiny Arctic Ice.*

It is my ledger without summation, so I revise the poem, again and again. I build it materially anew, creating new choreographies of reading. Early on, I built the poem as a teabag—Green Tea imported from China—one page per line, small pages, small gestures, the poem built from the far-flung trade of things.

At another point, I had traveled to Switzerland and read it at Cabaret Voltaire. Considering the extravagance of air-travel, I recast the poem as a series of paper airplanes, working with Kathrin Schaeppi to translate, and write new lines in Swiss German, and my daughter and Susana Gardner's daughter tossed the airplanes into the crowd. I've also recast this as a bouquet of local flowers, contrasted with the *airplanes of roses flown over Quito mountains* in the poem, and as an accordion of pages made from the *Financial Times* of London.

How might a poem continue to live in the world? To age as we age? To embrace new cities, new recessions, new scars?

As I write this essay, I turn back to "Tiny Artic," my faithful poem companion. A phrase I read recently from a scientist—"the swimming dead"—is seeding a new line, I know. He was referring to the salmon swimming to their death in too-warm

Oregon rivers. During my episodes that area kind of unsettled reverie, syntax shuffles and swishes, becoming a line.

That poem, finished in each moment, is changing in the next.

Note:

Some bits of this essay were developed in the *Jacket II* column I shared with Jules Boykoff, "Moxie Politic" and on the Ooligan Press blog.

Bibliography
Brutus, Dennis. "Longing." *A Simple Lust*. London: Heinemann, 1973

Coleman, Jen. "Census of the Fishes." Pacific Poetries Feature. *Jacket II.* 2011 *http://jacket2.org/poems/poems-jen-coleman*

Durback, Lara. *Hoarders*. Oakland: Made for Dusie Kollektiv with NoNo Press, 2011.

Teaiwa, Teresia. "crisis poem #1" *Burn This CD*. Produced by Alice Te Punga Somerville and
Maraea Rakuraku, New Zealand, 2007

Perceptual Challenge

Begin with the Wallace Stevens' line: "If all the green of spring was blue, and it is."
Borrow his syntax, begin to look around, and write:
If all of the cold of winter were a sun, and it is
If all the noise of the traffic were a whistle, and it is
If all the ache of my spine were a touch, and it is

——————————————————————

How might a detail from your immediate surroundings move you into the past? Or
across geography? Consider the chair you sit in, the bottle on the table, the sign
across the street....

————————————————

What odd (i.e. some stuff of poetry) lists might you keep? Obsessive lists. Quirky
lists. The crumbs & the crud & the crystallizations. This is not a neutral ledger. Just
as some people must "settle the accounts," you too see what is out-of-whack,
destructive, hopeful.

————————————

I created this poem as an Ars Poetic to begin *Remember to Wave*. How might you
poetically respond to these questions?

> How do I notice
> what I don't notice
>
> How do I notice
> what I don't know
> I don't notice?
> Inexpert, I
> notice with the attention
> and drifting inattention
> of poetry
> Inexpert, I
> investigate
> Inexpert, I
> walk, and walk

————————————

Consider how poetic forms or traditional tropes might be charged anew. How might a love lyric or elegy or lament respond? What intimate unknowns might you address?

———————

Return to something you have previously written, and think about how it might live as your contemporary. Perform it so that you sweep in the *now* of place or time. Maybe you change or add language. Maybe you witness how a new context changes the poem.

Kate Schapira

Kate Schapira is the author of six full-length books of poetry, most recently *FILL: A Collection* (Trembling Pillow Press, 2016), a collaboration with Erika Howsare. Her 11th chapbook, *Someone Is Here*, is out with Projective Industries. She lives in Providence, RI, where she teaches at Brown University and with Frequency Writers. Summer 2016 was her third summer offering Climate Anxiety Counseling: http://climateanxietycounseling.wordpress.com.

Works

NOTES FROM THE BOOTH: CLIMATE ANXIETY COUNSELING 2014

Day 8: Are the poles really melting, and it's gonna raise the seas? So we're gonna lose Manhattan, Nag's Head? It doesn't matter! There's no anxiety --you'll be dead, I'll be dead, and new life will come.

Everything will die
but where and when I care
doesn't matter what's matter
what's the matter darling
why are you crying
what does any of it matter
the sleep state of energy
butterflies with dreamy names
are they identical
what if one was lost
what if one was that same thing
named twice would you still
care would you care then
would you cry your eyes out
would it matter then
would you be in a state
would your eyes move

Day 11: Speaking for myself, I have huge climate anxiety. It's the biggest problem we're facing, and we should be devoting huge amounts of resources to it. Instead, they're still having debates about whether to give oil and gas leases in national parks. We're putting the Earth, the country, and the climate at risk by looking for oil and gas. It won't be helped by a piecemeal approach. And I'm not hopeful. I don't think governments have the guts to face up to oil and gas interests. I think we're doomed. And my biggest concern is not so much for humans--I'm worried that we'll make it impossible for anything else to survive. We don't begin to take this seriously enough. Most people are ignorant about it. It involves making sacrifices, using less water -- my parents lived in Southern California, and people moved there from the Northeast and the Midwest and brought their habits with them. They kept building houses, kept building golf courses, and development always won out over concerns over resources.

Do you talk to people about this?

People I know, or people I don't know?

Both.

To people I know, I talk about it a lot. I go to a Unitarian church, many of whose members are left-leaning. But the church can't even get recycling right. I'm discouraged on a personal and political and countrywide level. They say gas is cleaner, but if getting the gas requires the kind of stuff that's going on in Canada--I think if we devoted sufficient money to alternatives, in 10 years we could prevent a catastrophe, but we don't have the will.

I don't think we have
the guts but we do to
face but we have faces
up to the bottoms of our
hairlines the water we're
deepening in calling
out to us in the night
making us get up
there's no one to turn
to at the bend
of the intestines we share
with all vertebrates no one
to tighten the drip we say
it's how we're made
we're made end to end
the last body type standing
it's how we make ourselves
and where fear takes up
its home translucent and folded
up with the microfauna
their mouths to feed
their points to tip
us without knowing
their names into again
how intimate and how
transitory to be
moved this way a wave
washing up at the ends
the multiple ends of the earth

Day 19: The future is here. I don't have to imagine it. There are extreme environmental events right now that are happening to people I know. The flood in Boulder -- cataclysmic. Nothing like that had happened during my lifetime. I think in terms of water movement, flood water, estuarial water, and what I imagine is a worsening and a picking up of tempo. It happens gradually--though less gradually--and people adapt to it. It's not noticeable enough.

I go from the extreme cases
to the trembling water
where the edge is anything
that can happen to keep
us tipping and sickening
motion-sick murderers
clues to undoing
our own endemics
a dizzy spell overtakes
the upper air and the highest
highs and the lowest lows
aren't the best to look at
what does a good neighbor do
how does a good neighbor rule
on whether you shelter
them or let them slip
like the part of the net
I would grip if I could
I would pause for extremity
to bear down on me
to be borne like somebody's
undeniable body into the very house
do they even bring people home
when they die anymore who knows
I don't know I guess I'll find out
who has washed and who has ordered
who can teach me how to do it
who can take me under
the shadow of their wing

THE WEAKEST LINK: AN EELGRASS ASSERTION

Day 7: The environment itself. The water, the rise of the water. The climate shifting--just the climate changing. Is that all right? Do you have what you need?

My ecopoetics works. It labors to make the softest, the most vulnerable, into a site of protection instead of a site of violence. It's looking for a place to lean, to heave, our emphasis, our attention and our care into the service of the weakest link, the most easily dropped-out, shat-on, forgotten, believing that if we tend these, we tend the entire web. To do this, we have to listen--listen with all the senses and instruments available to us--and act on what we hear. My ecopoetics works to transform me into a listening instrument, an amplifying instrument. It works to reveal interdependence, mutuality, fragility, loss, and sustenance.

The poetics of many of our present systems serve the strongest links, the nodes with the most cushion, the greatest access, the most resources. These systems involve all people and things--they wrap around us, they run through us, they "want" us to believe that they are the only systems that do so. But they are not.

It's not accurate, even in poetry, to say that a system "wants", any more than it's right to say a tree is "helping" us by respirating carbon dioxide and exhaling oxygen. And yet we are helped, we inhale. The tree is not working for us, but its work reaches us; it counts. Systems of sustenance, of kinship, of stimulation, of care, involve us too. My ecopoetics works to reveal them, to tint them, to smell them out, to listen to them.

Listen to the water in the Narrow River, thick with sea lettuce fed by nitrogen runoff from people's lawns. The algae chokes off the eelgrass: thin rooted ribbons tearing loose. The algae is strong and numerous, it's doing fine at the moment. That won't go on forever, but we're not going to worry about the sea lettuce. We are going to worry about the eelgrass. We are going to listen to the eelgrass's problems.

The eelgrass would like cooler water with less nitrogen in it. Go up the slope of the watershed, then, where we'll need less lawn fertilizer to flow down. Go to the garden center. The people working there still need to eat; I need to take care of them too. They can sell no more fertilizer, because of the eelgrass. Don't I care about the people at the garden center? But the eelgrass and the people at the garden center are not nearly as much at odds, as far apart, as the people at the garden center are from the company that makes the fertilizer and sells it to the store where they work, the national gas company that heats their premises, and the computer company. To the computer company, the people at the garden center and the eelgrass have everything in common: they are material. They are casualties. They are fuel.

And so some of my poems are poems of grief and fury for the people and nonhuman creatures that the poetics of these greedy, hasty systems make use of, dispose of; to make room for weakness, for fragility, for loss. Against the systemic poetics of use, value and worth, the poetics of fuel, I propose and attempt a poetics of care and illumination, a poetics that tends and fosters and strengthens, that carves out new channels and runnels of habit, that allows care and sustenance to flow from those living beings who can best offer it to those living beings who need it most, on their own terms. Poetry is good at this--at recognizing and valuing multiple systems and relationships at once. Relationships of sound, of history, of similarity, of radiance, of devouring, of symbiosis, of accident, of complication, of comparison, of dissolution, of sustenance.

Eelgrass has plenty to do: rooting, shading, breathing. That's what it's good at. Humans can't do those things nearly as well, but we can be pretty good at tending, at taking into account, at responding quickly to stimuli, at moving around fast. The eelgrass, by doing what it would do anyway, holds our coasts together, it mingles the waters, it shelters the infancy of multiple species. It doesn't center us, but we can center it; what can we do, on purpose, that would offer fair exchange for what it gives us by accident? A person can write in words, "This is what I need in order not to die, in order to fully live." Listening to this person is the beginning, but only the beginning, of trying to meet that need, to mend the net.

My ecopoetics knows perfectly well that the eelgrass, the algae, and the people don't need the same things. It acknowledges that some parts of the web need more, but if they are tended, the web can be whole. We can extend our "we" without blurring it into sameness. My ecopoetics is sentimental, sensitive, limited, radial. That's why it needs your ecopoetics. Its edges are permeable, allowing it to fill with contamination and failure. It works to reveal what's already here.

Process

Day 23: Land use, the various ways it spirals down into other issues: agriculture, water quality, wildlife, urban living. I've been overwhelming myself by listening to climate news. I just want to curl up in my apartment and not do anything, I feel like I can't do anything. I don't even know what I would do. How do you narrow it down to a place where you can start?

I cried through the winter of 2014 about the effects of climate change, present and possible future. When spring came, I spent three hours a day, five days a week, Kennedy Plaza — opposite Providence's bus terminal, and just outside a big downtown park—with a Lucy-from-*Peanuts* style booth, inviting people who stopped to share their anxieties with me. "What is this?" they would say.

"So the thing I'm most anxious about right now is how the changing climate is gonna affect the world, and especially Rhode Island, because I live here and I love it here. So I wanted to find out if other people were anxious about that, or what they're anxious about. Is there anything you're anxious about, that's pressing on your mind?"

Sometimes they laughed or snorted and walked away, and sometimes they stayed to talk. I asked if I could write down what they said, and sometimes I responded, or asked more questions. When no one was talking with me, I wrote poems using their words as starting points, or make more cards to give away--little drawings of our fellow Rhode Island organisms on the front and a link to the project website and other ecologically engaged organizations on the back, including where I would send their 5-cent donations. Sometimes they recognized the plant or animal on the card, and got excited, and told me about it: a woodpecker whose noise annoyed them, a mushroom they had gathered in the woods, a plant they used as medicine. A place where they felt strong instead of helpless.

The poems I wrote during this time are the sites of their helplessness, fury, grief and fear, as well as mine. I wrote them fast, and I haven't revised them very much. While I listened and talked with other people, they kept me calm and kind, focused on the people I was listening to. People spoke to me about feelings they thought they had to shoulder by themselves, in addition to the real circumstances that brought the feelings out, and seemed to leave feeling that they weren't as alone as they thought they were.

From the project's beginning, I wanted to invite, listen and respond to any kind of anxiety, not just climate ones. Doing this work of listening, and the reading and listening and thinking I've done since, brought me to understand that many of the seemingly "non-climate" concerns--one person's need for a safe place to stay, another's shame at her need to use food stamps, a third's grief for a friend's suicide-- were also ecological: the fears and frustrations of people involved in and swamped by systems of use, profit, and violence.

The people who did speak to me directly about climate change and its effects revealed a stymied hunger for action. Destructive systems involved them and yet they had no access, could imagine neither gripping those systems in order to change them nor any other way of living. The next phase of Climate Anxiety Counseling will practice those imaginations. I'll ask people who talk with me to also respond to each other's fears with a restored, re-storied version of the future, to answer circumstances as well as feelings, to imagine stories with each other at the center.

Perceptual Challenge

Listen

with all the methods available to you. Listen by reading the Twitter timelines of Black women, trans women, disabled people calling out for basic, practical recognitions of their irreducible particularity and humanity, demanding to exist safely in public and in private. Listen by noting the yellowing of the spruce needles on the tree near your house, by researching what the causes might be if you don't already know. Listen in your city, noting who goes where freely, training yourself to see absences, holes; listen to what grows, what shades, what cracks, what crumbles. Listen to your own voice, how you speak to people, what you ask; listen to your silences and what fills them, what you make room for.

Take inventory

of yourself as a node, of where you are in the web, in the net, in the globe, in the cloud. Write your answers here:

Who and what sustains you? Who and what do you depend on?

Who and what do you sustain? Who and what depends on you?

What flows toward you? What do you have to strive for?

What flows away from you? What do you have to work to give?

What can you spare, share, offer? What do you do well?

What do you lack? Where do you need to learn?

What is closed to you? Where do you see dead ends?

Where do you have access? Where can you open a way?

Draw a map

of these connections. Show yourself yourself in context. Draw the lines of supply and the trajectories of harm: what bypasses you, stops with you, passes through you? Mark the absences, the zones of loss, the wounds in the map, the sites of protection, the possibilities for regeneration. Draw on what you've heard and what you know. Draw it on paper, or in mud, or with chalk on pavement. Make this version of the map physical. Let it be lumpy, textured, various, wet. Make a new kind of mark to show the relations and re-directions you want to work for. Send me a picture of your map, if you're willing: publiclycomplex@gmail.com.

Re-Story

by both writing and acting, using your map as a guide.

Follow the lines you drew toward the acts of resistance and restoration that are truly within your power.

Follow them toward people whose needs, as spoken by them, you can help to meet, and toward people with whom you can act in unison.

Follow them toward systems and structures that operate with care, in measure, in full knowledge of interlaced survival.

Follow them into the presence of the nonhuman world, along the movement of the air, at the meristems of growth, into the heat of decay.

Follow them like a watercourse, like a course of action, like a way of setting to work.

Here is one more anxiety that someone shared with me. Write the events and actions that protect this person, that meet their fears, that restore their portion of the web; keep them possible in science, but otherwise imagine everything you want.

Day 5: I'm worried about the environment in the big picture, but I don't have time to think about that in my own life right now. I have to hustle what I can to take care of my child and me.

Suggesteds

Day 25: My anxiety is that people don't realize it's real.

How did you come to realize that it's real?

Intergenerational feedback--people older than me telling me that things are blooming earlier, ponds you used to be able to skate on all winter melt after a couple of days.

My ecopoetics is flexible: it shifts, it learns, it correlates, it trusts. Who is on the other end of that sentence? Who is it turned to? Here is where I continue to learn: the words of Zahira Kelly (@bad_dominicana), Shaadi Deveraux (@TwittaHoney), b. binaohan (mxbees) and Doreen St. Felix (@dstfelix); Anne Boyer's writings on her own blog, some of which are also in *Garments Against Women* (Ahsahta Press); CAConrad's somatic poetry exercises in *A Beautiful Marsupial Afternoon* (Wave Books) and at http://somaticpoetryexercises.blogspot.com; Yoko Ono's instructions, collected in *Grapefruit;* Yayoi Kusama's naked boy and girl dancers on Wall Street; all of Bhanu Kapil's books, particularly *Schizophrene* and *Incubation: A Space for Monsters,* and a talk she gave on fragmentation, healing and the sacred at AWP one year; the visionary ecopoetics of Monica Mody in *Kala Pani* and Brenda Iijima, especially in *going blooming falling blooming* (delete press) and *Rev. You'll--ution* (Displaced Press); Rachel Schragis's flowcharts of waste, Lucia Monge's verdant parade *Planton Movil*, and Edie Fake's performances of gay utopia.

Jonathan Skinner

Jonathan Skinner is a poet, editor, and critic, best known for founding the journal *ecopoetics*. His poetry collections and chapbooks include *Chip Calls* (Little Red Leaves, 2014), *Birds of Tifft* (BlazeVOX, 2011), *Warblers* (Albion Books, 2010), and *Political Cactus Poems* (Palm Press, 2005). He has published critical essays on Charles Olson, Ronald Johnson, Lorine Niedecker, Mei-mei Berssenbrugge, and Bernadette Mayer, translations of French poetry and garden theory, essays on bird song from the perspective of ethnopoetics, and essays on horizontal concepts such as the Third Landscape. Skinner teaches in the Department of English and Comparative Literary Studies at the University of Warwick.

Works

Blackbird Stanzas

the whole woods
   connected
  naturally plucked
    roar
  pulling us into thin air
whether we like it or not

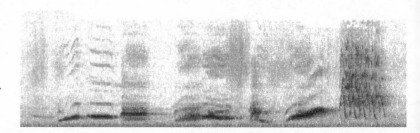

when you
 designated art
 an algorithm
    bayous
   bright chops
   accrete beats

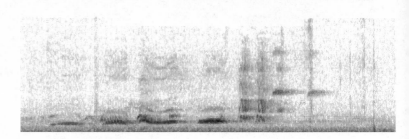

they can resolve
     degauss what
   animals cough up
 night flights
   arriving with rain
    recordings of ivory

organismally
there is a machine   a lyre
            a gasp
      insect chainsaws
       shredding the soundscape
           wing beats
       shaking the branches
so hard it is to see what we hear

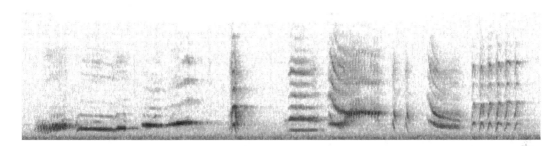

neurology
something   oceanic
interrupted by lemurs
        thrushes   in stereo
the three lek sounds

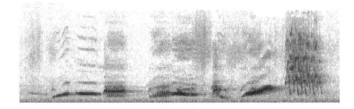

intuition
    married us to
  our tools
athletically
    grounded
who would complain
    peregrines, whales

difficult listening
    noisy   sound of air springs
        whack   jobs
eternally watching the pigeons
            we are so rife
        with nostalgia

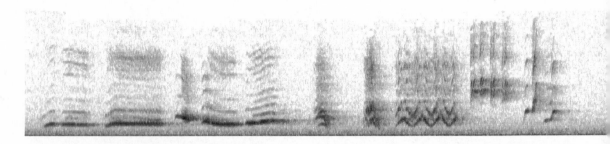

interpreting   graphs
        who are we to say
    YOU   are ANimal?
mwa'ahahaha   we don't know
        we'll eat you

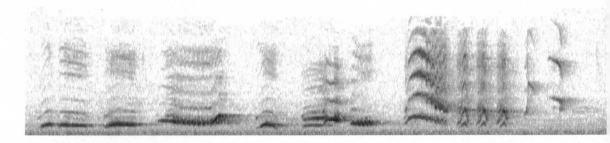

birdsong   bug music
    subsonics
            combusting
machines all make your chest cave
    in acoustically

like the homeless   who keep losing
                their lawn
                        furniture
        scanning a chunk of thunderstorm
                rifle   shots crack
                        bulge into echoing
            ivory's   market

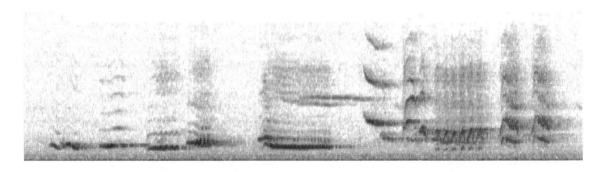

value   accumulates
                    inside
            a different kind of game
                    loon calls
                        syrinx
            boxing   our ears

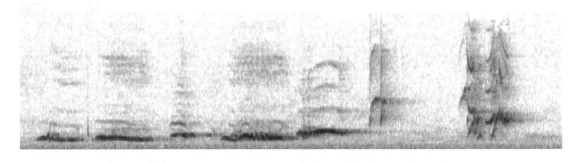

<http://soundcloud.com/ecopoetics/common-blackbird-newbold-comyn>

Vibrational Communication: Ecopoetics in the Seismic Channel

Magicicada septendecim emerge synchronously and in tremendous numbers every 17 years, to aggregate into chorus centers producing their distinctive "Pharaoh" calls to attract mates. They sing by vibrating their tymbals, or cartilaginous clickers, into abdominal resonation chambers. (Some derivations trace the name to the Greek *kikkos*, membrane + *aeidw*, singer, so, literally, "membrane singer.") These abdominal Helmholtz resonators also generate energy that travels through cicada bodies to induce strong vibrations in the substrate, what we might call the "seismic channel."

Tymbal

M. J. Raupp

Commenting on Keats's phrase "Hedge-crickets sing," in the third-to-last line of his ode "To autumn," poet Robert Grenier notes how, "everything still counts as one—frequency of vibration in crickets, locusts . . . no single note 'lost,' in nature . . . 'meaning' identical to physical fact of a sound . . . in series of discrete particles strung together . . . attention to extra-linguistic sound provokes awareness of like patterns in language." Grenier wrestles with a correlationist "mirror of nature" philosophy, a pursuit of likenesses. Yet in his own writing (the 'word drawings' in a book like *Rhymms,* for instance: the letters "I S A W/ I T/ W H E R E/ I S I T" overlapping in four different colors), Grenier demonstrates a vibratory practice of line and color that such philosophy cannot account for.

I propose "vibration" rather than correlation as the communication model for ecopoetics—which I define as the aesthetic part of house-making, to take the word at its Greek root, *oikos* + *poiein*. Better house-making, that is. Some say there's no point to house-making when the house itself is structurally unsound, that we're better off tearing it down and starting over. In which case ecopoetics comes after revolutionary poetics. Certainly, the house that capitalism has built is nothing if not destructive to household Earth. As Bruno Latour and other have shown, however, these houses are intertwined; the house is not ours alone to tear down. It may be that the same channel capitalists use to locate resources can be used to orchestrate resistance across the many different scales that constitute a house. A collective is a vibratory body, not one reproduced via imitation. The mass media, we know by now, will not induce mass movement, or not the kind that can save the Earth.

Vibration turns us toward what lies beneath our feet as well as what rises above our heads. "Vibrational communication" in the substrate is most dramatically rendered by the communication practices of the Treehopper species, picked up by inserting a phonograph needle into a leaf stem in (for instance) a Virginia field. Treehoppers communicate by literally vibrating the plant material on which they are perched: the moaning, churring, tapping, mewing sounds picked up by the scientist's probe are translations for human ears of the vibrations treehoppers feel through legs, thorax, and abdomen. If we stood in the Virginia field with our own ears, we would hear nothing: how much of what we deem to be "happening" is a matter of the scale to which we are attuned?

How might such a communication model apply to prosody—conceived as an art neither of the vocal apparatus nor of writing but of the substrate? What would that substrate, or those substrates, be, and what would be sung through them? What would it mean to orient these substrates *pros odos,* toward song? To sing the membranes?

Subsonic

    only hearing the upper registers
    we look for elephant calls
    investigating the given sounds
    of upland sandpipers' slurred whistle
    the impact of commerce on the oceans
    the system that crosses species groups
    putting our electronic skills to work
    in the service of nature

    duetting is a major component
    in the upstate NY gorge country
    where the cardinals we never recorded
    are backed up on tape

to create space outside a human construction
a whale song in a wooden boat hull
changing in the same way at the same time

it's so loud you can hear
Homer with his rosy-fingered dawn

how the two organs of his syrinx
were overloaded and damaged
how absolute the law of impermanence
like him we can stop listening stop
putting our microphones under the water
our mice into the floorboards

This dual role of sound waves—to communicate but also to echo back and in so doing to sound the substrate, in the submarine sense of "sounding"—has been exploited by the hydrocarbon industry to map the subsurface lay of its prospects. Integral to seismic prospecting is the percussive generation of controlled seismic energy sources: explosives, air guns, sparker, thumper trucks, seismic vibrator, boomer sources.

The seismic channel also vibrates at the heart of our "social media." A proof mass that deforms a spring in an accelerometer is sometimes called the seismic mass. Inside every touchscreen smartphone is an accelerometer, and in every accelerometer, you'll find extremely tiny springs made of silicon, which oscillate back and forth between contact points. As they move, those microscopic springs create a small charge which can be measured and used to determine how your device is oriented—an MEMS (Micro-Electro Mechanical System) sensor, about 1mm across. Such "inertial sensors" also orient our drones. And they virtually flex our pop stars' vocal cords. Auto-Tune was initially created by Andy Hildebrand, an engineer working for Exxon. Hildebrand developed methods for interpreting seismic data and subsequently realized that the technology could be used to detect, analyze, and modify the pitch in audio files.

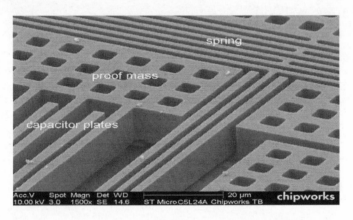

Systems can message one another without communicating, or communicate without messaging one another. Sociologist Niklas Luhmann once described ecological communication as communication of ignorance—social networks linked in the blind spots our seeing constitutes. What if the language abyss between humans and other-than-humans, or the unbridgeable gaps between disciplines, were precisely what make communication not only possible but necessary? In noisy, obstructed, over-determined environments we might practice seismic communication, trading directionality for reach, and short loop, closed-circuit communication for "earth magnitude" signals. Communication in the seismic channel reaches beneath the message to vibration. The "social network" is vibrational to the extent that its devices interface with bodies, with Earth's gravity and with the surrounding magnetosphere. It is not vibrational when it withdraws from this reach. Communication in the seismic channel means attending to distant bodies, absent bodies, difficult bodies, prosthetic bodies, beyond the echo chamber and groove of eros—in the promising if darkened reach of the manifold body of Earth and its open circuits. There are, of course, other models for ecopoetics. Much can be accomplished within the high fidelity, sharply encoded signals of closed circuit communication: birds sing there too. You can reach bodies that speak your language with very specific instructions. Vibrational communication does not, however, reach from abilities and fluencies but from the disabling interconnections that constitute the very possibility (and necessity) of communication. Locate your membrane and flex it.

North Atlantic Right whales die from two major causes: collisions with ships and entanglement in fishing gear. While fewer than 400 individuals remain, Massachusetts Bay sees more than 1,500 ship visits per year. The Right Whale Listening Network hopes to reduce vessel strikes using an array of auto-detection buoys. The buoys feed information to the Northeast U.S. Right Whale Sighting Advisory System, sending vessel captains the signal to slow down when whales are present. A team of acoustic technicians scans the incoming sound, converted into a spectrogram's endless scrolling strip, for the "Nike logo"-shaped signature of Right Whale calls. Technicians also are at work writing code to automate the recognition process. All of this is vibrational communication.

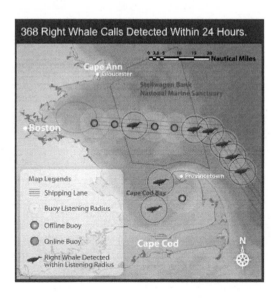

A poet in black holds a dying sunflower to the oil company's roadsign, a poet travels by car across America sleeping in Wal-Mart parking lots and speaking with the homeless, 70,000+ kilometers of poetry are written in resistance to the oil company's pipeline and scrolled across our screens, a poet unfurls a core sample from Pablo Neruda's "Great Ocean" across the congressional representative's office floor, a poet sings her prairie dog translations to the coral reef scientist at the National Center for Atmospheric Research, a poet filling her tank moans at the gas pump, a poet's verse is unpacked in court for a description of how the barricade was constructed, defending the snake mound a poet sings of genocide to the game fish & parks department, a poet teaches children in Paradox Valley how to think climate change with metaphor, a poem is installed in a zoo facing *into* the gorilla enclosure, a poet fills a city hall with dead leaves, a poet translates the radial syntax of bark beetles, a poet writes an autobiography of plastic cleaning the shoreline as she walks, a poet composes lines with the words we throw out: "It rises and falls through the repercussions of songs of birds. . . . Thoreau heard his stretched from first dark sparrow to last dog baying moon."[9]

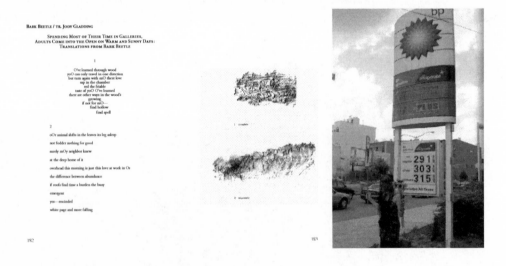

[9] See the work of Kristin Prevallet, CAConrad, Enpipe Line, Jonathan Skinner, Jaclyn Hawkins, Brenda Hillman, Stephen Collis, Allison Hedge Coke, Jack Collom, Gary Lawless, Cecilia Vicuña, Jody Gladding, Allison Cobb, Ronald Johnson. Also see "Offshore: Poetics, Catastrophe, Peak Oil," guest ed. Jonathan Skinner, *Interim: the eco issue*, ed. Christopher Arigo, vol. 29, nos. 1-2, 2011.

In their reverberation and repercussion, non-representational activist poetries might open up contact zones, generative spaces and times not bound to the apocalyptic doom of human lifeworlds. When political and scientific discourses reverberate in such active poetry, and when poetry repercusses beyond humanist and beyond human channels, what Niklas Luhmann has called the "ecology of ignorance" might begin to communicate, disrupting efforts to sustain an illusion of control with the shared knowledge of ignorance.

References

Grenier, Robert. "10 Pages from RHYMMS." 2000. <http://www.thing.net/~grist/l&d/grenier/lgrena00.htm> Accessed 26 Aug. 2015.

"Hedge-crickets Sing" in *The L=A=N=G=U=A=G=E Book,* eds. Bruce Andrews and Charles Bernstein. (Carbondale and Edwardsville: Southern Illinois University Press, 1984)

Hill, Peggy S.M. *Vibrational Communication in Animals.* (Cambridge, MA: Harvard University Press, 2008)

Johnson, Ronald. *ARK* (Chicago: Flood Editions, 2013)

Joyce, Christopher and Bill McQuay. "Good Vibrations Key To Insect Communication." 27 Aug. 2015. <http://www.npr.org/2015/08/27/432934935/good-vibrations-key-to-insect-communication> Accessed 27 Aug. 2015.

Kahn, Douglas. *Earth Sound Earth Signal: Energies and Earth Magnitude in the Arts.* (Berkeley: University of California Press, 2013)

Luhmann, Niklas. *Ecological Communication.* Tr. John Bednarz Jr. (Cambridge: Polity Press, 1989)

Right Whale Listening Network. < http://www.listenforwhales.org/>

Rothenberg, David. *Bug Music: How Insects Gave Us Rhythm and Noise.* (NY: St. Martin's Press, 2013)

Skinner, Jonathan. "Animal Transcriptions: Listening to the Lab of Ornithology." 21 March 2013. < http://soundstudiesblog.com/2013/03/21/skinner-podcast/> Accessed 26 Aug. 2015.

Wikipedia. "Reflection Seismology" 25 Aug. 2015. <http://en.wikipedia.org/wiki/Reflection_seismology> Accessed 26 Aug. 2015.

Process

"Blackbird Stanzas" is lyrics to a performance, a translation or transcript of eleven vocalizations of a European Blackbird (*Turdus merula*) that I recorded singing at the edge of town on a golf course in the English Midlands. I slowed the recording down to one fourth its "natural" speed and generated a spectrogram for each vocalization, using the Raven Lite software developed by Cornell Lab of Ornithology. The slowed down spectrograms reveal the distinctive parts of each vocalization, modeling variety, density, and rhythm for the five to eight lines of each stanza. The words come **from interviews conducted with Lab of Ornithology, Bioacoustics Research Program, and Macaulay Library staff**—interviews I spent a month transcribing and composing into lyrics before attempting this translation: **see "Animal Transcriptions: Listening to the Lab of Ornithology.**

<http://soundstudiesblog.com/2013/03/21/skinner-podcast/>

When I perform, the recording provides the backing track for my attempt to vocalize, karaoke style, the blackbird's song. Ideally, software would allow me to scroll through and follow the spectrogram as I sing, but we're not there yet. If in the interviews and associated poems I listen to listening, the performance of "Blackbird Stanzas" brings this listening back as echo.

Perceptual Challenge

Slow Listening

With the physical equipment we have evolved as human beings, we move through a particular bandwidth of the material and spiritual sensorium—narrower, with regards to any one given sense, than our combinatorial brains might admit. (The ultrasonic and the subsonic, the ultraviolet and the infrared, for instance, remain beyond our immediate sonic and visual ken.) Our limited overlap with the way our other-than-human neighbors see and hear the world, which includes our ability to take in what they might be telling us, constrains our appreciation of their brilliance and impacts our understanding of their needs. As the noisiest, neediest (and nosiest) residents on the block, it may be our job to stop and listen, not theirs. Some of the constraint is attentional. Can we, for instance, expand our listening to encompass more of what we hear? To a point: despite transcendental claims, enlightenment will never be more than human.

As Thomas Nagel lucidly argued, we won't in this life experience what it is like to be a bat, but there nevertheless remains something it is like to be a bat. Just as translation makes opportunities of the constraints our language encounters in another's hearing, slow listening can turn our lumbering ears into instruments for unwinding the musical microcosm inside a sparrow's ear. We at least begin to hear what we aren't hearing. Our algorithmic manipulations of space and time might offer a probe into the seismic channel of perceptual distance between us and those we share the planet with. Finding ways to see what we hear offers a purchase into translations that become ways of performing other than human being. We will listen differently after a journey into the sparrow's ear, and we might act differently if we can become sparrows, speaking or singing into what we hear, even briefly.

This prompt works best with a recording device and access to audio editing and visualization software. Record a minute or two of a bird singing, a song that interests you or perhaps a song you hear every day, one you never stopped to listen to before. (You can use your phone or a digital memo device or a laptop or even a tape recorder if it has a headphone jack—you'll need a "male to male" cable to connect to your computer's input jack.) It might be a song you walk past or one you hear out your window. Larger birds tend to sing more slowly, so the smaller the bird the greater the challenge. The ambient environment should be quiet enough that you have a clear recording of one bird's song. Transfer the file to your computer, and open it in a free audio editing program like Audacity, Raven, Sonic Visualiser or Garage Band (more complicated). Slow the song down to one quarter its "natural" speed (in Audacity, Effect > Change Speed > -75%). With some species, like the wren, you may need to slow it down to one tenth its natural speed (-90%) to hear more of the notes. Notice how every space seems filled with a sonic fractal of yet more material to zoom. You can then shift up the pitch (Effect > Change Frequency > +75%) to get the slowed down song back into "normal" hearing range.

Some software packages, like Raven, allow you to display a spectrogram of the sound file. This is different from the two-dimensional waveform view that shows only amplitude; a spectrogram uses a Fourier transform to generate a three-dimensional view of the spectrum of frequencies in the sound as they vary over time, with amplitude represented by intensity of color. The images can be beautiful and useful as they yield a visual signature for specific vocalizations (like the "upsweep" call acousticians look for to detect the presence of Right Whales in ocean soundscapes). For our purposes, the spectrogram allows us to see the different parts of a bird vocalization and especially how radically they differ—some parts are continuous with upsweeps and downsweeps, some jagged as a series of staccato strokes, some are smeared and some are sharp, some zigzag and some straight, some compressed and some spread across the spectra, some complex and some relatively clear. There are as many forms as there are shapes in the visual domain.

Play around with your software, tweaking its parameters, until the spectrogram shows clearly defined shapes, shapes pleasing to you. Looking at such spectrograms might seem like a fast kind of listening, bypassing the durational aspect of sound, but it also slows listening, when a stretched-out graph can show in one view events happening too quickly for the human ear. (Research has shown that a bird's minimum unit of attention is much smaller than the minimum unit of human attention. Or as Ronald Johnson put it, "I know the housefinch singing outside the window just now heard its own song with slower and lower ear than mine.") Visual representation also allows us to parse sounds that are, due to intricacies of the avian syrinx, too complex to discriminate by ear.

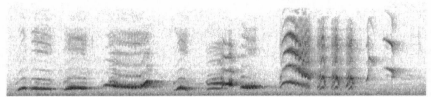

Spectrogram of the vocalization of a European Blackbird, generated using Raven Lite.

A spectrogram is a good crib for translating bird song. If you don't have access to audio analysis software capable of generating a spectrogram, try drawing, making graphic representations of the sound, as you listen to the slowed-down song. You can invent your own system of marks to represent the different kinds of vocalization.

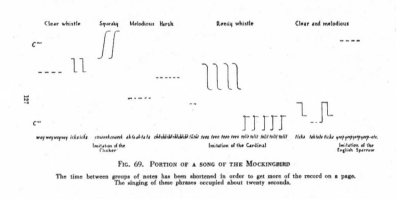

FIG. 69. PORTION OF A SONG OF THE MOCKINGBIRD

The time between groups of notes has been shortened in order to get more of the record on a page. The singing of these phrases occupied about twenty seconds.

Aretas A. Saunders, *A Guide to Bird Songs* (New York: Appleton-Century Company, 1935), p. 127

If you are capable of slowing your brain cycles down through meditation, it may even be possible to do this exercise without the aid of any technology, though I suspect there are limits.

The next step in your slow listening exercise is to use the spectrogram or drawing to model the lines and stanzas of a poem that translates the bird song you hear. The language of the poem can be taken from almost any source, since birds and humans, let's face it, don't speak the same language. We nevertheless communicate—a vibrational communication that should be the focus of your translation, one that doesn't end with the writing. But if language about birds, about your relationship to and feelings about birds, helps you activate this communication, by all means use those words. However you go about it, listen, over and over again, to the bird's song, using your crib as a guide. Take the song in parts, but write straight from the song. You can be as impressionistic or as precise about this as you want to be. An upper limit for precision might be writing a text that you could perform ("karaoke" style) along with the slowed-down birdsong. A different limit might be addressing your feelings as you listen and look. Surely many other directions emerge from this listening exercise. The important thing is what happens when you are done with the poem.

Suggesteds

Vibrational Communication

H.D. Thoreau, Journal, October 12, 1851
The Journal of Henry D. Thoreau, Volumes I-VII,
eds. Bradford Torrey and Francis H. Allen
New York: Dover Publications, Inc., 1962

Ronald Johnson, *ARK*, "BEAM 7"
Chicago: Flood Editions, 2013

Thomas Nagel, "What is it like to be a bat?"
The Philosophical Review LXXXIII, 4 (October 1974)

Peggy S.M. Hill, *Vibrational Communication in Animals*
Cambridge, MA: Harvard University Press, 2008

David Rothenberg, *Thousand Mile Song: Whale Music in a Sea of Sound*
New York: Basic Books, 2008

Douglas Kahn, *Earth Sound Earth Signal: Energies and Earth Magnitude in the Arts*
Berkeley: University of California Press, 2013

Niklas Luhmann, *Ecological Communication*
Translated by John Bednarz Jr.
Cambridge: Polity Press, 1989

Cecilia Vicuña

Cecilia Vicuña is a poet, artist and filmmaker born in Santiago de Chile. The author of twenty-two poetry books, she exhibits and performs widely in Europe, Latin America and the United States. Vicuña's work deals with the interactions of language earth, text and textile. Her site specific performance installations begin as a poem, an image or a line that morphs into a film, a song or a collective performance. These transformative acts, she calls the *precarious,* bridge the gap between art and life, the ancestral and the avant-garde.

A precursor of conceptual art in Latin America, she founded 'Tribu No' in l967, a group that created anonymous poetic actions in Santiago. Exiled in London, she co-founded 'Artists for Democracy' in l974 to oppose dictatorships in the Third World. She arrived in New York in l980 and joined the Heresies Collective that published *Heresies: A Feminist Publication on Art and Politics.* In 2010 she co-founded oysi.org, a website for artists/poets and oral cultures around the world.

Her most recent books are: *Kuntur Ko,* Hueso Records, Chile, 2015. *El Zen Surado,* Catalonia, Chile, 2013. *Chanccani Quipu,* Granary Books, New York, 2012. Her *Spit Temple: Selected Performances of Cecilia Vicuña,* Ugly Duckling Presse, New York, 2012, was Runner-up to the 2013 PEN Award for Poetry in Translation. *SABORAMI,* ChainLinks, 2011. *Instan,* Kelsey St. Press, 2002. *The Precarious / QUIPOem: The Art and Poetry of Cecilia Vicuña*, Wesleyan University Press, l997. She co-edited *The Oxford Book of Latin American Poetry*, New York, 2009.

She was appointed Messenger Lecturer 2015, at Cornell University, N.Y.
She lives in New York and Chile.
www.ceciliavicuna.org, www. konkon.cl

Works

The poem
is the animal

Sinking its mouth
in the stream.

Translated by Eliot Weinberger

UNUY QUITA

Water
and its thirst
are one

Mist is the semen of the mountains
where the streams are born

Mist is the semen of the forest
where coolness is born

Curving soundulating
magmatic stream

Pacha Pacarina
flashflood sphere

You are one
Waterrrrr

Zig zag meander

Who filled you with filth?

Chicha gone
around the bend

Playing splashing

Your sack
my span

One thirst!

*

The round spring
its own silence
the sylvan key
will end

It will all end!

Where will the fog go?
The life-giving mist?
Where it will go?

Cool, fresh

The earth's sustenance
the tear filled branches

Our hearts extinguished
the fog is gone!

translated by Suzanne Jill Levine

Death of the pollinators

the pollen touches the stigma

feels

the

                            fe   faith

female

and unleashes   cun

                      dándolo

                                  spreads

a strand

of love   dating   pain

thread   it

"Territories of pollen
are sensitive to sound"

"Playing their trumpets,
the Desana precipitate
pollination"

"The particles
of masculine pollen
then fall on
the feminine
part of the palm"

Polen
Pulvis
Powder

"Death of the pollinators"

Bee   bat   moth   bird   butterfly

all dying out

                              Penetrate
                              Little Pollen
                              Dust

who will come?

who will feed us?

                    Polvito
                    Polen
                    Polvar

The miriti palm
hears the blare
and gets excited.

                    (the palma and the trumpet
                    are bisexual
                    and are always played
                    in pairs)

                              In Europe, women
                              displayed their privates
                              to flax

At the sight of vulvas
the plants grew
with great velocity

Down with dresses!
up with plants!

To Hear is to Strike Gold

(A response to Pascua Lama)*

Glacier is the origin of the word "cool" and the first "chill," the slow-moving ice of an inner music that dies when no one wants to hear it.

As it breaks the glacier moans, releasing a cow's alveolar lament.

The nearly extinct condor is the glacier: water messenger, intermediary between two worlds.

Kauri Paqsa, the boy-condor, guardian of the glacier, was buried alive at the source of the Mapocho River, El Plomo's glacier peak, to ensure the valley we now call "Santiago" would never lack water.

Buried and forgotten for 500 years, he was then discovered and torn from his sleep by miners in 1954. They located him only to dislocate him, turning him into a "trophy," an "archaeological object." They called it "mountain worship," and with that phrase situated him in the past. They called him "El Plomo Mummy," and that name separated him from life. But the boy continues to sleep, and when someone listens to the water his sleep forms part of the present.

The boy returns now to national consciousness, the glaciers at risk of being sold, contaminated, lost. He reappears at this moment when Chile must choose between hearing and not hearing the music of an ancient connection between the earth and the glacier, the specific tone of a place.

Place is sound, and a form of hearing it.
A weave of interrelations, interactions between people and land,
the space of naming.

To change the meaning of a name is to change the world.

In Alto del Carmen, situated in the Huasco Province, land of Gabriela Mistral's ancestors, Chile is choosing one meaning. Alto del Carmen can become the place where Chile places, on high, its poetry. Or, it could be the end of poetry.

Today, shepherds from Valle del Huasco, descendants of the Diaguita, are the guardians of an ancient vision of the glacier as life-giving, sacred. We can choose to listen to the music of the place, in all its potential, or put an end to life by surrendering the glacier and the mines to the neocolonial powers.

But do we hear its voice? Our own interior voice? Or do we hear the voice of the system, which says, "The dollar is what counts" "What do you know" "Now we are the owners of these mines, and cyanide is the new guardian of the waters."

Water is gold
Manquemilla, Gold Condor
The blood of the glacier
listening to us.

The ice slowly shifting is testimony to an ancient relationship with earth and water, and ritual conservation of its fluidity is our true cultural patrimony. The future inheritance of a music that sustains the earth and human life simultaneously.

In Australia, indigenous peoples have recovered their dignity and land rights through poetry: the ritual conservation of their history in the landscape is their "songline."

In Chile, the condor and the water of legends, the memory of the people, is the line of song that enters the earth to fecundate it.

The intangible quipu of our continuity.

(2006)

---

* *Pascua-Lama* is an open-pit mining project in the Andes mountains, south of the Atacama desert, at an altitude of over 4,500 meters. A Toronto-based gold mining company is developing the project, which has caused irreparable damage to the glaciers, as well as contamination.

Translated by Rosa Alcalá

Poetics

Eco poetics:

Our home is awareness.

Poetics, its doing.

> *"La poesía es la única evidencia de la humanidad de lo humano."*
> *"Poetry is the only evidence of the humanity of humans."*

> Juan Sánchez Peláez

Process

Com Position is a mysterious force, a contradiction in terms: *com* is 'with' (all encompassing) and *position* is 'placing' (a limit), the tension we inhabit.

The body and the cosmos are com positions and history, *histos,* is a web we com pose, aware or unaware of our role. History is not just 'written', it is performed in a cosmic field, the quantum memory of Earth.

We may emit only weakly, but our acts form a parallel script that the Earth reads. The air, struck by lightning, becomes a network to transmit electricity. That is why efforts to erase the voice of the underdog fail; what is erased is never lost.

My sense of com position was born from a desire to respond to the sun and the sea. A moment came when I felt they sensed me, as much as I sensed them. I bent down in awe and gathered sticks and feathers placing them like little dolmens in the sand for the high tide to erase. Thus, my precarious art began as a com position *with* the elements. (January, l966)

To res pond, is to offer again, to perform a rite.

The ancient particle '*rēs*', gave birth to the word '*real*', what arises from shared awareness. To acknowledge the beauty of the exchange, transforms the *res*, into response ability.

I learnt my sense of com position with history the violent way.

The day before the opening of my exhibition *Otoño/Autumn* in Santiago (June 9, 1971), a political murder took place setting the stage for violence. The beauty of Chile's spirit, its chance to fullfill the peaceful revolution already underway was destroyed. The violence unleashed that day led to the military coup of September 11, 1973. National mourning was declared, and the Museum closed. My work and our participatory democracy were symbolically erased in one stroke.

Otoño/Autumn–a room filled with leaves at the National Museum of Fine Arts –was a metaphor in space, a poem performed as a collective act: many people gathering leaves; the gardeners of the big parks, my family and friends. It was dedicated to joy.

"joy could make people aware of the need to fight for joy. the urgency of the present is the urgency for revolution."

The erasure of the *Autumn* event showed me that our democratic revolution was the true art of Chile and 'my' art was only part of the *com* position: the collective wave of *com* munal creativity.

.

The idea of com position as participation is at the core of the Indigenous worldview. I remember a scene from the film, *También la lluvia/ Even the Rain* when the Indians in Bolivia are about to be massacred by the police. They are fighting for their water rights and are terrorized until one man shouts: "Acabémonos pues", "Let's come to our end". His willingness to sacrifice himself. transforms everything. The people find their strength and charge ahead unarmed until the police, the government and the corporations back away. As a result, the people retain their water rights and privatization fails.

Water and life rejoice in the beauty of sacrifice!

.

The com position com poses itself through us. When writing, I remember Mark Twain saying: "lightning does the work." And Nikola Tesla: To resonate at the same frequency, tuning is the key". The poem is a powerful resonator.

What is the com position the Earth wants from us now?

Perceptual Challenge

-Go outside and observe a cloud, a bee or a plant.

-Enter their perspective.

-Find a meeting point between your perspective and theirs.

-You will notice a tension (perhaps between your belief and disbelief in the non-human ability to perceive.)

-Engage that tension.

Buckminster Fuller said "tension is the great integrity."

-Write from the perspective of the exchange.

Suggesteds

-*How Forests Think, Toward an Anthropology beyond the Human*
Eduardo Kohn

-*A Foray into the Worlds of Animals and Humans with a Theory of Meaning*

Jakob von Uexküll

-*The Metamorphosis of Plants*
Johann Wolfgan von Goethe

-*Pollen and Fragments: Selected Poetry and Prose of Novalis*

Novalis

Amy King's latest book, *The Missing Museum*, is a winner of the 2015 Tarpaulin Sky Book Prize. She is on the executive board of VIDA: Women in Literary Arts, received the 2015 WNBA Award, co-edits the series, Bettering American Poetry, and is a full professor of creative writing and English at SUNY Nassau Community College.

Heidi Lynn Staples' debut collection, *Guess Can Gallop*, was selected by Brenda Hillman as a winner of the New Issues Poetry Prize. She is author of three other collections, including *A**A*A*A,* forthcoming from Ahsahta, and her writing has appeared widely. She teaches in the MFA program at the University of Alabama in Tuscaloosa.

SMCL

3 5151 00261 4907

**RESERVE
4 HR NO N/O**

DATE DUE

3/5/19	5:29PM		
GAYLORD			PRINTED IN U.S.A.

57379869R00163

Made in the USA
San Bernardino, CA
20 November 2017

F R A M E W O

A Developer's Han

MW00606735

FRAME
WORK
™

Editor: Richard Pressler

Text Editor: Brenda Johnson

Text Designer: Thomas Clark

Cover Design: D.A. Gray

Production Manager: Bruce Miyake

Managing Editor: Robert Hoffman

Illustrations: Commercial Graphix

Published by Ashton-Tate Publishing Group

10150 West Jefferson Boulevard, Culver City, CA 90230　　　ISBN: 0-912677-24-4

ASHTON·TATE

FRAMEWORK

ACKNOWLEDGEMENTS

My hope is that this book will fill you with the excitement I have felt in writing it, as I watched a flexible, powerful language unfold its many potentials. One of the reasons this book carries so many examples is that I wanted to show you what a creative programming adventure FRED has to offer. Writing about FRED just isn't enough.

But write I did. And with a lot of help. All that stuff you hear about the importance of a team effort is true. So, I begin this book by thanking the team of people who have so fully supported my efforts.

Robert Carr, President and CEO of Forefront, along with my editors, Bill Jordan, Robert Hoffman, and Richard Pressler at Ashton-Tate Publications, deserve great thanks for saying "We want a high quality book" and meaning it.

Then there are the Forefront programmers. Some innocently answered the phone on weekends. Others strolled out into the hallway, thinking they were just getting coffee. All got bombarded with questions and responded with amazing patience and helpfulness.

Thanks to

Dan Altman   Hal Schectman
Steve Aubrey   Greg Stikeleather
Samuel Feldman

David Helms, co-author of the FRED language, spent a lot of time explaining the mechanics of the language and its finer points. His discourse on debugging? I should've taped it.

Chris Kirkpatrick, co-author of the FRED language, took on the role of official FRED tour guide. The hours he spent in patient exegesis of the language, providing insights into how to write more efficient code and editing each manuscript page, and his koan-like advocacy of "thinking FRED" instilled in this book the quality that all of us sought.

Alice. I didn't know there was that much love and patience in the entire world.

Bill Kling

DEVELOPER'S HANDBOOK

CONTENTS

DEVELOPER'S HANDBOOK

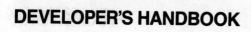

DEVELOPER'S HANDBOOK

DEVELOPER'S HANDBOOK

DEVELOPER'S HANDBOOK

INTRODUCTION

What level of programming skill should you have attained to profit from this book? Who is FRED? What's the premise behind this book? What are good programming techniques in FRED? What typographical conventions does this book employ? Where do I begin? Read this Introduction and find out.

EXPERIENCE REQUIRED

To profit from this book, you should, at the very least, feel completely comfortable with elementary programming concepts like variables, loops, subroutine calls, controlling flow of execution, and the like. Additionally, you should have a sound knowledge of Framework's elements and techniques.

Are you senior programmer (you cut your coding teeth on FORTRAN compilers)? A DP programmer supporting a senior decision-maker (Graphs! He wants more graphs!)? A ''power-user'' (you like to write programs and are determined to know your software inside out)? A hacker (at 3:30 AM, your only friends are a can of flat soda and half a carton of cold Szechwan beef)?

Naturally, some experience is necessary, but what really counts is not your current position, but your degree of interest and readiness to ''think FRED.''

REQUIRED READING

If you have not already done so, work through the on-line tutorial and the *Framework Tutorial* book. Then plunge into the *Framework Reference Manual* and *Framework: A Programmer's Reference*. If you're relatively new to programming, be sure you've read *Framework: An Introduction to Programming*. All are available from Ashton-Tate.

How much time should you spend with these books? If you show up at social events and are greeted with, "Ah. I see you've brought those gray books with you again," you're approaching an impressive level of diligence.

WHO IS FRED?

Why all this emphasis on Framework? Because from a programming standpoint, Framework is a part of the FRED language; it is also the environment in which FRED exists. Think of it this way: You may never have to write a sort routine again. The reason? Framework's powerful database facility gives you impressive sorting power. The key is to think in *system* terms. In many ways, the Framework-FRED system is a collection of *software tools* including:

- Outlining for top-down program design.

- Word processing for easy coding, editing, and reporting.

- A spreadsheet for arrays, tables, and calculating.

- A database for organizing, storing, and manipulating data.

- Graphics for illustrating the meanings of numbers.

- Telecommunications for sending and receiving data.

- A DOS window to link FRED with other languages and programs.

- Macros and filtering to turn an individual key into an entire program.

With FRED, you can write your own functions and store them in a library file to use with other programs. You can go so far as to write functions and macros that assist you in writing further functions and macros. This extensible quality also means that you can turn FRED into the kind of language you find most useful—a telecommunications language, a financial analysis language, an accounting language, and so on.

Ultimately, extensibility means that Framework and FRED exist only as an environment in which to develop your application ideas. With relatively little effort, you can write a turnkey application that gives no hint of any relationship to FRED. It has its own screens, menus, prompts, and functions.

As an experienced programmer, you've developed your own ways of doing things. Before you try to apply these techniques across the board, work at deepening your understanding of FRED and Framework. This new system may very well offer you easier, more efficient structures than those allowed by the language(s) you're most familiar with.

THE PREMISE BEHIND THIS BOOK

You may want to call this book "FRED Illustrated" or "Favorite FRED Modules." Why? Because one program is worth a thousand words, and you'll find this book liberally laced with small programming models, many only a few lines long. Each model illustrates some programming principle. When you want a guide in your own programming, you may well find a model to help you move your own efforts along.

Another excellent source of models are the programs on your Framework Utilities disk. These are well written in terms of style and efficiency. Print them out and study them. Consider how you can apply them and the principles they illustrate to your work. Many are directly adaptable to other applications. Why re-invent the wheel?

GOOD PROGRAMMING TECHNIQUES

You can make programming a difficult task in any language by approaching the task in a haphazard manner. Maybe you heard all this before in Algorithms 152A. But just in case you didn't....

Design before You Code

Once you have an idea for an application, write a description of the application. What does it do? What kind of input does it take? Keyboard? DOS files? Telecomm files? Will the program have to filter that data in any way? What sort of error handling does the input demand? What form will you (or your client) want the output to take? The screen? Printed reports? Files? What kind of data structures would best suit the project?

As you work through these and other questions, talk to potential users. What are their needs? What features would they like? What don't they want?

Make the concept as graphic as possible. Draw pictures of screens, sketch your report format. Make it as real as possible. Use Framework's word processing and outlining facilities to clarify your ideas. Both are great tools for thinking, for "seeing" your ideas.

Build in a Top-Down Manner

Once you have a good picture of your application, draw upon the Framework Outline facility to describe the highest level tasks—the basic input, processing, and output modules. Then describe the next level of modules that support the highest level. Once you have the second level modules under control, describe the third level, and so on. This first level involves no coding, just structuring and naming your subroutines and variables.

Code in Logical Subroutines

Don't try to make a single module do too many things. Keep it to the point. Nest subroutines. The simple, logical module as a coding unit makes debugging and program maintenance a lot easier than "do-it-all" style modules. A corollary of this is to avoid confusing control structures. If your code looks like a plate of spaghetti, find the source of confusion and re-write it in clearer units. (See "Think Small," below.)

The Framework-FRED system encourages working with small units. For example, instead of working with one huge spreadsheet that fills all of memory, unite several small spreadsheets with FRED.

Think Small

Particularly when you are new to a language, you may find yourself in the middle of a complex module. The more you code, the worse things become. The solution is to think about exactly what it is you're trying to do. Then go off and write a "toy program" that does the job—something you can experiment with and beat around without worrying about damaging your masterpiece. When you have created your own programming model, return to the actual program and bring your newly acquired knowledge to bear.

Make your Programs Speak for Themselves

This means that you should:

- Write clear, meaningful names for modules (frames) and variables.

- Comment frequently.

- Indent and prettyprint as appropriate to demonstrate the logic of your code.

The ability to comment at length means that you can write formulas and understand them months later—and so can your users. Comment your cell formulas, too. It's nice to have an intelligent reply when your boss asks you how you got the figures on which he's basing a decision.

Test, Test, Test

Test your modules as you develop them. When the application is complete, test some more. Get dirty. Try to break your own program. What happens when you enter an alphabetic character instead of a number? What happens when you put in a value that is too small or too large? Rest assured that if you don't find the weak points, someone else will—perhaps a complete novice, perhaps one of your peers with an ugly sense of humor. ("Did you know I can make your program lock up the keyboard?")

Distribute the program with as much documentation as you can muster and an evaluation form. What other features would users like to see? What do they like or dislike? How can you improve the documentation? Be specific wherever possible, but allow for general comments.

When the results come back, analyze them, fix the bugs, and test again.

THE KEYBOARD AND TYPOGRAPHICAL CONVENTIONS

Because you're an advanced programmer, this book assumes that you know how to use your computer's keyboard; for example, you press <Shift> to get uppercase characters. Also, be aware that this book works according to certain typographical conventions.

Bracketing of Non-Alphanumeric Keys

Non-alphanumeric keys are always surrounded by the "less than" and "greater than" symbols. The name of each key is exactly the same as FRED's key names. Here are a few examples:

- <Alt> for the Alt key

- <Backspace> for the key with the fat arrow

- <Ctrl> for the Control key

DEVELOPER'S HANDBOOK

- <Dnlevel> for the gray plus key

- <Uplevel> for the gray minus key

- <Return> for the key with the bent arrow

- <Esc> for the Escape key

- <F1> for function key F1, the Help key

- <Shift> for the (hollow arrow) Shift key

- <Tab> for the Tab key with its two arrows

The cursor-moving (arrow) keys are symbolized as:

<Uparrow>

<Dnarrow>

<Rightarrow>

<Leftarrow>

INTRODUCTION

Keystroke Combinations

Whenever you must press two or more keys simultaneously, you will see the keys linked with a hyphen. For example:

> \<Alt>-N
>
> \<Ctrl>-\<Alt>-\<Del>
>
> \<Ctrl>-\<Break>
>
> \<Ctrl>-C
>
> \<Shift>-\<Tab>

> **Note:** Wherever lists of items have no particular tradition or logic, items appear in alphabetical order.

When you must press two or more keys serially, the key symbols appear separated only by a single space character. For example:

> Change the margin to 10; type **\<Ctrl>-W L 10** \<Return>

Notice two things about this example. First, everything you must enter is in bold type. Bold type, except in FRED function names (which are always written in bold type), means you are to type the characters involved. Here, you would press \<Ctrl>-W, then type an ''L'' followed by ''10.'' Finally, you would press the \<Return> key. Second, notice that the example sentence does not end with a period. The reason is that extraneous characters like the period or quotation marks can confuse readers.

DEVELOPER'S HANDBOOK

xix

Program Style

This manual ~~follows~~ the prettyprinting style established in previous Framework books. These guidelines ~~are~~ the following:

- Frame names and user-created functions appear in initial and mid-caps—Looper, Err Check, TimeTest, @GetInput, @Again

- Framework functions appear in lowercase, boldface type—**@quitmenu**

- Functions like loops, If-Then statements, etc., are indented by one tab character per level. For example:

```
COUNT := 0,
@while(COUNT <> 10,
    @GetInput,
    @if(SUM < 100,
        @ReDo, TOTAL := TOTAL : SUM
    ),
    COUNT := COUNT :1
),
@TestTotal
```

- Variables appear in all caps—COUNT, SUM, TOTAL

- Spaces, though not necessary, separate operators from operands for easier reading—COUNT := 0 instead of COUNT:=0

> **Note:** Because of typographical practices, the programmer has modified listings so that no line exceeds 60 characters in length. This most often happens when concatenating strings and writing macros. FRED's syntax places no such restriction on line length. However, FRED programmers generally break lines at logical points to make listings easier to read. For example, you'll often see an **@if** statement written on three lines—one for the If clause, one for the Then clause, and a third for the Else.

THE REST OF THE BOOK

The first two chapters get you up to speed in FRED. Chapter One gives you an introduction to the programming environment by taking you step by step through the process of creating a frame, typing a toy program, running it, saving it, and printing it.

The second chapter, "FRED Programming Structures," puts your current knowledge of programming together with FRED's way of doing things. You'll find it all here—how to declare variables, get input, display output, do calls, the works.

With the basic structures in hand, you'll learn how to create macros, menus, and libraries. You'll also learn about debugging, error trapping, changing formulas on the fly, and a host of other good things along the way. Included in this programming cavalcade are plenty of everyday, highly practical programming tips, techniques, and shortcuts, all discovered in the real world by the folks who bring you Framework and FRED—the folks at Forefront Corporation.

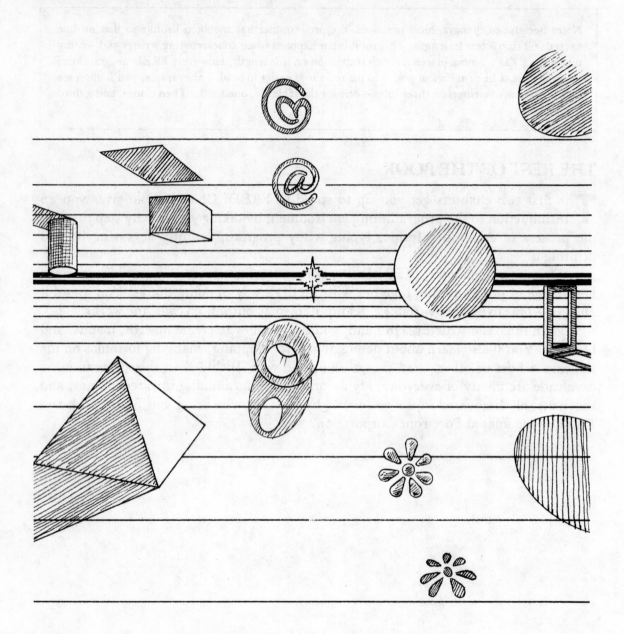

FRAMEWORK

CHAPTER ONE

THE FRED PROGRAMMING ENVIRONMENT

This chapter introduces you to the FRED programming environment. You will create a frame, type in a brief program, recalculate it, save it, and print it. If you're already familiar with these basic aspects of FRED programming, skip to Chapter Two.

ENTERING, RECALCULATING, AND SAVING A PROGRAM

To enter a FRED program, all you need is the Framework desktop on your screen. Follow these steps:

1. To create an empty word frame, type **<Ctrl>-C E**

2. With the frame on your desktop, give it a name; type **First <Return>**

3. To get into the formula portion of the screen, instead of the content portion, press **<F2> <F9>**

<F2> puts you in the formula editing mode (a program is a formula). <F9> performs a zoom so that you can work with the whole screen, instead of just with the edit line at the bottom of the screen. This key combination is known simply as ''Edit Zoom.''

4. Type the program in Figure 1-1.

```
; First
@printreturn,
@local(NAME, CHARS),
NAME := @inputline("What's your name?"),
CHARS := @len(NAME),
NAME & " is a nice name." &
" It has " & @integer(CHARS) & " letters."
```

Figure 1-1. Program listing for First

5. To leave full-screen editing, press <F9>

6. To conclude, you can press <**Return**>, which causes recalculation, or <**Esc**>, which won't. Press <**Return**>

   After a moment of disk access, the program recalculates and your prompt (''What's your name?'') appears at the bottom of the screen.

7. Type a response and press <**Return**>

   The programmed message appears in the contents area of the frame. Want to see it again? Press <**F5**> to recalculate.

8. You save a program just as you would any frame; press<**Ctrl**>-<**Return**>

As a general rule, type your programs into the formula area of the frame, not the contents area of a frame.

   Look at the listing for a moment. The semicolon (;) is FRED's *comment character*. FRED ignores anything typed after a semicolon.

You place a *comma* at the end of a line only when you're separating either parameters inside of functions (as inside the **@local** statement) or individual functions. FRED programmers prefer to write one function or statement to a line, breaking only for readability. Be careful, however, of breaking in the middle of a string; FRED will "print" the carriage return, just as it prints the rest of the characters in the string.

PRINTING A PROGRAM LISTING

Check to see that your printer is connected, turned on, and on-line; then follow the steps below.

1. With First's frame selected; press **<Ctrl>-P**

2. Open the Output Options menu; press **O**

3. Turn the *Formulas Only* feature on; press **F**

    Also make sure that *Print Frame Labels* is on.

4. Press **<Rightarrow>** to return to the main Print menu.

5. Start the print process; press **B** to begin. When printing ends, Framework advances the paper to the top of the next page.

There are a couple of things you should know about printing. The **@printreturn** function sits at the top of the program to keep FRED from executing your program before it prints it. Normally, the Print command executes a formula (even a memo) to find any relevant print functions. Placing **@printreturn** at the top of a program tells Print that the rest of the formula carries nothing of interest. Many programmers prefer to write a small print routine at the top of a program to format their listings with page numbers, dates, and so on. If you choose this route, conclude your print formula with **@printreturn**.

This concludes Chapter One. Before reading any other portions of the book, read Chapter Two. It discusses FRED programming structures and serves as a gateway to the rest of the book.

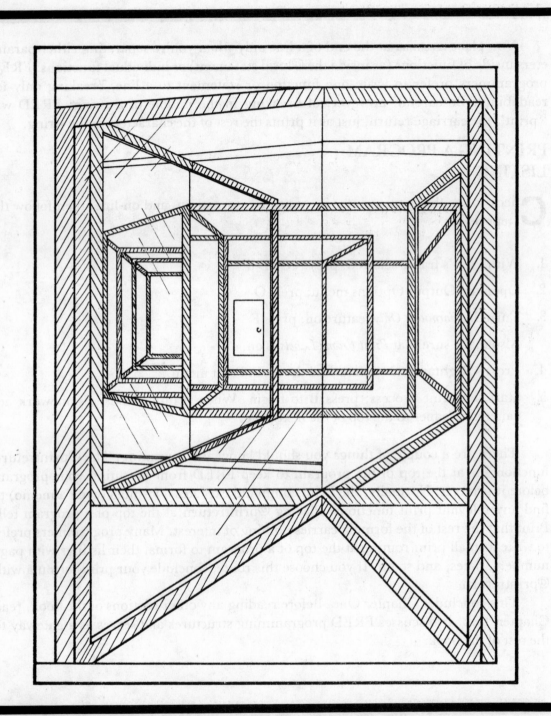

CHAPTER TWO

FRED PROGRAMMING STRUCTURES

This chapter illustrates how common programming structures work in the FRED language and will *acquaint* you with typical ways of doing things in FRED. The chapter discusses the following items:

- Facts about frames
- Variables
- Subroutines and formulas
- Operators and value types
- Flow of control
- I/O

For a concise syntactical discussion of the language see the *Framework Reference Manual* and *Framework: A Programmer's Reference.*

PROGRAMMING WITH FRAMES

Frames are the central fact of a FRED programmer's life. Indeed, FRED programming is "frame work." This section deals with the parts of a frame and the types of frames.

Frame Facts

Any Framework frame has four parts as Figure 2-1 shows. The *label* is the frame's name. It rests in the upper-left corner of the frame *border*. The *contents area* displays either any "text" (whether numerals or characters) that you type in, or the results of formula recalculations. The *formula area* resides "behind" the frame. You enter the formula area by pressing <F2> and, optionally, <F9> to zoom to full screen.

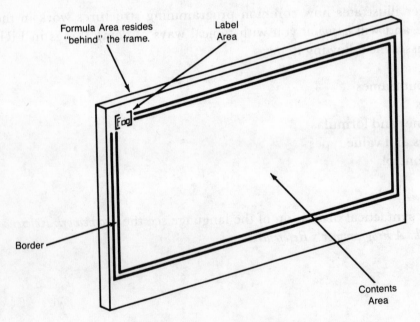

Figure 2-1. Portrait of a Frame

You create frames by going to the Create menu and selecting the type of frame you want. You can then modify its size, shape, and, where appropriate, the number of rows and columns and display formats (for example, word alignment and justification or style of numeric representation).

Types of Frames

Framework makes five types of frames available to the FRED programmer. Think of each type of frame as a *tool* for achieving a different kind of programming purpose.

The Outline Frame.   The Outline is indispensible for laying out programs in a well-structured, top-down manner. You can control the types of frames that you nest within the outline structure to show your subroutines and global variables in a graphic manner. You can also use outlines to structure data in the same way as *records* in other languages.

The Spreadsheet Frame.   Spreadsheets are ideal for programming values into a cell format and for storing values you want to graph. They can also serve as array structures.

The Database Frame.   A database frame assumes that any formula written in its formula area is a data filtering formula. Select this type of frame only for data management and filtering. This provides dynamic access to subsets in a pool of data.

The Graph Frame.   The Graph commands can create a frame to display a graph or draw the graph in an empty frame. Choose Graph for chart displays of spreadsheet and database data.

The Empty/Word Frame.   This is the general purpose programming and display frame. It is also used for containing other frames.

Note: When this book speaks of a frame without specifying its type, it refers to an Empty/Word frame.

An Empty/Word frame can contain data or other frames, but never both. Thus, you can write a memo in a word frame or put other frames inside it, but you can't do both. However, a frame can contain a frame that contains information (see the Outline frame in Figure 2-3). Also, a frame can contain a formula in its formula area and other frames (with or without formulas). This is an important consideration when outlining.

Labels: Naming Frames

Meaningful labels or frame names become increasingly important when you use frames as subroutines and variables. Writing a label is simple. A label can include any insertable character and can be of any length. When a label is over eight characters long, Framework clips it for the desk tray and for DOS, while remembering the entire label for frames and references.

Labels are one form of *identifier*. The rules of naming become more restrictive when you make references to other identifiers, such as variables and subroutines, in a program. These rules, however, do not invalidate any frame name. They are the following:

- The first character of a constant or variable must be an alphabetic character (upper- or lowercase), the underscore (__), or the tilde (~).
- Subsequent allowable characters include numerals, the space, and the tab.
- To reference a frame or cell whose name includes "illegal" characters, place the characters inside square brackets. For example:

    Pressure.[Lb/Sq.In]

    [1985].Fiscal Year

Keep the following in mind:

1. Never put square brackets within any portion of a frame name; only place them where needed in references.

2. When placing tabs and/or spaces in a name, keep their position(s) and number identical in any reference to the name.

3. FRED ignores *case* in matching frame names to references.

FRAMES AND VARIABLES

A frame is an information container. As such, it can act like a variable, a location for storing values. The capacity to bear an executable formula can also make a frame act like a subroutine, not just a passive data receptacle. Before looking more closely at frames as containers of information, take a look at the types of data that frames contain. The "Operators and Value Types" section below discusses these values in greater detail.

FRED Values

FRED recognizes three kinds of values:

*   Numeric values (including reals and integers)
*   Strings (text values)
*   FRED constants

FRED can store and manipulate numbers with exponents as small as -64 or as large as +64. Numbers can have up to 15 significant digits and enjoy display in a number of formats. Examples include:

```
3
10.2%
$1,234.56
7.95623E-29
```

The maximum length for a text string is 32,000 characters. Any string can take advantage of any of the features in the Words menu—attributes (normal, bold, underline, and italic), alignment, and justification. For example:

Normal

Bold

Italic

<u>Underlined</u>

<u>***Bold, Italic, Underlined***</u>

FRED constants are named values that have special meaning within a FRED program. Examples:

```
#TRUE
#NULL!
#N/A!
```

Global Variables

When you discuss frames as variables, you're talking about global, not local, variables. Any frame on the desktop can work with a value in a global variable. To create a *global variable*, you create a frame and label it. That's it. The label or frame name acts as a variable name. Global variables require neither declaration nor type statement, just creation.

To enter a numeric value into a frame, you can either type the value into the formula area or assign it to the frame from another frame. When you assign a value to an empty word frame, the value appears immediately in the contents area. If you type a numeric value into the contents area, FRED treats it as a string, not a numeric value.

To enter a string value into a frame, you can assign it from another frame or type it in. If you type it directly into the contents area you don't need double quotation marks. But if you type the string value into the formula area, you do need them.

> **Note:** You can edit string values as displayed in the contents area of a frame, even when generated by a formula. However, FRED won't let you enter the contents area of a frame in which a formula has written a numeric value.

The best way to see these facts at work is to open a couple of frames and experiment.

Local Variables, Assignments, and Declarations

Local variables differ from global variables in four ways.

1. A local variable is known only to the frame in which you have declared and assigned it. You can, however, pass its value to another subroutine with FRED's parameter passing statement, **@item** (see the "Parameter Passing" section below), or assign its value to a global variable.

2. You must *declare* a local variable before putting it to work, preferably near the top of the program. The declaration statement is the **@local** statement. For example,

   @local(COUNT, PHONE, NAME),

   declares the three local variables COUNT, PHONE, and NAME.

3. You must assign the variable a value with either of FRED's assignment statements: The "gets" sign (:=) or the **@set** statement. For example:

   ```
   COUNT := COUNT + 1
   @set(NAME, "Fred")
   COST := @value( @inputline("Type item cost")
   @set(COST, @value( @inputline("Type item cost"))
   ```

Note that **@set** and := accomplish exactly the same thing, as shown by the last two examples. Here, the values typed in response to a request for input are converted to numeric values and assigned to the COST variable. FRED initializes any unassigned local variables with the value of zero each time the formula is recalculated.

4. Local variables are ephemeral creatures. FRED creates them when he encounters their **@local** declaration and throws them away when he exits their formula (subroutine).

> **Note:** FRED does not require you to declare a variable's type. Type only becomes an issue when you put a variable to work. For example, an arithmetic expression will give you an error message if you try to apply it to a string.

FRAMES, FORMULAS, AND SUBROUTINES

The programmer who wants to enjoy a successful relationship with FRED needs to "think FRED," not BASIC, not Pascal, not FORTRAN. One of the fundamental things to understand about the FRED language is that it evolved from spreadsheet formula languages. As a result, any valid FRED statement (including flow of control statements) yields a *value*. Let's take a look at some of the implications of FRED's formula orientation.

Because of the formula orientation, FRED tends to blur distinctions between programs, subroutines, formulas, and even variables. First, any valid FRED function is a formula. And when you run a group of functions together in a frame, FRED programmers describe that frame as containing "a formula." Even in a multi-frame program, each frame is considered an individual formula. Is it a program or a subroutine? That depends on whether it does the calling or gets called—a fragile distinction at best.

This vagueness of definition becomes an important tool in the hands of the creative programmer. When you work out your program designs, consider how formulas can free you from some of the restrictions of classic structures and make your programs run more efficiently.

Calling Subroutines and Variables

Physically, a subroutine is a formula in its own frame. You call it by using @ to preface the frame name. For example, if you write the statement

    @Postal Expense,

you send program execution to the frame named ''Postal Expense'' for recalculation. When FRED finishes recalculating Postal Expense, execution returns automatically to the next statement in the calling formula (or program).

This ability to call formulas is the essence of *user-defined functions*. FRED does not limit you to a pre-defined set of functions; you can create your own functions and call them just as you call built-in FRED functions. This is the core of FRED's extensibility. Now you can shape a language to your exact requirements. (Chapter Five discusses creating libraries of routines.)

> **Note:** If you find it necessary to type a program into the contents area (you should avoid this practice), use the syntax @@<reference>, instead of the usual @<reference> to call the formula. FRED still evaluates the formula, but has no place to store or display the result.

You can also treat a frame with a formula as a variable. It depends on whether you call it by prefacing its name with @ or treat it as a value container. For example, the statement

    UPDATE COST := Postal Expense * 1.07

assigns to UPDATE COST the value that Postal Expense most recently calculated, multiplied by 1.07.

FRED is fully re-entrant and supports recursion. Note, however, that FRED restricts recursion to a call depth of 32 calls.

Top-Down, Structured Programming

Through its subroutine formulas, variables, and parameter passing, FRED invites writing structured code in a modular fashion. As you begin to write in FRED, you'll find yourself able to accomplish a great deal with small subroutines.

FRED enhances this capability with its outline frame. Figure 2-2 shows an empty outline frame as it first appears on the desktop.

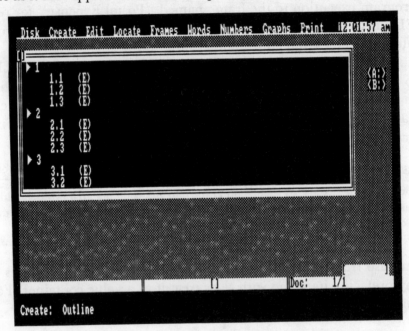

Figure 2-2. An Empty Outline Frame

With it, you can conveniently lay out a program, subroutines, and global variables without writing any code. With the structure in place, you can continue with the technique of step-wise refinement of modules.

Figure 2-3 shows an outline frame named Payment with its subroutines and global variables (in all caps). Note the nesting of the StgTest and NumTest routines under the GetInput routine that calls them for error checking. With one exception, all the frames in the outline are the default frame type, word frames (symbolized by the ''(W)'' at the end of each line). The Report subroutine is a spreadsheet to report the program's data in table form.

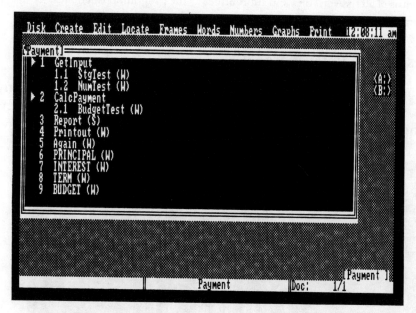

Figure 2-3. The Payment Program Outline

Note that a word frame can contain both a formula and other frames, as long as you write formulas in the formula area and not in the contents area. Once you've written a formula in a frame and recalculated it, Framework will not let you create sub-frames within it.

However, you can reserve a blank subsection before writing and recalculating a formula in the containing frame. When it comes time to add a subroutine, copy the blank subsection, name it, and continue programming. The only cost involved in nesting subroutines in an active formula frame is that you lose the ability to treat the containing frame as a variable. Note that spreadsheet and database frames cannot contain other frames.

> **A Tip:** When working with a program in outline form, you can take a frame view, opening up all the frames and organizing them like a control panel. By taking a control panel approach, you can watch the status of all the variables and subroutines as the program recalculates.

Pathnames: Frame References

Nesting brings up the issue of pathnames. Pathnames come into play any time one frame must reference anything other than a parent (or "grandparent") or sibling frame. Regardless of how deeply nested, a frame always knows its genealogy.

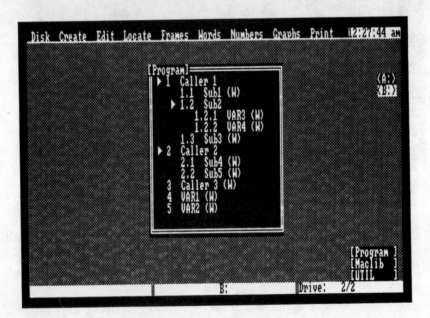

Figure 2-4. A Generic Program Outline

Parent frames are always containing frames. The frames they contain are their *children*. Similarly, when two frames share a parent and exist at the same outline level, FRED programmers refer to them as siblings. For example, in Figure 2-4, Caller 1, Caller 2, Caller 3, VAR1, and VAR2 exist at the same section level and are all siblings. They can refer to each other or Program (their parent frame) without pathnames. For example, Caller 1 could make the following statements:

```
@Caller 2
VAR1 + 3
VAR2 := @Program + VAR1
```

No pathnames are necessary, just frame names. Similarly, nested frames can call on their parents and siblings. For example, Sub1 could contain the formula Sub3 + @Caller 1.

> **Note:** A parent or containing frame has no frame in which to store its value. Therefore, you must recalculate it to read its value. Here, because Caller 1 contains frames, the programmer had to recalculate it by preceding it with @.

However, to reach a sibling's children, pathnames come into play. You construct a pathname by listing each frame name in descending order until you reach the desired frame. Each frame name is separated by the pathname delimiter, a period (.). The point of reference is always the *current frame*. For example, to reach VAR4, Sub1 needs to use a statement like:

```
Sub1 := Sub2.VAR4 - VAR1
```

Because Sub1 and Sub2 share a common ancestry (Program and Caller 1), you needn't include these names. Because VAR1 is also a child of Program, no pathname is necessary. When two frames fail to share a common parent, like Caller 3, VAR4, and Sub4, you must include the parent's name. For example, Caller 3, might contain a statement like:

```
VAR1 := Caller 1.Sub2.VAR4 - Caller 2.Sub4 + VAR2
```

Because VAR1 and VAR2 are Caller 3's siblings (they share Program as a common parent), no pathnames are necessary. A call from a nested frame must also take these rules into account. Sub5 could contain the formula

```
Sub4 + Caller 1.Sub2.VAR3 * VAR2
```

What about Program, the containing frame name? You would only need to include it if you were calling from a sibling of Program, another desktop frame. However, for Program to call one of its own children, it must use itself as part of a pathname. For example:

```
@Program.Caller 2.Sub4
```

The reason is that without Program in the pathname, Program would look for a sibling on the desktop named Caller 2. With no Caller 2 on the desktop, you would get a reference error message. Similarly, if another frame on the desktop wanted to call Sub4, it would have to use the full pathname given above.

> **Note:** The above pathname is calling frame Sub4. Whenever you call via a pathname, @ goes in front of the pathname, not in front of the frame name. For example, *do not* write:
>
> ```
> Program.Caller 2.@Sub4
> ```

If you want to practice with pathnames and outlines, bring up an outline frame, name it "Program," and practice entering simple assignment and arithmetical statements. The values don't matter at this point—just that you don't get a reference error when you press <F5> to recalculate.

Parameter Passing (@item)

FRED supports parameter passing between formulas. This means that frames can share values stored in local variables. It also means that user-defined functions have all of the capabilities to receive and manipulate values that built-in functions have. The function that references parameters is **@item**. You can pass up to 16 parameters to a subroutine by numbering each item; for example, **@item1**, **@item2**... **@item16**. Note that FRED passes parameters by *value*.

To set up a subroutine call with parameter passing, start with the name of the frame the formula will call and then, in parentheses, place each parameter separated by commas. In a second frame, place the necessary **@item**(s) with the functions and/or operators needed to do the job.

As an example, write a formula that generates a random integer between 1 and 10. In FRED it looks like this:

@int(@rand∗10+1)

Follow the steps below to see parameter passing in action.

1. Create two frames. Label the first Fa and the second Fi. Then type the following formula into Fa.

    ; Fa

    @Fi(@rand,10,1)

2. Recalculate it. A "Not Available" (#N/A!) message will appear because the formula tells FRED to call Fi and pass it the three parameters in parentheses—a random number, 10, and 1. But Fi has no formula and, therefore, no values to return.

3. Now select Fi, type the following formula, and recalculate it.

    ; Fi

    @int(@item1∗ @item2-@item3)

    Because the **@item**'s do not have a value until Fi is called by Fa, Fi will display #VALUE! and the error message "Operand must be numeric." Both will disappear as soon as you recalculate Fa (#FUNCTION will replace #VALUE!).

4. Reselect Fa and recalculate it. Fa will call Fi and pass a random number to its corresponding item (**@item1**), then 10 to **@item2**, and 1 to **@item3**. With all the values in place, **@int** will do its work. Then Fi will pass the calculated integer back to Fa for display.

That's all there is to it. Far more complex formulas follow exactly the same principles. FRED also has the **@itemcount** function to keep track of the number of parameters passed.

OPERATORS AND VALUE TYPES

As mentioned earlier, FRED has three types of values: numeric, string, and constant. This section explores these values and their operators.

Arithmetic and Relational Operators

Fred enjoys a full complement of arithmetic and relational operators. Table 2-1 shows these operators and their order of precedence (that is, the order in which they execute). Place parentheses wherever you want to override precedence.

Strings and String Operators

FRED strings take fairly conventional treatment. When composing strings, put the string characters in double quotation marks (''). To concatenate strings, place an ampersand (&) between strings. For example, to concatenate ''Dear'' with the string variable NAME, type:

    "Dear" & NAME

To print double quotation marks, put two double quotes together *within* the string that is already surrounded by double quotation marks. For example, each of the two strings:

    "Hello is not " & """Jello"""

    "Hello is not """"Jello"""

yields:

Table 2-1. FRED's Operators

Operator	Description	Precedence
-	Unary minus	1
+	Unary plus	1
%	Percentage	2
^	Exponentiation	2
*	Multiplication	3
/	Division	3
@mod	Modulo	3
+	Addition	4
-	Subtraction	4
=	Equal	5
<	Less than	5
<=	Less than or equal	5
>	Greater than	5
>=	Greater than or equal	5
<>	Not equal	5
@not	Not	6
@or	Or	7
@and	And	7

Hello is not "Jello"

FRED's relational operators can make either string comparisons or numeric comparisons. The logical operators do not differentiate between upper- and lowercase characters. FRED considers one string "less than" another when one contains earlier letters ("A" is less than "B"), and when one string contains fewer characters than another. (See the "String Functions" chapter in *Framework: A Programmer's Reference* and Chapter 11, "Programming within Framework," of the *Framework Reference Manual* for details.)

Beyond formatting numbers, FRED has some powerful string-handling functions.

@chr converts an ASCII value to its character.

@int converts a string character to its ASCII value.

@len returns the number of characters in a string.

@mid parses strings.

@rept repeats a given string.

@textselection returns the currently selected string.

FRED also has string functions for converting and formatting numbers. See the "Storing and Formatting Values" section below.

Constants

FRED has six categories of constants, as given in Table 2-2. Certain functions return constants rather than numeric or string values. For example, the result of a completed loop is #FALSE, meaning that the condition that kept the loop going is no longer true. You can also include many constants as values in formulas.

Table 2-2. FRED's Constants

Error	Graphing	Macro
#DIV/0!	#BAR	#OFF
#N/A!	#COLUMN	#ON
#NAME?	#LINE	
#NULL!	#MARKEDPOINTS	
#NUM!	#PIE	
#REF!	#ROW	
#TBD!	#STACKEDBAR	
#VALUE!	#XY	

Formula	Logical	Position
#FILTER	#FALSE	#AFTER
#FUNCTION	#NO	#BEFORE
#GRAPH	#TRUE	#BOTH
#KEY	#YES	#EVEN
#MACRO		#ODD
#NAT		
#PICTURE		
#PRT		

> **Note:** FRED has one other constant, #PRT; it appears only when printing while **@trace** is on. (See Chapter Eleven, ''Debugging and **@TRACE**,'' for details on **@trace**.) The *Framework Reference Manual* and *Framework: A Programmer's Reference* describe the other constants in more detail.

Storing and Formatting Values

The FRED programmer needs to make a distinction between those functions that change the way a value is stored and the way it is displayed. Selecting any of the formats in the Numbers menu to format spreadsheet cells only changes the way numbers are displayed. The Numbers menu functions do not change the fact that FRED stores all numeric values as reals with 15-digit precision. Similarly, the *tailoring functions* like **@nationalize** and **@pound** also change a number's display without affecting the way it's stored.

FRED has four functions that change both the form a number takes when stored and the way in which it's displayed. The first three of these convert reals to integers. The fourth, **@round**, has an optional decimal place argument to convert the number of decimals to a given number of places. Table 2-3 shows the four operators that can change the way a number is stored and displayed.

Table 2-3. Number Changing Functions

Function	Description	Example
@ceiling	Round up to integer	@ceiling(5.2) = 6
@floor	Round down to integer	@floor(5.9) = 5
@int	Truncate	@int(5.5) = 5
@round	Round to nearest integer	@round(5.5) = 6

The difference between **@floor** and **@int** arises when you apply them to negative numbers. For example, **@floor**(-5.6) yields -6, while **@int**(-5.6) yields -5, the greater value.

Note: Because FRED takes care of arithmetic housekeeping, you derive little, if any, benefit from reassigning reals to integers.

Fred has five functions that convert numeric values into string values. Each takes a numeric expression as an argument. Here are the functions with an example of how each treats the number 7662.625:

@business	7,662.63
@currency	$7,662.63
@decimal	7662.63
@integer	7663
@scientific	7.66E+3

Don't confuse these with the formatting options in Framework's Numbers menu, the tailoring functions, or with the numeric functions given above, none of which convert numbers to strings; they affect only numeric *display*.

FLOW OF CONTROL

FRED has numerous commands for controlling the flow of program execution. This section discusses the four most commonly used statements: If-Then-Else, cases, loops, and formula exits.

If-Then-Else (@if)

FRED's If-Then-Else statement takes the form:

    @if(expr, then, else)

If FRED evaluates the initial expression as true, it executes the Then parameter. If false, FRED executes the (optional) Else parameter. When the expression evaluates as false and no Else statement exists, the entire statement evaluates as #FALSE.

You can nest FRED's If-Then-Else statements. Nesting takes the following form:

```
@if(expr1,
    @if(expr2,
       @if(expr3,
          then-expr3,
          else-expr3
       ),
       else-expr2
    ),
    else-expr1
)
```

If you want either Then or Else to perform multiple activities, use the **@list** statement.

```
@if(SPEND >= BUDGET,
@list( @beep, @return("You're over budget")),
BUDGET := BUDGET - SPEND
)
```

Here, if SPEND is greater than or equal to BUDGET, FRED will beep, end recalculation of the formula, and print the ''over budget'' message. If SPEND is less than BUDGET, BUDGET is readjusted by SPEND.

To begin an **@if** expression with multiple conditions, you can use **@and** or **@or**. Figure 2-5 shows one way of accepting either a lower- or an uppercase ''Y'' as a response to a prompt (''To continue, press Y''). Although intended as a fragment, the listing in Figure 2-5 would work if entered in the formula area of a frame labeled Init.

```
@local(ANSWER),
ANSWER := @inputline("To continue, press Y"),
@if (@or(ANSWER = "y", ANSWER = "Y"),
    @Init,
    "Thanks for playing"
)
```

Figure 2-5. An @or Example

Here, either ''Y'' response will call the frame labeled Init. Notice that **@or** and **@and** statements need their arguments stated in full. The following syntax, missing the second ''ANSWER ='', would not work.

```
@if( @or(ANSWER = "y", "Y"),
    @Init,
    "Thanks for playing"
)
```

A similar way of testing a prompt is:

```
@if( @or( @nextkey = {Y}, @key = {y}),
    @Program)
```

See the "Input and Output" section below for details on **@nextkey** and **@key** and a program example.

> Note: Besides **@and** and **@or**, FRED has a negative logical operator, **@not**.

Case (@select)

FRED's case statement is **@select**. Syntactically, it looks like this:

> **@select**(index, expr, expr, expr, ...)

The index, a numeric expression, acts as a pointer to select and execute one of the expressions that follow the index.

To see **@select** in action, open a word frame and name it Casey. Then, enter the program listed in Figure 2-6 and recalculate it. The purpose of the program is to convert the numbers 1, 2, 3, or 4 into words.

```
; Casey
@local(NUM,SPELL),
NUM := @value( @inputline("What number? ")),
SPELL := @select(NUM,"one","two","three","too big"),
Casey := "The number is    " & SPELL
```

Figure 2-6. Case Statement Example

Case statements have their boundaries. The "too big" item is not a catch-all; it is the *fourth* item. When you try to push the index beyond that, the program must fail. With Casey, any number less than one or greater than four will garner an error message. Keep this in mind when writing case statements and bomb-proof your work accordingly.

Loops (@while)

FRED has only one loop structure, **@while**. **@while** needs an expression to evaluate as true or false. Any activities that follow end with a closing parenthesis which tells FRED he has reached the last task in the loop.

The default number of times a loop can run is 2048, the minimum number is 1, and the maximum 32000. You can modify your system by changing the default in the CONFIG.FW file. You can nest loops to a depth of 32.

Figure 2-7 gives the listing for a very simple loop program called Loop1 (its frame name). Loop1 prints out the value of its index as the loop increments the index. When the test (COUNTER < 50) finally fails, #FALSE results. Because the programmer assigned no value to COUNTER, FRED initializes it at zero.

```
; Loop1
@local(COUNTER),
@while(COUNTER < 50,
    Loop1 := COUNTER,
    COUNTER := COUNTER + 1
)
```

Figure 2-7. Program listing for Loop1

Whether your loops exit at the top or bottom is determined by where you place your incrementing (or decrementing) statement and by statements inside the loop that influence the counter, such as **@return** and **@result** (see the "Formula Exits" section below.)

You can create a non-finite loop by assigning the #TRUE constant to the test variable and changing the variable to #FALSE only upon a certain condition. Or you can test for a keystroke and not exit the loop until the user presses it. Figure 2-8 shows the listing for a frame labeled Loop2. In Loop2, a loop gathers data in a primitive adding machine. Pressing <Esc> quits the program.

```
; Loop2
@local(TOT,NUM),
Loop2 := " ",
@while( @key <> {Esc},
@if( @iserr(NUM := @value( @inputline("Type number or Esc "))),
   0,
   TOT := TOT + NUM
   ),
   Loop2 := TOT
),
TOT
```

Figure 2-8. Program listing for Loop2

The **@iserr** statement filters any non-numeric input. This keeps the program from bombing when the user types letters, punctuation, or <Esc>.

Formula Exits
(@return and @result)

FRED also has two ways to exit from the middle of a formula: the **@result** and **@return** statements. Going over budget will cause the **@result** statement to force execution out of Program's loop, assigning text to the Messages frame when COUNT equals MANY:

```
@if(COUNT = MANY, @result(Messages := ...
```

Both **@result** and **@return** cause an immediate exit from the current formula. The function's parameter becomes the formula's value. Note that this parameter is *not* optional. If you don't want to give a specific value, give a zero as a dummy argument.

The only difference between these two functions is that **@return** causes #FUNCTION to appear in the current display area, whereas **@result** displays the formula's value. As a general rule, choose **@return** when you're not interested in displaying an intermediate value.

> **Note:** If you interrupt a subroutine recalculation with an **@result** or **@return** statement, only the subroutine, as a discrete formula unit, ceases recalculation, not the main program (formula).

To see the difference at work, create two word frames. Name one Caller and the other Sub. Then type the listings as shown in Figures 2-9 and 2-10 respectively.

```
; Caller
Sub := " ",
Caller := "Hello",
Caller := @Sub
```

Figure 2-9. Program Listing for Caller

```
; Sub
@local(COUNTER),
@while(COUNTER < 100,
   COUNTER := COUNTER + 1
),
@result(COUNTER),
Sub := "Done"
```

Figure 2-10. Program Listing for Sub

When you recalculate Caller, it calls Sub. With the **@result** statement in Sub, Sub will evaluate to 100. This result will also appear in Caller, the result of the **@Sub** statement. Because **@result** halts evaluation of Sub, you'll never see "Done."

Next, change **@result** to **@return.** Again, Caller will display 100, while Sub will show the constant #FUNCTION.

INPUT AND OUTPUT

This section discusses FRED's input and output statements.

Assignment to Frames (:=)

As shown in the discussion of frames and variables, the most straightforward way to display a value to a frame is to assign it to a frame with FRED's assignment operator (:=). For example:

```
Foo := "The answer is " & @decimal(NUM)

Net.Profit.G43 := GROSS - COST

@if(BUDGET < 10000,
   @return(Message := "Sorry. Value out of bounds"))
```

You can assign to the current frame or other frames on the desktop as long as you obey pathname syntax. Trivial though it might seem, assignment is a potentially sophisticated mechanism for a program to display information. Do not underestimate its power.

Displaying Output (@display)

Consider the problem of providing help screens for an application user. How can you cause a table of keystrokes or a list of abbreviations to appear at the touch of a key? The answer is the **@display** statement which calls a frame and displays it.

To create a "pop up" effect, programmers prepare their display frames so that the frames are the same size and stacked in the same position on the desktop, like a deck of cards. To "hide" the deck, you can either position all the frames under the program frame or disguise them. You can create a "cover" frame textured with the desktop character (ASCII 176) in either of two ways: by hand or under program control. The advantage of the latter is that it saves bytes. First, here's how to do it by hand:

1. Create a frame and size it to the desired dimensions. Then place the cursor in the contents area of the frame.

2. Type the desktop character by holding down <Alt> and typing *on the numeric keypad* the number 176. When you release the <Alt> key, the desktop character will appear.

3. Copy the character with <F8> until you fill the top row of the frame.

4. Copy the row as many times as necessary to fill the rest of the frame.

5. Save the frame and reproduce it whenever you need a cover. When working with the frame in a program, you get the best effect by selecting the Frames commands Hide Borders on and Display Labels off.

And now the program version:

1. Create a frame and size it to the desired dimensions.

2. Press <F2> <F9> to enter the formula area of the frame.

3. Begin the formula by typing **@rept("**

4. Type the desktop character (see above) and copy it enough times to fill the width of the frame.

5. When you have the correct number of characters, press <**Return**> and complete the formula by typing a closing quotation mark, a comma, the number of rows in the frame less one, and the concluding parenthesis.

6. Press <F5> to recalculate the formula and fill the frame with desktop characters.

If you select any frame other than one of the display frames, it will fade into the desktop and appear only when called by **@display.** Display frames are usually called from menus or through an indexing system such as you might set up with **@select.** You can also use **@display** to animate displays by calling frames in rapid succession.

Getting Input (@inputline)

FRED has two ways to get keyboard input: **@nextkey** and **@inputline.** Choose **@inputline** when you want the user to be able to edit input. Usually, you'll reserve **@nextkey** for single keystroke input, even though you can write a loop to take multi-character input with **@nextkey.** The "Capturing Keystrokes" section below discusses **@nextkey.**

@inputline has five parameters; each is optional. They are:

- The prompt string (''How many calculations'')
- The default text acting as starting text to edit
- Cursor pointing allowed— # YES or # NO
- Auto-deletion of the default text— # YES or # NO
- Select first character— # YES or # NO

For example:

```
@inputline("How many of item? ","1",# NO, # YES, # NO)
```

The prompt string appears in bold, centered on the bottom line of the screen. The default string value, ''1'', appears on the editline. The user can type another number, automatically deleting the 1, edit the 1, or press <Return> to enter the value on the edit line. If the user makes no changes, the string value is 1. **@inputline** passes its parameter and control back to the program only when the user presses <Return>.

@inputline always returns a string. To convert the string to a number, process the input with **@value.** You may want to do this after testing the input. For example, you could convert the input to a numeric value immediately with:

```
MANY := @value( @inputline("How many of item? "))
```

Or, if you had a frame named ErrTest that would check for input errors (like alphabetic characters), you might write:

```
MANY := @inputline(''How many of item?''),
@ErrTest(MANY),
MANY := @value(MANY)
```

See the *Framework Reference Manual* and *Framework: A Programmer's Reference* for details on the optional parameters.

Prompting for Input
(@prompt and @eraseprompt)

Besides the prompt carried in the **@inputline** statement, FRED makes another provision for placing and erasing prompts. You can use **@prompt** to ask for input before an **@nextkey** statement (see the next section) or simply to advise the user. For example:

@prompt(" Now recalculating data table ",29)

@prompt(" Type " "Y" " to continue. Any other key quits ",22)

Notice two things about these prompts. First, the prompt string is bold, so that it will appear in bold when executed. Otherwise, it would print in normal type. You can also choose the italic or underline type styles for prompts. Second, you specify the string's horizontal position. The optional numbers tell FRED the character position at which to begin the prompt string. The default is 1, the leftmost position.

Prompts appear on the bottom line of the screen. FRED does not support multi-line prompts. Depending on how your prompts progress, you may want to force the erasure of a prompt with **@eraseprompt.** Because **@prompt** does not automatically erase its text, you can build a prompt with multiple prompt statements.

As a general rule, precede each **@prompt** with an **@eraseprompt** to clear any FRED messages (like RECALCULATING) from the prompt line. To see the importance of **@eraseprompt,** type this formula listing in Figure 2-11 into a frame labeled Foo and recalculate it.

```
; Foo
@eraseprompt,
@prompt(''Press a key'',38),
@nextkey,
@eraseprompt,
@prompt( @keyname( @key),38)
```

Figure 2-11. @eraseprompt Example

It should run smoothly, taking your keystroke and displaying it. Edit the formula by placing a semicolon in front of each **@eraseprompt.** Recalculate it a few times. The program still runs, but with **@eraseprompt** deactivated, the prompts remain and get tangled up with FRED's prompts.

Unless followed by an input statement, a keystroke will erase a prompt, making **@eraseprompt** unnecessary. Keep this in mind as you design your prompts. The next section discusses the three ''key'' commands in the above formula.

Capturing Keystrokes (@nextkey, @key, and @keyname)

FRED's **@nextkey** command is excellent for capturing *single keystroke* input when no editing is necessary. You can control how long FRED waits for input by including the optional time parameter, any expression that evaluates to a number. For example,

@nextkey(15)

waits as long as 15 seconds for a keystroke. The number is the number of seconds you want FRED to wait. Omitting the parameter or issuing a negative parameter sets up an indefinite wait.

The **@key** statement gets the last key pressed; it does not wait. Thus it can look at the same keystroke that **@nextkey** captured. Programmers often combine **@nextkey** with **@key** to create decision branches. To see the two statements at work, type the formula in Figure 2-12 into a frame named Yesno.

FRAME WORK

```
; Yesno
Yesno := " ",
@eraseprompt,
@prompt("Press ""Y"" to continue",38),
@if( @or( @nextkey = {Y}, @key = {y}),
    @Yesno
                        ),
@eraseprompt
```

Figure 2-12. Key Functions at Work

When you recalculate, pressing "Y" causes Yesno to call itself. Pressing "N" or any other key ends execution. Yesno uses **@nextkey** and **@key** to test for an upper- or lowercase Y character. The reason the program uses **@key** instead of a second **@nextkey** is that a second **@nextkey** statement would cause a second wait for a second keystroke.

    @nextkey and **@key** work with *keynames*, not characters as such. The appropriate delimiters for keynames are the curly braces ({ }). The normal string delimiter, the double quotation marks, won't do the job. They delimit *characters*, not keynames. To view a key's keyname, address **@key** or **@nextkey** with the **@keyname** function, as in the example from the previous section:

```
@eraseprompt,
@prompt("Press a key",38),
@nextkey,
@eraseprompt,
@prompt( @keyname( @key),38)
```

Besides returning alphanumerics, **@key** can recognize <Return>, <Esc>, and other "non-insertable" keys.

Region-Walking (@get, @put, and @next)

As pointed out earlier, assigning a value to a word frame or to a single cell in a spreadsheet is simple. However, assigning a series of values to a series of cells requires *region-walking*. Region-walking requires you to define a *region*.

A region is range of cells (a solid rectangle in shape) defined by its pathname and its first and last cells. For example, a 15-cell region in a spreadsheet labeled SS that begins with cell A1 and ends with cell C5 takes the region definition SS.A1:SS.C5 as in Figure 2-13.

```
; SS
@fill(SS.A1:SS.C5, " "),
@while( @get(SS.A1:SS.C5) <> # NULL!,
   @put(SS.A1:SS.C5, @rand),
   @next(SS.A1:SS.C5)
)
```

Figure 2-13. An Example of Region-Walking

Note that you must write the full pathname on each side of the colon character (:). The colon acts as a delimiter between the two cells that define the region. An expression like

```
@next (SS.A1:C5)
```

will not work.

The purpose of the formula in SS is to place a random number in each of the region's 15 cells. It does this in a loop that works this way:

@get goes to the currently selected cell in the region and gets its value. If the value is not # NULL! (no further cells), **@put** puts a value, generated by its value argument, **@rand,** in the tested cell. Finally, **@next** moves the region pointer to the next cell in the region and the process begins again. Without **@next,** FRED would put each value in A1. **@get,** paired with **@next** is excellent for getting data from one spreadsheet and moving it into another. **@fill** blanks the spreadsheet by writing a space character to each cell in the region.

Disk I/O
(@writeframefile and
@writetextfile)

Disk I/O in FRED is utter simplicity. You don't have to worry about setting the number of open files, creating buffers, or any of the rest. Just choose either the **@writeframefile** or **@writetextfile** function and give the appropriate filename. **@writeframefile** writes a frame to disk; **@writetextfile,** a text file.

To retrieve a frame, you need to create a keyboard macro. Macros, which add astounding power to FRED, give you a whole new dimension of capability. As a sample, here's a macro to retrieve a frame labeled Foo:

```
@performkeys("{Ctrl-D}gFoo.fw{Return}")
```

A more generalized formula, allowing loading of different filenames would be:

```
@performkeys("{Ctrl-D}g" & @item1 & ".fw{Return}")
```

Whatever string value is assigned to **@item1** will become the filename.

This is an appropriate end for this chapter. Chapter Three begins a discussion of programming the keyboard with macros and key filters.

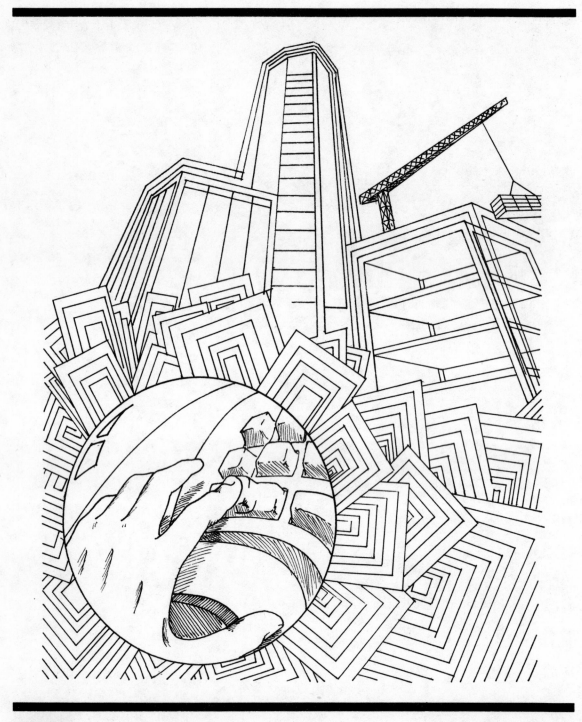

ASHTON·TATE

FRAMEWORK

CHAPTER THREE

MACROS AND MACLIB: THE PROGRAMMER'S TOOLBOX

This chapter introduces macros and the programmer's toolbox— the Maclib frame. Why program with macros? Because macros open up whole new vistas of programming power. For example, none of the FRED functions will create a frame, put column C of a spreadsheet into Currency format, or turn on bold type. In this chapter, you'll learn:

- How to program with macros.
- How to write your own software tools with macros and some of the utilities in Maclib.
- How to put your newly created tools to work forging new tools.
- How to use macros and the /X command to automatically load your tools and the frames you're working on at boot time.

AN OVERVIEW: AUTOMATIC KEYSTROKES IN FRED

Macros and key filtering are two aspects of the same activity: modifying keys to perform functions that they would not normally perform. This usually amounts to having a single key executing numerous keystrokes automatically.

DEVELOPER'S HANDBOOK

The major difference between macros and key filters is that macros assign activities to an <Alt>-key combination, whereas key filters assign them to non-Alt keys. Chapter Four introduces key filters with a program that creates a fast food keyboard.

A third form of automatic keystroking is the /X command. It comes into play when loading files from DOS and is excellent for turnkey applications. This chapter shows you how to write a program that loads your tools and current projects automatically with /X.

WRITING MACROS

Writing a macro takes two steps and two frames. The first step assigns an <Alt>-key combination (like <Alt>-Z) to a frame that contains the keystroke(s) the macro will perform. The assignment function is **@setmacro**. The formula below assigns <Alt-Z> to a frame labeled Name.

@setmacro({Alt-Z},Name)

The second frame (in this case Name) contains the keystrokes that you want the macro to perform. The function that causes FRED to type your keystrokes is **@performkeys.** You must place the **@performkeys** argument (a string) in double quotation marks. If you wanted Name to type the name Nigel Featherweight IV, Name would contain:

@performkeys(''Nigel Featherweight IV'')

To install the macro, you must recalculate the assignment frame. Thereafter, any time you press <Alt>-Z, FRED will perform the keystrokes in Name and print the name Nigel Featherweight IV.

This single macro example assigns only one macro. However, an assignment frame can assign numerous macros, just as the referenced frame can perform numerous **@performkeys** functions. You can also intersperse these functions with non-macro FRED functions, as the example in Figure 3-1 shows.

To turn off a macro, you issue the **@setmacro** function without a frame reference:

@setmacro({Alt-Z})

Note that the keys to which you can assign macros include the alphabetic, numeric, and function keys. Upper- and lowercase alphabetic keys are the same as far as macros are concerned.

The real power of macros lies not so much in typing alphanumeric strings as in carrying out command keystroke functions, such as control key commands and cursor movements. Figure 3-1 shows a program that includes a macro that creates a memo form, complete with the current date and proper cursor position at which to type the recipient's name.

The entire **@performkeys** sequence consists of user keystrokes. These can also be captured by Maclib's Record macro (discussed in the next section). For the moment, just get an idea of the power macros offer by reading the listing of a frame called Letter in Figure 3-1.

```
; Letter
@local(DATELINE),
DATELINE := @date1( @today),
@performkeys("{Ctrl-C}eMemo{Return}{Dnlevel}" &
"{Ctrl-W}L40{Return}123 Easy St.{Return}" &
"La Placebo, CA 99990{Return}" & DATELINE & "{Return}" &
"{Return}{Ctrl-W}L0{Return}Dear ,{Ctrl-4}{Return}" &
"{Ctrl-W}L40{Return}Sincerely,{Return}{Return}{Return}" &
"Ima Littleweird{Return}{Ctrl-W}L0{Return}" &
"{Ctrl-8}{Uparrow}{Ctrl-5}{Rightarrow}")
```

Figure 3-1. A Letter-Generating Macro

FRAME WORK

Notice the frequent use of <Ctrl>-key sequences—to create the word frame, to set margins with the Words menu, and to generate multiple keystrokes. The only element in the **@performkeys** sequence that was not recorded is the DATELINE string variable, inserted later.

> **Note:** Instead of calling Framework command menus with the <Ins> key, always choose the quicker <Ctrl>-key sequence method when writing macros.

A complete table of keystroke symbols ({Return}, {Ctrl}, etc.) appears in Appendix A, "Key Names." Both macros and key filters use these symbols.

INTRODUCING MACLIB

Maclib (pronounced "Mac libe") is a library of macro utilities, located on the Framework Utility disk. Think of it as a software tool box, waiting for you to supply it with even more tools. The wise FRED programmer will have it on the desktop at all times. At the very least, have it on your desktop while reading this chapter.

About Maclib

Maclib contains a collection of programming tools. It also provides space in which you can put the macro programming tools you create for your own work. As of the completion of this book, two versions of MacLib have been issued. Differences are minor—a couple of functions have been replaced and there are some <Alt> key reassignments. For this reason, this book refers to some macros by name rather than by their <Alt> keys (namely, Cut and Paste).

The utilities discussed in this chapter include:

- <Alt>-F1 The "Help" macro that describes the macros already available in Maclib.

- <Alt>-F2 The "Record" macro that records and stores keystrokes as you type them.

- The "Cut" macro for making copies of text in the formula area of a frame.

- The "Paste" macro for retrieving text stored with the "Cut" macro.

Before continuing, get a *copy* of Maclib on your desktop and recalculate it to install its macros. Do not modify the version of Maclib on your Utilities disk. Make a working copy and modify it.

For a brief tour of Maclib, follow the steps below:

1. Select and open the Maclib frame.

   Notice that the left section of the status panel shows the Maclib frame calling @Maclib.setm. Just like any other macro, Maclib must install its macros.

2. Take a look. Press **<Dnlevel> <Ctrl>-<End>** to get to the bottom of the frame. Then select frame 51, setm, and press **<F2> <F9>**

3. Scroll around and you'll see all assignments. Maclib installs all possible macros. What's it all about? Take a look at your collection of tools; press **<Alt>-<F1>**

4. This help frame is an example of the **@display** command. When you're through reading, go to the top of the Maclib frame. Press **<F9> <Esc> <Ctrl>-<Home>**

5. Frame 1, *Description of Maclib*, provides more extensive documentation. Press **<F9>** and look it over. When you're through, zoom out and look at the outline. Notice that it includes nested frames and container frames, just like the outline frames you write. You can see each frame's type by turning on "Reveal type." **Press <Ctrl>-F R**

6. When you're through, press **<Uplevel>** and get ready to add to your software toolbox.

Toolmaking: The Record Macro

This section shows you how to create two macros which come in handy when writing programs. The first turns on bold type, the second turns on normal type. In the next section, *Advanced Toolmaking*, you'll put these two macros to work building other macros. If you haven't recalculated Maclib, do so now. Then follow these steps:

1. As Maclib itself warns, don't invoke the Record macro when Maclib is selected. Create a work area and get into it. Press **<Ctrl>-C E <Dnlevel>**

2. Invoke the Record macro; press **<Alt>-<F2>**

3. A prompt asks you to, ''Type ALT-key to associate with the macro.'' Press **<Alt>-B**

4. A new prompt asks you to, ''Begin entering macros {ALT-B}.''

5. Type the sequence for turning on bold type; press **<Ctrl>-W B**

   As you work, you'll see the message, ''Creating macro {ALT-B}. To end macro, type the {ALT-B key}.'' If you make a typing error, it's simpler with a short macro to conclude and restart. With longer macros, correct your mistake and keep going. Then edit out the unnecessary keystrokes after you have finished editing the macro.

6. To conclude, obey the prompt and press **<Alt>-B**

7. Follow the steps above, but make a macro that turns on normal type. Name the macro **<Alt>-N** and type the sequence **<Ctrl>-W N**

8. When you're finished, try out your tools. Press **<Alt>-B** and type **This is bold** followed by **<Alt>-N and this is normal.** You should see:

   This is bold and this is normal

Congratulations. You will save a keystroke every time you change type faces. Further, you have created a macro that you can put into other macros (as you will see in the next section). Is this easier than creating three frames and hand typing the macro sequences? You bet. To see your macros, select Maclib and check the frames 26 (B) and 38 (N).

Keep your work area frame around. You'll use it in the next section, ''Advanced Toolmaking.''

Advanced Toolmaking

This section takes the two macros you've already created and puts them to work creating further macros. Each macro types a FRED function along with its parameter area and positions the cursor to type the parameter. These two macros will type:

```
@performkeys(""),
@setselection(""),
```

Both functions show up in the fast food program in Chapter Four. To create these macros, follow the steps below.

1. Jump back into the work frame you created earlier and start the Record macro; press <Alt>-<F2>

2. To create the **@performkeys** macro, type <Alt>-P

3. (The spaces in the following string are there only for ease of reading. Don't include them.) Now type <Alt>-B **@performkeys** <Alt>-N (""), <Leftarrow> <Leftarrow> <Leftarrow>

4. Conclude the macro recording process; type <Alt>-P

5. Test your work; type <Alt>-P

   Does the macro print all the characters and reposition the cursor under the second double quotation mark? You're in business.

Follow the next series of steps to create the **@setselection** macro.

1. With the cursor still in the work frame, start the Record macro again; press <Alt>-<F2>

2. To create the **@setselection** macro, type <Alt>-S

3. Again, don't include the spaces. Type <Alt>-B @setselection <Alt>-N (""), <Leftarrow> <Leftarrow> <Leftarrow>

4. Finish up; type <Alt>-S

5. Test your work; type <Alt>-S

Consider the savings that macros offer. First, you'll save a lot of keystrokes when you're coding. Second, macros save bytes. Compare these two strings:

@performkeys("{Ctrl-W}b")
@performkeys("{Alt-B}")

Two bytes. Not much if you only use it once, but again and again, it adds up. Consider, too, that a five- or six-character macro name could carry hundreds, even thousands of keystrokes. Quite a savings.

Consider Maclib yours to customize as you see fit. You may even want to make up several different Maclib's with different libraries of macros for different projects. Customize as you see fit, but work only with *copies* of the original.

The next section demonstrates major savings in programming time by showing you how to use the Record macro along with the Cut and Paste macros.

Cutting and Pasting

The Framework Copy key (<F8>) doesn't work when trying to copy material from a formula area to another formula area. To copy text, you need the Cut and Paste macros. Cut and Paste make it possible for you to record a macro and then retrieve it from Maclib for insertion in a formula. If you aren't sure which <Alt> keys carry Cut and Paste, press <Alt>-<F1> to see. This section symbolizes them as <Cut> and <Paste>.

To demonstrate these macros, this section has you create a simplified form of the memo maker in Figure 3-1. There are four basic tasks you must perform:

● Start the formula.

● Record the macro.

● Retrieve the macro and place it in the formula.

● Edit the macro.

Follow the steps below to create your own memo maker.

1. Start with a clean slate. Delete the old work frame and create an outline frame.

2. Label the frame MemoMake.

3. Label frame 1; type **Do <Return>**

4. Select the MemoMake frame and go into the formula area.

5. Enter the following lines of code:

```
; MemoMake
@printreturn,
```

6. Press **\<Return\>** and type

   @setmacro({Alt-z}, MemoMake.Do)

7. Go to the formula area of Do and type

   ; Do
   @local(DAY),
   DAY: = **@date4**(**@date**),
   @echo(# **OFF**),

   @echo(# **ON**)

The containing frame, MemoMake, calls the Do frame. Do does all the work. By sending the current date to a variable, instead of using the string-producing \<Alt\>-2 macro, your memo will always show the current date.

Note: In Framework versions before 2.0, all macros, including those inside of programs, demand an **@setmacro** function. To recalculate the program, you must press both \<F5\> and press the appropriate \<Alt\>-key combination (in this case, \<Alt-Z\>). In later versions, however, you can issue a straight subroutine call. Recalculate a version 2.0 (or later) program by pressing \<F5\> only.

The **@echo** function turns the screen display off and on. By turning the display off, you won't see the menu frames and cursor moves as the macro executes. You can go into Maclib and surround your own macros with the **@echo** pair. *Always* turn **@echo** back on. When it's off, you can't see your own keystrokes. Also, pressing \<Ctrl\>-\<Break\> not only halts program recalculation, but turns echo on.

The space between the two echoes waits for a string of keystrokes. You'll record that next and then cut and paste the string from Maclib into the waiting space.

To record the keys that will create the memo, follow these steps. Again, spaces between keystrokes are for easier reading.

1. With MemoMake selected, press <Alt>-<F2> to record.

2. Type <Alt>-Z to name the macro.

3. Create, name, and enter the frame. Type <Ctrl>-C E MyMemo <Return> <Dnlevel>

4. Center the date, type in the date variable, left-align the margin, and start the salutation; type <Ctrl>-W C & <Space> DATE <Space> & <Return> <Return> <Ctrl>-W A Dear <Space>

5. Now, go down a couple of lines, set the margin for the closing, type the closing, and reset the margin; type <Return> <Return> <Ctrl>-W L 40 <Return> Cordially, <Return> <Return> <Return> your name <Return> <Ctrl>-W L 0 <Return>

6. Return the cursor to the space after ''Dear.'' Press <Uparrow> five times and conclude with a <Leftarrow>.

7. Conclude the recording session; press <Alt>-Z

8. You won't need the MyMemo frame you created for recording purposes, so delete it.

Now it's time to retrieve your macro string from Maclib.

1. Select Maclib and go into the formula area of the Z frame. You'll see the string you typed, ready to run, complete with @performkeys.

2. Select the entire string; type <F6> <Ctrl>-<End> <Return>

3. Invoke the Cut macro; press <Cut>

   While Cut works, you'll see the message:

   Cutting selected text to clipboard

This may take awhile. Cut has to check each delimiter as it works. When Cut finishes, you'll see the message:

Selected text cut to clipboard

4. Leave Maclib and take the cursor to the empty line between the two **@echo** statements. To paste in the string, press **<Paste>**

Paste will print the entire string. Notice that Paste does not accommodate bold type; **@performkeys** now appears in normal type.

At this point, you could recalculate MemoMake and everything would work but the date constant. However, by editing, you can save bytes and make the macro string more readable. Begin by breaking up the string so it looks like the listing in Figure 3-2.

```
@performkeys("{ALT-C}EMyMemo{RETURN}{DNLEVEL}{CTRL-W}C
& DAY &{RETURN}{RETURN}{CTRL-W}ADear {RETURN}{RETURN}
{Ctrl-W}L40{RETURN}Cordially,{RETURN}{RETURN}{RETURN}
your name{RETURN}{CTRL-W}L0{RETURN}{UPARROW}{UPARROW}
{UPARROW}{UPARROW}{UPARROW}{LEFTARROW}")
```

Figure 3-2. Chopped up Macro String

Note: Maclib's Record macro records non-alphanumeric keynames in uppercase letters.

The first editing task is to save bytes with the **<Ctrl>**-*number* function. For the time being, cut the five {Uparrow} statements near the end of the program to:

{Ctrl-5}{Uparrow}

Then change the three {Return} statements to:

{Ctrl-3}{Return}

If you want, you can also save a couple of extra bytes by changing the double {Return}s to {Ctrl-2}{Return}, but at this point, it's not necessary. To make the macro work on multiple lines, you need to make each line a concatenated string. Use Figure 3-3, a listing of the completed Do formula, as a guideline.

```
; Do
@local(DAY),
DAY := @date4(@date),
@echo( # OFF),
@performkeys("{ALT-C}EMyMemo{RETURN}{DNLEVEL}{CTRL-W}C" &
DAY & "{RETURN}{RETURN}{CTRL-W}ADear " &
"{RETURN}{RETURN}{CTRL-W}L40{RETURN}" &
"Cordially,{CTRL-3}{RETURN}your name{RETURN}" &
"{CTRL-W}L0{RETURN}{CTRL-5}{UPARROW}{LEFTARROW}"),
@echo( # ON)
```

Figure 3-3. Completed Do Formula

Note: DAY, a string variable, is not surrounded by double quotation marks. If you were to surround it, the macro would print the variable name, instead of the date. Recalculate MemoMake and watch your fresh memo form pop up ready for use. If you plan to use a program like MemoMake without Maclib present, you should re-write Maclib-dependent statements.

You could have issued the <Ctrl>-*number* command while recording the macro. However, you'll probably run into cases where it's easier to press an arrow key several times than to try to guess or count the number of keystrokes necessary.

The next section gives guidelines for a self-opening programmer's toolbox, an example of the /X command.

THE SELF-OPENING
TOOLBOX (/X)

Framework has a command that will automatically load a frame and execute its formula at boot-time. For example, to boot Framework and load and execute a frame named Loader.fw, you would type:

```
FW Loader.fw/X <Return>
```

You can also include this command string in a DOS AUTOEXEC.BAT file:

```
TIME
DATE
FW Loader.fw/X
```

There are three things to remember: First, you must separate any frame names after FW with a space character. Second, don't forget the filename extension (.fw). Third, only the final frame in the list will be executed.

```
FW MyFrame.fw YourFrame.fw TheirFrame.fw/X
```

With /X, you can write turnkey applications very easily. You can also create a self-opening programmer's toolbox. Look at the listing for Loader in Figure 3-4.

Once on the desktop, Loader loads three frames: Maclib, Chap3, and FF1. It then selects Maclib and recalculates it so that Maclib's macros are ready to run. Finally, Loader puts up a prompt (for three seconds) to press <Del>. Why not have loader delete itself?

FRED code is always "live." When you ask a program to delete itself, you're playing with fire. As a general rule, you should never ask a macro to act on itself. The results range from unpredictable to disastrous.

```
; Loader
@performkeys("{Ctrl-D}ga:Maclib.fw{Return}"),
@performkeys("{Ctrl-D}gb:Chap3.fw{Return}"),
@performkeys("{Ctrl-D}gb:FF1.fw{Return}"),
@setselection("Maclib"),
@performkeyst("{F5}"),
@setselection("Loader"),
@prompt("Press <Del> to erase Loader",24),
@beep(20,300),
@eraseprompt
```

Figure 3-4. Listing for the Loader Program

> Note: The **@setselection** command selects the frame designated in its argument. You'll see a lot more of **@setselection** in the next chapter.

Whether you choose to set up your own loader and how you do it depend on your system configuration and work preferences. It does, however, save a lot of time and keystrokes. Here's how one intrepid programmer set up a self-opening toolbox:

1. He made a *working copy* of his System Disk #2 and deleted its Help files to make room for Maclib.

2. He copied Maclib onto the disk.

3. He wrote his Loader program and saved it onto the disk.

4. He wrote a version of the AUTOEXEC.BAT file referred to earlier and saved it on the System Disk #1 disk to boot Framework and load Loader.

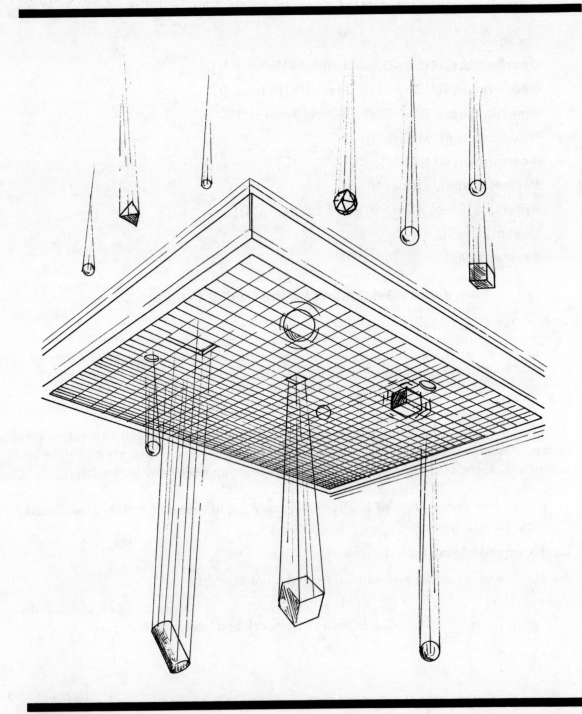

FRAMEWORK

CHAPTER FOUR

KEY FILTERS

Key filters alter the results of typing individual keys. You can make a single key perform a string or execute a formula. You can even turn off an entire group of keys so that a user can't bomb an application by pressing <Return> or an arrow key at the wrong time. For example, the program in this chapter filters six function keys so that they represent fastfood entries—"Hamburger," "Cheeseburger," "Fries," and so on. When the user presses one of the function keys, the program filters the keyboard so that the user can enter only numeric input (for example, the number of burgers or sodas).

Before proceeding to the program, let's look at how you assign a key filter and how FRED maps the keyboard into groups of keys.

ASSIGNING KEYS FOR FILTERING (@keyfilter)

Like macros, installing a key filter also requires at least two frames—one in which to assign the key filter to a key definition (formula) frame, and a second to bear the formula of the new key definition. For example, to cause <F1> to print the string ''Hi. I'm F1'', you could write the following formula in a frame called Assign:

@keyfilter({F1}, Greeting)

In Greeting, the key contents frame, you would write:

@performkeys(''Hi. I'm F1'')

@performkeys does the work, just as it does in macros. You turn off a key filter similar to the way in which you turn off a macro: type the **@keyfilter** function, naming the key without a corresponding frame:

@keyfilter({F1})

FRED doesn't let you assign individual filters to each key on the keyboard. The next section discusses how FRED maps the keyboard for filtering.

KEY CLASSES AND {char}

FRED divides the keyboard into six different classes of keys for filtering purposes. These are:

- The function keys (<F1> to <F10>) — individually assignable

- The navigational keys and ''other'' keys — the arrows, <Home>, <End>, <Pgup>, <Pgdn>, <Uplevel>, <Dnlevel), <Del>, <Ins>, <Tab>, <Backtab>, <Esc>, <Return>, <Backspace>, <Scroll-Lock>, and their <Ctrl> versions (<Ctrl>-<Uplevel>) — individually assignable

- The insertable keys — the alphabetic, numeric, and punctuation keys — treated as a group

- The macros — all <Alt>-key combinations — treated as a group

- <Ctrl>-alphabet keys (<Ctrl-C>, etc.) — treated as a group

- <Ctrl>-numeric keys (the repeat keys) — treated as a group

You can filter only the first two classes, the function keys and the navigational and other keys, as *individual keys*. With the last four groups, if you filter one, you filter all the keys in its class. For example, if you were to write

> **@keyfilter**({x},Awesomely)

pressing the x key would execute the contents of a frame labeled Awesomely. But so would pressing S, b, 3, or ;. In other words, pressing any of the insertable keys executes Awesomely. But pressing <Ctrl-M>, <Ctrl-7>, or <Alt-G> won't. They're not members of the insertable class.

A pair of statements like

> **@keyfilter**({x},Awesomely),
>
> **@keyfilter**({k},Awesomely)

is redundant, whereas

> **@keyfilter**({x},Awesomely),
>
> **@keyfilter**({k},AhGosh)

is wrong. The assignment of the insertable class to AhGosh would overwrite the assignment to Awesomely. You can assign only one frame to a class *at a time*.

To avoid confusion, substitute the {char} symbol for any insertable characters. For example, instead of

> **@keyfilter**({x},Awesomely),

write

> **@keyfilter**({char},Awesomely)

{char} refers to any and all members of the insertable class.

Note: {char} does not change the functionality of the statement in any way.

You do not always have to deal with one class at a time. FRED has another symbol that acts on the entire keyboard.

MASKING THE KEYBOARD WITH {all}

Masking is an important filtering technique. It consists of turning off the entire keyboard with the {all} symbol and then enabling only those keys you want the user to press. Here's a typical masking statement:

    @keyfilter({all},ErrKey)

where the Errkey frame formula is

    ; ErrKey
    @beep,
    @eraseprompt,
    @prompt("Sorry! Key not active", 33),
    @beep(20, 100),   ; pause 1 sec
    @eraseprompt

Errkey beeps and displays its message for one second before going away. (**@beep** is given an inaudible frequency for the pause.)

Once you have disabled the keyboard, you can selectively enable specific keys. One FRED programmer describes this process as ''laying a floor and cutting trapdoors in it.''

The {all} symbol acts on all keys, regardless of class. To re-enable the entire keyboard, you write this statement:

@keyfilter({all})

Errkey is one of the subroutines in the fast food program that take advantage of this "floor" and numerous trap doors — turning off the keyboard and enabling a group of keys — and then turning off the keyboard again only to enable a different group of keys, as different input needs arise. The next section shows you how to set up the fast food program, FF1, and run it.

SETTING UP THE FAST FOOD PROGRAM

This section gives you an overview of the fast food keyboard program, FF1. Read the overview to see how the pieces fit together. Then, type in the outline and code.

Program Overview

FF1 turns the computer keyboard into a fastfood keyboard for a very small store (only five items on the menu) with pretty decent prices (only a buck for a burger). When FF1 is running, it requires only two inputs—the item being purchased and the number of items (input default is set to 1). Because only five items are available, FF1 automatically totals the bill after you've entered five items.

FF1 filters five function keys as food items with a sixth key set to force a total calculation:

    <F1> Hamburger

    <F3> Cheeseburger

    <F5> Fries

    <F7> Regular-size beverage

    <F9> Large-size beverage

    <F10> Calculate total for customer

Although this is a sample program for illustrating keyfilters, you could add routines for printing the receipt, subtracting from inventory, and registering sales in a database that keeps track of the number of each item sold at what date and time.

If you would like to practice with FRED's tailoring functions, you could convert FF1 for a British crumpet shop, a French boulangerie, or a Japanese tofu store.

Here's how FF1 does its stuff: FF1 is really two programs— the initialization group and the input and calculation group. The initialization formulas set the ROW variable to 1, erase the previous contents of Receipt, and prompt for an item (that is, a function key). At this point, the program actually ends. Pressing an item key starts the rest of the input and calculation routines.

Each food item key supplies the cost and name of the item and calls DoItem. DoItem prints the item name in Receipt and then calls GetNum. GetNum prompts for the number of items and prints this number and the item cost in Receipt. GetNum then returns control to DoItem, which calls SubCalc.

SubCalc calculates a subtotal for the line. It also increments the row number. If you've entered five items, it automatically calls TotCalc to calculate the subtotal, tax, and grand total and print these items. TotCalc calls Again to see if you want to take another order.

These calls become more obvious as you look at the well-nested outline that follows. As mentioned earlier, a good outline serves as a structural skeleton to guide your programming efforts.

The Outline

Figure 4-1 contains the outline for FF1. Bring up an Outline frame and label it FF1. Then, type in the entire outline before coding. When you get to the Receipt frame, create a spreadsheet frame with four columns and 12 rows. You can size the columns after running the program. All other frames are Empty/Word frames. (To create extra Empty/Word frames, just press <Ctrl>-C E. To create a lower level subsection, press <Ctrl>-<Dnlevel>)

FF1

1 Init

   1.1 Cleanup (E)

   1.2 Receipt (S)

   1.3 GetItem (E)

2 Food

   2.1 Hburg (E)

   2.2 Cburg (E)

   2.3 Fries (E)

   2.4 RgBev (E)

   2.5 LgBev (E)

   2.6 Action

      2.6.1 DoItem

         2.6.1.1 GetNum

            2.6.1.1.1 AcceptNum (E)

      2.6.2 SubCalc

         2.6.2.1 TotCalc

            2.6.2.1.1 Again (E)

3 Errkey (E)

4 GetOut (E)

5 ROW (E)

6 MANY (E)

7 COST (E)

Figure 4-1. Outline for FF1

When you have typed in the outline, save it, and continue to the listing section.

The Listing

Figure 4-2 contains the listings for all the formulas that make up the fast food program, FF1. Type each formula into the appropriate frame's formula area. For example, FF1 goes in the formula area of the containing frame; FF1.Init goes in the formula area of the Init frame, and so on.

> **Note:** Take a look at the last two lines in FF1, the first formula. If you have a Framework version prior to 2.0, type the **@setmacro** statement. If you have a 2.0 or later version, type the second line to call the Init formula, instead. In versions prior to 2.0, you can only execute a macro (even within a program) by pressing the appropriate <Alt>-key.

Two frames are container frames only; they serve to structure the outline and carry no formulas. These are Food and Action.

Don't recalculate formulas by pressing <F5> or <Return> to exit. Exit with <Esc>, because a FRED program can bomb when all its subroutines aren't in place.

```
FF1:
    ; FF1 -- Fastfood Keyboard

    ; Print listing routine
    @tm(2),
    @bm(4),
    @po(5),
    @ll(75),
    @fl("FF1 Listing"),
    @fc(@date1(@today) & " : " & @time1(@today)),
    @fr(@pn),
    @printreturn,

    ; Call initialization routine and set macro
;   @setmacro({Alt-F},FF1.Init)
;   @FF1.Init
```

Figure 4-2. Listing for FF1

```
FF1.Init:
   ; Init

   ROW := 1,
   @Init.Cleanup,
   @setselection("Init.Receipt.A3"),
   @Init.GetItem


FF1.Init.Cleanup:
   ; Cleanup Receipt and print date and time

   @setselection("FF1.Init.Receipt"),   ; needs complete path!
   @performkeys("{Dnlevel}{Ctrl-Home}{F6}{Ctrl-End}{Del}" &
       "{Ctrl-Home}@scientific(@date){Return}{End}" &
       "@time1(@today){Return}{Home}{Dnarrow}{Dnarrow}")


FF1.Init.GetItem:
   ; GetItem

   @keyfilter({all},ErrKey),
   @keyfilter({Esc},GetOut),
   @keyfilter({F1},Food.Hburg),
   @keyfilter({F3},Food.Cburg),
   @keyfilter({F5},Food.Fries),
   @keyfilter({F7},Food.RgBev),
   @keyfilter({F9},Food.LgBev),
   @keyfilter({F10},Food.Action.SubCalc.TotCalc),
   @eraseprompt,
   @prompt("Select item (F1=HB F3=CB F5=Fr F7=RS F9=LS F10=TOT)",15)


FF1.Food.Hburg:
   ;Hburg

   @Action.DoItem(1.00, "Hamburger")


FF1.Food.Cburg:
   ; Cburg

   @Action.DoItem(1.25, "Cheeseburger")
```

Figure 4-2 continued.

FRAME WORK

```
FF1.Food.Fries:
  ; Fries

  @Action.DoItem(0.75, "Fries")


FF1.Food.RgBev:
  ; RgBev

  @Action.DoItem(0.50,"Regular soda")


FF1.Food.LgBev:
  ; LgBev

  @Action.DoItem(0.65, "Large soda")


FF1.Food.Action.DoItem:
  ; DoItem

  COST := @item1,

  ; Type in item name and cost
  @performkeys(@item2 & "{Tab}"),

  ;Find how many items and calc line subtotal
  @Action.DoItem.GetNum,
  @Action.SubCalc


FF1.Food.Action.DoItem.GetNum:
  ; GetNum

  ; Turn off everything except 3 edit keys, Esc, and cr
  ; AcceptNum tests for and Returns 0-9 only

  @keyfilter({all},ErrKey),
  @keyfilter({Esc},GetOut),
  @keyfilter({char},Action.DoItem.GetNum.AcceptNum),
  @keyfilter({Return}),
```

Figure 4-2 continued.

```
@keyfilter({Leftarrow}),
@keyfilter({Rightarrow}),
@keyfilter({Backspace}),
@keyfilter({Del}),

MANY := @inputline("How many of item?", "1", #NO, #YES, #YES),
@performkeys(MANY & "{Tab}" & @business(COST) & "{Tab}"),

@keyfilter({all},ErrKey)


FF1.Food.Action.DoItem.GetNum.AcceptNum:
  ; AcceptNum

  ; if keystrokes are numeric, type them in.  Else error.
  @if(@and(@key >= {0}, @key <= {9}),
        @performkeys(@keyname(@key)),
        @Errkey
  )


FF1.Food.Action.SubCalc:
  ; SubCalc -- Calcs end of line total

  ROW := ROW +1,

  @performkeys("+{Uparrow}{Leftarrow}*{Uparrow}{Leftarrow}" &
      "{Return}{Return}{Dnarrow}{Home}"),

  ; if receipt has all 5 items, calc total
  @if(ROW < 6,
      @Init.GetItem,
      @result(@SubCalc.TotCalc)
  )


FF1.Food.Action.SubCalc.TotCalc:

  ; TotCalc adds subtotal, calcs tax, sums bill, asks again?

  @keyfilter({all},ErrKey),
```

Figure 4.2 continued.

FRAME WORK

```
@performkeys("Subtotal{Tab}{End}" &
    "@sum({Uparrow}{Uparrow}:D2){Return}" &
    "{Dnarrow}{Home}Tax{Tab}{End}" &
    ".06*{Uparrow}{Uparrow}{Return}{Return}" &
    "{Dnarrow}{Home}Total{Tab}{End}" &
    "+{Uparrow}{Uparrow}+{Uparrow}{Uparrow}" &
    "{Return}{Return}{Dnarrow}{Dnarrow}{Home}{Tab}" &
    "Fred's thanks you{Return}{Ctrl-Home}{Ctrl-Uplevel}"),

@keyfilter({all}),      ; Turn off all filters
@TotCalc.Again          ; Asks for another order


FF1.Food.Action.SubCalc.TotCalc.Again:
  ; Again

@while(@nextkey(0) <> {null},
    0
),
@eraseprompt,
@prompt("[Esc] quits.  ""Any"" other key continues.",23),
@if(@not(@nextkey = {Esc}),
    @FF1.Init,
    @eraseprompt
)


FF1.Errkey:
  ; ErrKey for filtered out keys

@beep,
@eraseprompt,
@prompt("Sorry! Key not active",33),
@beep(20, 100),      ; pause 1 sec
@eraseprompt


FF1.GetOut:
  ; GetOut turn off all filters and go to containing frame

@keyfilter({all}),
@performkeys("{Ctrl-Uplevel}")
```

Figure 4.2 continued.

When you finish coding, go to a Frames View (<F10>), and move the cursor around until the containing frame displays the Receipt frame. Go into Receipt and format the columns from the Numbers menu as follows:

Column B in Integer format

Column C in Business format

Column D in Currency format

While you're in Receipt, move over to column A and type the word Cheeseburger. Then size the column for a comfortable fit. You may also want to shrink column B down to a four-character width and expand D (will you ever sell $9,999.99 worth of food or is $999.99 enough?).

You can also contract the Receipt and FF1 frame so that they display only your four columns. Before running FF1, sharpen up the display:

Turn off Number Labels

Turn off Reveal Type

Turn off Display Labels

Turn Hide Borders on

You may also want to close all frames except Receipt. Use Figure 4-3 as a guideline. Remember, creating a good display is as much an art as a part of programming science. Play around with your displays. Try different things. For example, you could also force the display to go full screen by inserting

```
@performkeys(''{F9}'')
```

just before the @Cleanup call in the Init frame.

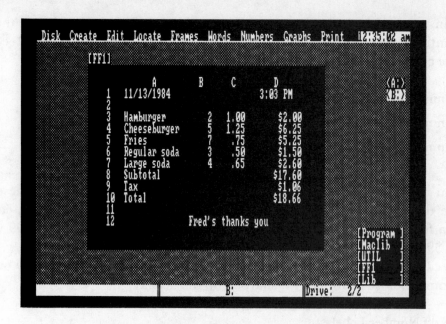

Figure 4-3. FF1 after Entering an Order

To recalculate the program in a Framework version prior to 2.0, select the container frame, FF1, and press <F5> followed by <Alt>-F For 2.0 or later, just press <F5>

HOW TO FILTER FUNCTION KEYS

Take a look at the filter portion of the GetItem formula, shown in Figure 4-4.

This listing shows how to turn off the keyboard— @keyfilter({all},ErrKey)—as discussed earlier. At this point, pressing *any* key will cause a beep, an error message, and that's it. You can't type, can't move, can't do a <Ctrl>-<Break>. In fact, the only thing you can do is <Ctrl>-<Alt>-<Del> to reboot.

```
@keyfilter({all},ErrKey),
@keyfilter({Esc},GetOut),
@keyfilter({F1},Food.Hburg),
@keyfilter({F3},Food.Cburg),
@keyfilter({F5},Food.Fries),
@keyfilter({F7},Food.RgBev),
@keyfilter({F9},Food.LgBev),
@keyfilter({F10},Food.Action. SubCalc.TotCalc),
```

Figure 4-4. Listing for GetItem's Filters

That's why the first trap door opens the <Esc> key to the GetOut formula. GetOut is a safety valve for the programmer and user:

```
@keyfilter({all}),
@performkeys("{Ctrl-Uplevel}")
```

It turns off all keyfilters and moves you to the highest level, FF1, freeing you to resume. Always have access to the outermost frame while programming.

The remaining six function keys define calls for food entries and the TotCalc function. Take a look at what the individual Food frames do. Hburg, the hamburger frame, carries the following listing:

```
@Action.DoItem(1.00, "Hamburger")
```

Instead of typing in the word Hamburger and the cost, this frame packages this data for parameter passing, thus saving bytes by taking advantage of **@item**. Otherwise, each food item would have to follow this pattern:

```
@performkeys("Hamburger{Tab}{Tab}1.00{Return}{Leftarrow}"),
@Action.DoItem.GetNum
```

@performkeys can continue to type even when filters are on. Filters inhibit the *keyboard*, not character generation from other sources. DoItem calls GetNum, the formula that prompts for and takes user input. This calls for another set of filters.

HOW TO FILTER
NUMERIC KEYS

To begin, take a look at the filters in GetNum, shown in Figure 4-5.

```
@keyfilter({all},ErrKey),
@keyfilter({Esc},GetOut),
@keyfilter({char},Action.DoItem.GetNum.AcceptNum),
@keyfilter({Return}),
@keyfilter({Leftarrow}),
@keyfilter({Rightarrow}),
@keyfilter({Backspace}),
@keyfilter({Del}),
```

Figure 4-5. Listing for GetNum's Filters

The first two elements are the same as those in GetItem. The last four turn the individual keys on again so that the user can edit the number of items. The third line is the most interesting. Here, the {char} symbol tells FRED to send all members of the insertable key class (to which numerals belong) to the AcceptNum routine for processing.

Figure 4-6 contains a listing of AcceptNum. AcceptNum tests to see if a keystroke is a numeral. If it is, then AcceptNum types it into the edit line. If not, AcceptNum calls ErrKey. is a numeral. If it is, then AcceptNum types it into the edit line. If not, AcceptNum calls ErrKey.

```
@if( @and( @key >= {0}, @key <= {9}),
@performkeys( @keyname( @key)),
@Errkey
)
```

Figure 4-6. Listing for the AcceptNum Formula

To do this, AcceptNum checks to see if the value of the last key pressed (the one that activates this filter formula) is greater than or equal to zero and less than or equal to nine. It types a numeral by converting the **@key** value into a character representation with **@keyname**. In fact, AcceptNum, not the user, types in the value representing the number of items. This is an example of how you filter a group of items from an entire class—a trapdoor within a trapdoor.

OTHER PROGRAMMING COMMENTS

Frame Navigation

To select a frame, FF1 relies on the **@setselection** command. This command appears in the Cleanup formula and in the Init formula where it sets the cursor position to A3 for the first GetItem. When working with macros and key filters, **@setselection** can take an argument, as it does here. You can also use **@setselection** to return the current selection. For example,

```
CURRENT := @setselection
```

would place the name of the current selection into the variable CURRENT. FF1 does not use this form.

Avoid using arrow keys to select frames in macros, especially if your program creates frames as it recalculates. As programs grow, their component frames have a tendency to get moved around. Havoc awaits the programmer who selects frames with arrow keystrokes alone.

When using arrow keys within a cell frame, always begin with a {Ctrl-Home} statement. This gives you an absolute reference point from which to venture out into other cells. Cleanup does this with its

@performkeys("{Dnlevel}{Ctrl-Home}{F6}...")

statement. This is important, because FRED always remembers the cell from which you exit and wants to return to it. Thus, if you were to stop the program with the cursor on D4 and jump out, the cursor would return to D4 upon re-entry into the cell frame. An absolute point becomes all the more important if a program allows the user to move freely within a cell-based frame.

> **Note:** The FRED programmer has a number of choices for how to do things. For example, in Cleanup, instead of the {Dnlevel}{Ctrl-Home} move, you could change the **@setselection** statement to **@setselection**("FF1.Init.Receipt.A1"). This would take you directly to the "home" cell, A1.

Another note on Cleanup: Each time Cleanup recalculates, it writes in the current date and time of day. You could "hardwire" these two elements into the Receipt spreadsheet and protect them from Cleanup's deleting activities with the Edit menu's Protect from Editing command.

The Value of Recording Keystrokes

Three frames (Cleanup, SubCalc, TotCalc) take advantage of <Alt>-<F2>, the Record macro in Maclib. Take a look at Figure 4-7.

Now, honestly, would you want to figure that out and assemble it by hand? Nah!

```
@performkeys("Subtotal{TAB}{END}" &
  " @sum({UPARROW}{UPARROW}:D2){RETURN}" &
  "{DNARROW}{HOME}Tax{TAB}{END}" &
  ".06*{UPARROW}{UPARROW}{RETURN}{RETURN}" &
  "{DNARROW}{HOME}Total{TAB}{END}" &
  "+{UPARROW}{UPARROW}+{UPARROW}{UPARROW}" &
  "{RETURN}{RETURN}{DNARROW}{DNARROW}{HOME}{TAB}" &
  "Fred's thanks you{RETURN}{CTRL-HOME}{CTRL-UPLEVEL}"),
```

Figure 4-7. Recorded Portion of TotCalc

The Transportable Time-Out

A common way to slow down execution or to create a pause is to write a null loop, like:

```
@while(COUNT < 300
    COUNT := COUNT +1
)
```

However, FRED programmers have found that the processing speeds of different computers make this a bad idea. What seems like a restful, one-second interlude on one machine is a 100-millisecond flash on another. To remedy this situation, create pauses of absolute length with the **@beep** function. Give it a sub-sonic frequency and a duration—one second per 100. For example, Errkey holds its message on the screen for one second with:

```
@beep(20,100)
```

Maximum duration is 32767, 328 seconds.

Clearing the Typeahead Buffer

Framework has a typeahead buffer. The buffer's job is to hold characters for processing. Occasionally, this can create problems. Take a look at the Again formula in Figure 4-8.

```
@while( @nextkey(0) <> {null},
    0
),
@eraseprompt,
@prompt(" [Esc ] quits. ""Any"" other key continues.",23),
@f( @not( @nextkey = {Esc}),
    @FF1.Init,
    @eraseprompt
)
```

Figure 4-8. Listing for the Again Formula

Again will quit FF1, if you press <Esc>. Any other key calls the Init formula. This decision makes the state of the *typeahead buffer* crucial, because **@nextkey** looks into the typeahead buffer for a character. If someone had pressed an extra key during the TotCalc routine, its character would be waiting for **@nextkey**. And it might not be the character the user wants.

Therefore, you need to clear the typeahead buffer, and that's what the little **@while** loop does. This is how it works: **@nextkey's** zero parameter (wait zero seconds) keeps **@nextkey** from accepting any key presses and forces its attention to the typeahead buffer. The loop causes **@nextkey** to pull characters out of the typeahead buffer until the buffer is empty, returning a {null}. The second zero is a "do nothing" argument; its only purpose is to provide **@while** with its required second parameter. The loop, then, keeps sending **@nextkey** back to the typeahead buffer until **@nextkey** has sucked the buffer dry.

Formatting Notes

Perhaps you noticed that Cleanup formats its date with a function not mentioned in the books as a date/time function, **@scientific.** **@scientific** will turn an **@time, @today, @date,** or **@datetime** argument into the ''slashed'' date format. For example, if the date is November 5, 1985, **@scientific(@today**) would return:

11/5/85

There are two other ''new'' date/time formatting functions which double as string formatting functions. **@business(@today**) would return a display like **@date4:**

November 5, 1985

And **@integer(@today**) returns the string:

19851105

Earlier, you read that to print a number as part of a string, you had to format it as a string, i.e, **@integer**(MANY). In the GetNum routine, the following line types in how many items are being purchased and their cost (COST):

@performkeys(MANY & ″{Tab}″ & **@business**(COST) & ″{Tab}″),

Here, the **@business** function serves one purpose: to convert COST into a string. The reason is that the data is being printed in a spreadsheet. In spreadsheets, the format of the individual cell (set with the Numbers menu) determines the format of the number, not a string function like **@business.** Functions like **@business** have a formatting effect only in a string-oriented environment—word frames. The programmer uses **@business** here strictly to remind himself which format the number should ultimately appear in.

CHAPTER FIVE

LIBRARIES

This chapter discusses libraries and how to create and work with them. The library example belongs to a program named Currency1. Currency1 also serves as the model for menus (Chapter Six) and tables (Chapter Seven).

CURRENCY1: A PROGRAM OVERVIEW

When you look at the tables of currency values in a U.S. newspaper, you normally see two columns: foreign currency in U.S. dollar equivalents and currency per U.S. dollar. This means that to buy yen with francs, for example, you have to calculate an intermediate dollar factor. Currency1 takes care of this task and multiplies the factor by the desired number of monetary units. All conversions are menu driven, as is the option to change a currency's value.

Because Currency1 is a model, it handles only five currencies—the American dollar, the British pound, the French franc, the West German mark, and the Japanese yen. However, with a few changes, you could expand it to a professional level with 40 or 50 currencies.

Currency1 stores its currency per dollar constant in a library along with its input routines and a global variable. As the chapter progresses, the value of libraries will become evident.

WHAT EVERY LIBRARIAN
SHOULD KNOW

A library is a frame that can contain constants, variables, and/or user-defined functions. Regardless of what a library contains, it must always bear the three-character label ''Lib'' (pronounced ''libe'') in any combination of upper- and/or lowercase characters. Only available memory limits the size of a library.

Any frame on the desktop can use the routines and data stored in Lib (as long as Lib is also on the desktop), without referencing by pathname. In fact, several programs can take advantage of one Lib. FRED treats all library entities as if they were built-in. For example, instead of calling a calculation routine with @Lib.CalcNum, a frame need only call @CalcNum.

FRED's extensibility draws heavily on libraries. By storing your ''greatest hits'' in appropriate libraries, you can shape FRED into a vertical language—a word-processing language, a scientific language, a statistical language, and so on. In fact, many FRED programmers keep various libraries—WordLib, SciLib, StatLib—available for different projects. Just change the library's name to Lib when you get it on the desktop.

> **Note:** Although MacLib is a library, it is not a ''Lib'' library. Its name is different, and as a result, any calls to a MacLib formula must include a complete pathname.

How does FRED know to look in Lib for a called element? As a last resort. Whenever you make a call, FRED first searches for the element according to standard pathname rules. If this search fails, he looks for a Lib frame. If he finds a Lib, he looks for the element there. If no Lib exists or the element doesn't exist in the Lib, FRED returns an error message.

As you know, Framework tolerates the same label on multiple frames. If you have more than one frame labeled Lib on the desktop, FRED goes to the first frame and only the first in his search. If the search fails there, FRED doesn't bother to try the next Lib.

SETTING UP LIB, A LIBRARY

Currency1's library contains just eight items. Begin by setting up the outline and follow that with the code.

Outlining Lib

Create an outline frame and label it Lib. If you have a copy of FF1 on disk, type in the elements shown in Figure 5-1. You can copy routines you wrote for FF1 directly into the outline (as discussed in the next section). If you don't have a copy of FF1, type in the outline shown in Figure 5-2.

Note: Each frame is a word frame.

Lib:

   1 Lb
   2 Nf
   3 Dm
   4 Yn

Figure 5-1. Outline 1 for Lib

Lib:

  1 Lb

  2 Nf

  3 Dm

  4 Yn

  5 GetNum

    5.1 TestNum

  6 ErrKey

  7 GetOut

  8 MANY

Figure 5-2. Outline 2 for Lib

Coding Lib's Constants

The first four items are the constants that Currency1's Table uses to calculate currency values. They correspond to currency per U.S. dollar figures. Enter them in their respective frame formula areas.

Lb	.8107
Nf	9.42
Dm	3.0730
Yn	247.20

Now for the formulas, and several pleasant surprises.

Coding Lib's Formulas

If you don't have a copy of FF1, type the listings given in Figure 5-3 into the formula area of the appropriate frame. If you have a copy of FF1, you can enjoy FRED's extensibility. The four formulas are slightly modified versions of four formulas you've already written: GetNum, AcceptNum, ErrKey, and GetOut.

Here's how to copy (*not* move) these formulas from FF1 to Lib.

1. Bring up FF1 and put the highlight on the frame you want to copy, like GetNum. Note that you copy GetNum and AcceptNum as a unit by just selecting GetNum. You can bring ErrKey and GetOut back together by highlighting ErrKey and pressing <F6> <Dnarrow> <Return>

2. Once you've made your selection, press the Copy key, <F8>

3. Move the cursor to the FF1 frame; press <Ctrl>-<Uplevel>

4. Press the appropriate arrow key(s) to select Lib.

5. Press <Dnlevel> to get inside the Lib frame. Make sure the cursor is on the last item in the outline.

6. Press <Return> to finish copying.

Note: If you have turned off various items in the Frames menu, turn them on again with your copied frames selected. Otherwise, your copied frames may appear to be floating without outline numbers. You can wait until you've copied all your FF1 frames before following this procedure. Just select the copied frames as a group and go to the Frames menu. Then, make sure that:

- Number Labels is on
- Reveal Type is on
- Display Labels is on
- Hide Borders is off

Although this is a cosmetic touch, it can save a great deal of confusion later on.

---

7. Create an eighth frame and label it MANY.

Because you are copying whole frames and not formulas from the formula area of a frame, you can work with the <F8> key instead of Cut and Paste. When you have your formulas in place, edit them in accordance with the listings shown in Figure 5-3. If you don't have a copy of FF1 just type each formula into its frame.

```
Lib:
    ; Lib

    @printreturn

Lib.GetNum:
    ; GetNum

    @local(BOOL),
    BOOL := #TRUE,

    @keyfilter({all},ErrKey),
    @keyfilter({Esc},GetOut),
    @keyfilter({char},GetNum.AcceptNum),      ; note pathname
    @keyfilter({Return}),
    @keyfilter({Leftarrow}),
    @keyfilter({Rightarrow}),
    @keyfilter({Backspace}),
    @keyfilter({Del}),

    @while(BOOL,
        MANY := @inputline(@item1, @item2, @item3, @item4, @item5),
        ; items           "prompt", "1",    #NO,    #YES,   #YES
        BOOL := @iserr(MANY)
    ),

    @performkeys(MANY),
    @keyfilter({all}),
    MANY := @value(MANY)


Lib.GetNum.AcceptNum:
    ; AcceptNum

    ; if keystrokes are numeric, type them in.  Else error.
    @if(@or(
            @and(@key >= {0}, @key <= {9}),
            @key = {.}
            ),
```

```
            @performkeys(@keyname(@key)),
            @Errkey
    )


Lib.Errkey:
   ; ErrKey for filtered out keys

   @beep,

   @eraseprompt,
   @prompt("Please press a numeric key",30)


Lib.GetOut:
   ; GetOut turn off all filters and go to containing frame

   @keyfilter({all})
   ;@performkeys("{Ctrl-Uplevel}")
```

Figure 5-3. Lib Formula Listings

The next section discusses the important differences between the FF1 and Lib versions.

THE GENERIC, NUMERIC INPUT ROUTINE

Currency1's input routine must handle decimal figures, not just integers as FF1's did. It must also take numbers for different purposes. To fulfill these requirements, as well as make this library generic, you will have to make some changes.

The New GetNum Formula

```
; GetNum
@local(BOOL),
BOOL := #TRUE,
@keyfilter ({all},ErrKey),
@keyfilter ({Esc},GetOut),
@keyfilter ({char},GetNum.AcceptNum),          ; note pathname
@keyfilter ({Return}),
@keyfilter ({Leftarrow}),
@keyfilter ({Rightarrow}),
@keyfilter ({Backspace}),
@keyfilter ({Del}),
@while (BOOL,
   MANY := @inputline ( @item1, @item2, @item3, @item4, @item5),
   ; items              "prompt",  "1",    #NO,   #YES,   #YES
   BOOL := @iserr (MANY)
),
@performkeys (MANY),
@keyfilter ({all}),
MANY := @value (MANY)
```

Figure 5-4. Listing for the New GetNum Formula

Study Figure 5-4 for a moment. As you can see, the filters remain essentially the same. {char} still symbolizes the class of insertable characters that AcceptNum must filter for numerals (and now decimal points). The basic editing keys are also "de-filtered."

The two big differences involve the **@inputline** statement and what the program does with input. Compare it to the **@inputline** statement in FF1, shown in Figure 5-5.

```
MANY := @inputline (''How many of item?'', ''1'', #NO, #YES, #YES),
@performkeys (MANY & ''{Tab}'' & @business(COST) & ''{Tab}''),
```

Figure 5-5. Listing for FF1's @inputline Statement

The first major difference is that Currency1's **@inputline** is absolutely generic. Routines that call it must supply all five **@inputline** parameters. This makes it far more flexible. Figure 5-6 shows Currency1's GetMany routine, which sends all five parameters to Lib's GetNum statement.

```
; GetMany
@GetNum(''How many '' & WITHMONEY
& '' would you like to spend?'',''1'', #NO, #YES, #YES),
@GetMany.Look,
@GetMany.Show
```

Figure 5-6. Listing for GetMany

Compare it to the parameters sent by SetOne routine in Figure 5-7.

```
; SetOne
@GetNum(''Type constant for '' & @item1 ,
@business ( @item2,6), #NO, #YES, #YES),
```

Figure 5-7. Listing for SetOne

Here, SetOne is sending **@item** parameters sent it from the Reset Constants menu and passing them along to GetNum. The flexibility for input prompts and defaults is evident, but what about the #NO and #YES parameters? None of routines that call GetNum alter these settings. As a programmer, you have a choice about how generic you want a library routine to be in terms of a given program. This is a question of context and style. Here, the programmer has chosen an entirely generic statement, mainly for purposes of illustration.

The second major difference is that the **@inputline** lives inside a loop. The purpose of this loop is to trap illegal input. For example, in FF1, the user can erase the default value of 1 and press <Return>, effectively entering a null value. FRED doesn't like null inputs and the program bombs out.

The loop works this way. The **@iserr** function only returns a #TRUE when an error occurs. Therefore, if the user enters acceptable input, **@iserr** returns a #FALSE, the #TRUE condition that powers the loop turns #FALSE (by assignment), and execution leaves the loop. However, as long as the user persists in entering illegal input, the loop repeats the input statement.

Note that BOOL, the local boolean variable, doesn't need a comparison statement. Writing:

@while(BOOL = #TRUE,

is the same as saying:

@while(#TRUE = #TRUE,

because BOOL is first assigned #TRUE. When the #FALSE condition arises, the loop condition will fail.

What about the handling of the MANY variable? Instead of typing it into a spreadsheet as FF1 did, GetNum converts it into a value for Currency1's formulas to use. For example, the Show formula will multiply MANY times the conversion value found by Look. Likewise, SetOne causes MANY's value to be assigned to the appropriate currency constant.

The New AcceptNum Formula

```
; AcceptNum

; if key is numeric or dot, type it--else error.
@if (@or(
   @and (@key >= {0}, @key <= {9}),
   @key = {.}
   ),
```

```
@performkeys (@keyname(@key)),
@Errkey
)
```

Figure 5-8. Listing for AcceptNum

Because AcceptNum must accept both numeric and decimal point (or period) characters, the formula uses **@or** to link together numbers that are greater than or equal to zero and less than or equal to nine, and the decimal point.

> **Note:** Instead of typing insertable characters into the curly brackets, you can write the character's three-character ASCII code. For example, you could write {046} instead of {.}. FRED programmers generally reserve this ASCII argument for non-printable characters.

The New ErrKey Formula

The new ErrKey formula holds no surprises. The old formula had to warn against pressing different classes of keys so its message was generic, "Sorry! Key not active." In Currency1, you need only warn against non-numeric keys. See Figure 5-9.

```
; ErrKey for filtered out keys

@beep,
@eraseprompt,
@prompt (" Please press a numeric key ",30)
```

Figure 5-9. Listing for ErrKey

This ErrKey also leaves off the time out and **@eraseprompt** statement. They are no longer necessary. (The GetOut routine remains unchanged.)

Next, in Chapter Six, you will see more clearly how Lib works with the Currency1 program as you construct its menus and subroutines.

CHAPTER SIX

MENUS

The FRED menu system can improve program interface, speed data entry, and direct the user's choices efficiently. Best of all, you'll find designing and implementing menus easy; the basic structuring device is the Framework outline.

ABOUT MENUS

FRED's menu function turns an ordinary Framework outline into a menu system, complete with nested choices. This chapter discusses menus in terms of Currency1's menu system. It also takes you through Currency1's non-menu formulas.

Menus and Outlines

Figure 6-1 shows a menu—for a restaurant—written in a Framework outline frame.

If you were to execute this as a menu, FRED would display the three highest level menus—Entrees, Desserts, and Beverages. As you move the cursor from one item to the next, you would see the sub-categories. For example, selecting Beverages would bring up the Coffee, Tea, and Sodas menus.

```
Diner Menu:
    1 Entrees
        1.1 Steak (E)
        1.2 Chicken (E)
        1.3 Trout (E)
    2 Desserts
        2.1 Cake (E)
        2.2 Pie (E)
        2.3 Ice Cream (E)
    3 Beverages
        3.1 Coffee (E)
        3.2 Tea (E)
        3.3 Sodas (E)
```

Figure 6-1. A Restaurant Menu

To see this restaurant menu in action, create an outline frame, name it Diner, and then type

@menu(Diner)

in Diner's formula area. Press <**Esc**> to exit the formula area and <**F5**> to see the menu at work.

FRED displays menu frame names as choices at the bottom of the screen, unless you turn on *full-screen* menus. Full-screen menus blank out the screen and display only menu items. When you want the user to see desktop frames, choose *bottom-line* menus.

To change between these formats, first select the outermost menu frame and then go to the Frames menu and turn Number Labels off for full-screen format. When Number Labels is on (the default value) menu items appear at the bottom of the screen.

Although a well-chosen frame name can act as a prompt, you can also write prompts that appear on the bottom line of the screen. The next section discusses prompts.

As a general rule, resist nesting sub-menus beyond a depth of 32. Figure 6-2 shows sub-sub-menus added to the original Diner menu.

Diner Menu:

  1 Entrees

    1.1 Steak

      1.1.1 NY Cut (E)

      1.1.2 Porterhouse (E)

    1.2 Chicken

      1.2.1 Fried Chicken (E)

      1.2.2 Roasted (for 2) (E)

      1.2.3 Breast in Wine Sauce (E)

    1.3 Trout (E)

  2 Desserts

    2.1 Cake

      2.1.1 Chocolate (E)

      2.1.2 Angel Food (E)

      2.1.3 Almond Torte (E)

      2.1.4 Devils Food (E)

2.2 Pie

  2.2.1 Berry (E)

  2.2.2 Cherry (E)

  2.2.3 Apple (E)

  2.2.4 Pumpkin (E)

  2.2.5 Ala Mode (E)

2.3 Ice Cream

  2.3.1 Selected flavors (E)

  2.3.2 Sundaes (E)

3 Beverages

3.1 Coffee

  3.1.1 Regular (E)

  3.1.2 DeCaf (E)

  3.1.3 European Blend (E)

3.2 Tea (E)

3.3 Sodas (E)

Figure 6-2. Menu with Additional Categories

As you will see in Currency1, you can call different sets of menus at different times within the same program. Table 6-1 shows the different levels that different **@menu** calls would produce in the Diner program.

Table 6-1. Table of Menu Calls

@menu(Diner)	All menus and levels
@menu(Diner.Entrees)	Steak, Chicken, Trout and their sub-menus only
@menu(Diner.Desserts.Pie)	The selection of pies only

A FRED menu follows the same control rules as built-in Framework menus. You can select items by letter (where each item has a unique first letter), or you can move the cursor to an item with cursor-navigation keys and press <Return>.

> **Note:** All menus are wrap-around. Similarly, you can navigate through menu levels with the <Uplevel> and <Dnlevel> keys.

The only two ways to leave a menu are by pressing <Esc> or selecting a menu item containing the **@quitmenu** command. Reserve **@quitmenu** for the lowest level menu items or *nodes*. Otherwise, you'll quit the menu system before reaching the lowest level on a branch.

Formulas work only in *terminal nodes* (frames that do not contain a lower set of frames). For example, in Figure 6-2, items like Porterhouse, Trout, and Berry could contain formulas, but Entrees and Pie couldn't; they contain further items and merely direct control. These rules apply when you either type the first letter of a menu item, or select the menu item and press <Return>. If another level of menus exists below the selected item, the menu descends to that level, ignoring any formula in the item. If the selected item contains no further menu calls, FRED executes the formula.

> **Note:** Although users can navigate between levels with <Uplevel> and <Dnlevel>, you can also outline your menu system so that quitting one menu level (through a ''Quit'' menu item) takes the user to a higher level. The Profit and Loss Generator example in Chapters Eight through Ten demonstrates this.

Prompting with a Frame's Contents Area

Like any Framework frame, a menu frame will display its value in the contents area. This, however, is not always desirable. For example, if you had a menu of metric conversion routines, every time you came back to a particular formula, you would see the result of the last recalculation below the name of the frame. Likewise, if you had an

@quitmenu command in a frame, you would see #TBD!, the constant that @quitmenu always leaves behind, as if it were a prompt.

To create a menu system with prompts, follow these steps *in order*:

1. Create an outline and type in the menu (frame) names.

2. Go to a frames view of the outline.

3. Enter the *contents area* of each frame and type the appropriate prompt.

4. Enter the *formula area* of each frame that should bear a formula and type in the appropriate formula.

Why is the order so important? Because FRED protects the contents area of a frame, once you have written and executed a formula in a given frame. If the frame generates a FRED constant or a numeric value, FRED won't let you enter the contents area at all. If the frame generates a string value, you can enter the frame and edit the string. However, if you recalculate the frame again, FRED wipes out the editing.

The best way to have control of the contents area of a frame is to insert text before the frame has a formula. (You will see this principle at work when you enter the prompts for the Currency1 program.) FRED remembers which frames are *his* (that is, frames in which he has stored values) and which frames are the *user's* (that is, frames in which the user has typed text). He will always feel free to store later values into his own frames, but he views the user's work as sacrosanct. The next section puts the four steps to work, beginning with the creation of an outline.

SETTING UP CURRENCY1'S MENUS

Currency1 has two sets of menus. The first, Choices, controls three actions: selecting the currency you'd like to buy, resetting currency constants, and exiting Currency1. The second menu set, With What, prompts you for the currency with which you prefer to pay.

Outlining Currency1

Create an outline frame, label it Currency1, and type in the items shown in Figure 6-3. When you reach item 7, Table, create a spreadsheet with seven columns and six rows. In Chapter Seven, ''Tables and Arrays,'' we'll come back to this spreadsheet and fill in the details.

```
Currency1:
    1 Starter (E)
    2 Init (E)
    3 Choices (E)
        3.1 Buy What
            3.1.1 American (E)
            3.1.2 British (E)
            3.1.3 French (E)
            3.1.4 West German (E)
            3.1.5 Japanese (E)
        3.2 Reset Constants
            3.2.1 Pounds (E)
            3.2.2 Francs (E)
            3.2.3 Marks (E)
            3.2.4 Yen (E)
            3.2.5 Reset All (E)
        3.3 Exit (E)
```

Figure 6-3. Outline for Currency1
(Continued on following page.)

Figure 6-3 continued.

It is important to note that a FRED program can have more than one menu system. Take a look at Figure 6-3. The first menu system is the Choices menu. It contains the Reset Constants, Buy What, and Exit menus. You must first choose a Buy What currency for the program to call the With What menu.

Figure 6-4 shows the flow of control through the major frames in Currency1. As a matter of programming style and interfacing technique, you could also incorporate the With What menu into the Choices menu. You would then see all four menus on the prompt line.

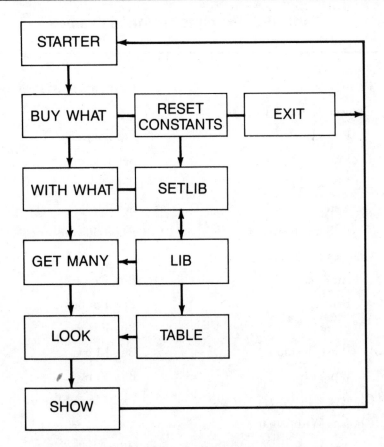

Figure 6-4. Flow of Control for Currency1

Supplying the Prompts

With the outline completed, it's time for the second and third steps—going to a frames view of each menu item and entering the appropriate prompts. Type the prompts, shown in Table 6-2, into the *contents areas* of their frames.

> **Note:** After entering the Buy What frames, you can copy (with <F8>) the whole group to create the With What group. Then edit as necessary. This saves a lot of keystrokes.

Table 6-2. Prompts for Menu Frames

Frame Name	Contents Area Prompt
Choices.Reset Constants:	
Pounds	Set Pounds
Francs	Set Francs
Marks	Set Marks
Yen	Set Yen
ReSet All	Reset all constants
Choices.Buy What:	
American	Buy Dollars
British	Buy Pounds
French	Buy Francs
West German	Buy Marks
Japanese	Buy Yen
Choices.Exit:	Exit Menu System
Choices.With What:	
American	With Dollars
British	With Pounds
French	With Francs
West German	With Marks
Japanese	With Yen

> **Note:** The menu titles have alphabetically unique names (American, British, etc.) so that the user can press the appropriate letter to select a menu item. The prompts are in a descriptive form (Buy Marks, With Yen) to cue the user. When the first letter of a menu item is not unique, typing a letter selects the first menu item beginning with that letter.

Entering Menu Formulas

The menu nodes carry choices and executable code. The Reset Constants menus send parameters to the SetLib subroutines. The Buy What menus assign an index value and a currency name to global variables. The With What menus assign an offset value and a currency name. The **@vlookup** function needs index and offset values to do its work.

Because of the similarity of formulas among menus, you may want to speed up entering of code with Cut and Paste (macros in Maclib) in each of the menu groups—Reset, Buy What, and With What. Figure 6-5 shows the listings for Currency1's menus.

```
Currency1.Choices.Buy What.American:
  ; Buy Dollars

  INDEX := 1,
  BUYMONEY := "Dollars",
  @quitmenu


Currency1.Choices.Buy What.British:
  ; Buy Pounds

  INDEX := 2,
  BUYMONEY := "Pounds",
  @quitmenu
```

Figure 6-5. Listing for Currency1's Menus

```
Currency1.Choices.Buy What.French:
  ; Buy Francs

  INDEX := 3,
  BUYMONEY := "Francs",
  @quitmenu


Currency1.Choices.Buy What.West German:
  ; Buy Marks

  INDEX := 4,
  BUYMONEY := "Marks",
  @quitmenu


Currency1.Choices.Buy What.Japanese:
  ; Buy Yen

  INDEX := 5,
  BUYMONEY := "Yen",
  @quitmenu


Currency1.Choices.Reset Constants.Pounds:
  ; Set Pounds

  ; send name and value of constant to SetOne
  @SetLib.SetOne("Lb",Lb)


Currency1.Choices.Reset Constants.Francs:
  ; Set Francs

  ; send name and value of constant to SetOne
  @SetLib.SetOne("Nf",Nf)


Currency1.Choices.Reset Constants.Marks:
  ; Set Marks

  ; send name and value of constant to SetOne
  @SetLib.SetOne("Dm",Dm)
```

Figure 6-5 continued.

```
Currency1.Choices.Reset Constants.Yen:
   ; Set Yen

   ; send name and value of constant to SetOne
   @SetLib.SetOne("Yn",Yn)


Currency1.Choices.Reset Constants.Reset All:
   ; Reset All

   ; call loop to get values for all currencies
   @SetLib.SetAll


Currency1.Choices.Exit:
   ; Exit

   ; set flag to true causing exit at init routine
   FINISHED := #TRUE,
   @quitmenu


Currency1.With What.American:
   ; With Dollars

   OFFSET := 2,
   WITHMONEY := "Dollars",
   @quitmenu


Currency1.With What.British:
   ; With Pounds

   OFFSET := 3,
   WITHMONEY := "Pounds",
   @quitmenu


Currency1.With What.French:
   ; With Francs

   OFFSET := 4,
   WITHMONEY := "Francs",
   @quitmenu
```

Figure 6-5 continued.

```
Currency1.With What.West German:
  ; With Marks

    OFFSET := 5,
    WITHMONEY := "Marks",
    @quitmenu


Currency1.With What.Japanese:
  ; With Yen

    OFFSET := 6,
    WITHMONEY := "Yen",
    @quitmenu
```

Figure 6-5 continued.

CURRENCY1'S NON-MENU FORMULAS

With the menu system and library in place, it's time to type in the non-menu formulas. These formulas belong to the following frames:

Currency1 (the containing frame)

Starter

Init

SetLib (the container for SetOne and SetAll)

GetMany (including its subframes Look and Show)

Once you've finished typing in these formulas, you'll have everything you need except the Table spreadsheet frame, the subject of Chapter Seven. Just type the listings given in Figure 6-6.

```
Currency1:
   ; Currency1

   ; Print listing routine
   @tm(2),
   @bm(4),
   @po(5),
   @ll(75),
   @fl("Currency1 Listing"),
   @fc(@date1(@today) & " : " & @time1(@today)),
   @fr(@pn),
   @printreturn,
   @Currency1.Starter


Currency1.Starter:
   ; Starter
   ; starts Currency1 and allows repeated use

   @printreturn,
   @local(BLUE),
   BLUE := #TRUE,

   @while(BLUE,        ; run loop as long as BLUE is TRUE
      @eraseprompt,
      @prompt("Press any key to continue; <Esc> ends",15),
      @if(@nextkey = {Esc},
          BLUE := #FALSE,      ; TRUE causes loop to end
          @Currency1.Init      ; FALSE calls Init
      )
   ),
   @eraseprompt


Currency1.Init:
   ; Init

   FINISHED := #FALSE, ; FINISHED is quit flag. TRUE quits

   @keyfilter({Esc},Choices.Exit), ; Esc set to Exit menu
   @menu(Choices),       ; call 1st menu

   ; check to see if user wants to quit
   @keyfilter({Esc}),              ; turn Esc filter off
   @if(FINISHED, @return(0)),   ; if TRUE, back to Starter
```

Figure 6-6. Listing of Currency1's Non-Menu Formulas

```
        ; if not, call with what
     @menu(With What),    ; get purchasing currency

     @GetMany     ; get amount of currency, calc, and display


Currency1.SetLib.SetOne:
  ; SetOne

  @local(EXEC),

  @GetNum("Type constant for " &  @item1, ;constant name
  @business(@item2,6), #NO, #YES, #YES),  ;constant value

  EXEC := @item1 & " := MANY",
  @EXEC,
  @Currency1.Table


Currency1.SetLib.SetAll:
  ; SetAll -- resets all constants in lib

  @local(SELECTOR,CONST,EXEC),

  @while(SELECTOR < 4,
      SELECTOR := SELECTOR + 1,
      CONST := @select(SELECTOR,"Lb","Nf","Dm","Yn"),
      @GetNum("Type new constant for " & CONST,    ; const name
          @business(@CONST,6), #NO, #YES, #YES),  ; const value
      EXEC := CONST & " := MANY", ; build formula on the fly
      @EXEC        ; write new value to constant
  ),

  @Currency1.Table     ; recalc table to set new values

Currency1.GetMany:
  ; GetMany

  @GetNum("How many " & WITHMONEY
  & " would you like to spend?","1",#NO,#YES,#YES),
  @GetMany.Look,       ; lookup value
  @GetMany.Show        ; calc & display value


Currency1.GetMany.Look:
  ;Look
```

Figure 6.6 continued.

```
@vlookup(INDEX,Table.A2:Table.G6,OFFSET)

Currency1.GetMany.Show:
  ; Show

@business(MANY,6) & " " & WITHMONEY & " buys " &
@business(MANY*Look,6) & " " & BUYMONEY
```

Figure 6.6 continued.

At this point, you should drag and size frames so that you can display Show, the frame in which the answer appears. Figure 6-7 shows Currency1 set up in "control panel" fashion so that the programmer can watch Show, the global variables, and spreadsheet. Of course, your spreadsheet remains blank.

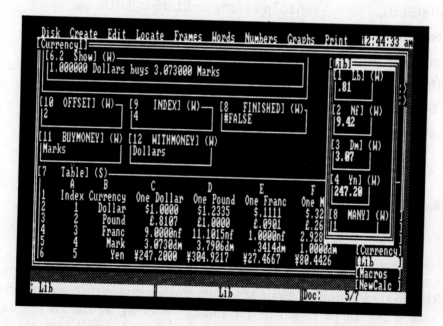

Figure 6-7. A Control Panel View of Currency1

Before you bolt to Chapter Seven (Tables), read the discussions of the formulas you have just entered; they offer a wealth of FRED programming techniques.

DEVELOPER'S HANDBOOK

Starter: An Example of Pseudo-Recursion

Beyond carrying the usual instructions for printing a listing, Currency1 only calls Starter. With that, the program begins. See Figure 6-8 for a listing of Starter.

```
;Starter
;Starts Currency1 and allows repeated use

@printreturn,
@local(BLUE),
BLUE := #TRUE,
@while(BLUE,          ; run loop as long as BLUE is TRUE
   @eraseprompt,
   @prompt(" Press any key to continue; <Esc> ends ", 15),
   @if( @nextkey = {Esc},
      BLUE:= #FALSE,          ; TRUE causes loop to end
      @Currency1.Init          ; FALSE calls Init
   )
),
@eraseprompt
```

Figure 6-8. Listing for Starter

Like the new GetNum formula, Starter takes advantage of a local boolean variable, BLUE, to keep running. Again the programmer makes no comparison to BLUE, because such a statement would be redundant. As long as BLUE is true (the user presses any key but <Esc>), the Starter loop continues to call Init, the Frame that drives the menus and GetMany.

But why do this? Why not have a routine called Again, at the end of the program, that asks the user whether to continue and then calls Init if the user says yes?

The reason is that such a use of recursion can create problems. FRED allows recursion, but not beyond 32 successive calls. A currency trader could exhaust such a limit and crash the stack. Here, the loop has no such stack impact. The moral: a good program, like good sourdough, always begins with a good starter.

Init: Filtering for an Exit

The Init formula calls the two menu systems, Choices and With What, and then calls GetMany. It also sets a key filter so that the user can exit either by pressing <Esc> and <Return> (one way to abandon a menu system) or by selecting the Exit menu item. This is an example of bullet-proofing a menu system—the user can only exit through the system. No bailing out in the middle of a subroutine. Figure 6-9 is the listing for Init.

```
; Init

FINISHED := #FALSE,              ; FINISHED is quit flag.  #TRUE quits
@keyfilter({Esc},Choices.Exit),  ; Esc set to Exit menu
@menu(Choices),                  ; call 1st menu

; check to see if user wants to quit
@keyfilter({Esc}),               ; turn Esc filter off
@if(FINISHED, @return(0)),       ; if #TRUE, back to Starter

; if not, call with what
@menu(With What),                ; get purchasing currency
@GetMany                         ; get amount of currency, calc, and
                                   display
```

Figure 6-9. Listing for Init

To set up the exit route, the programmer created a global variable (global because FRED must see the variable from a formula other than Init) and set its flag to #FALSE. The @if statement, after the call to Choices, tests this flag. If #TRUE, the

@return (with a dummy argument) pushes execution out of Init and back to the calling frame, Starter. But how does the flag get set to #TRUE? That is the job of the Exit formula, @keyfilter's second parameter. Take a look at Figure 6-10, the Exit listing.

```
; Exit

; set flag to true causing exit at init routine
FINISHED := #TRUE,
@quitmenu
```

Figure 6-10. Listing for Exit

The @keyfilter statement filters any pressing of <Esc> to Exit. Exit sets the flag to #TRUE and leaves the menu system to return to Init where it encounters the @if statement.

SetOne: Passing Passed Parameters

You can pass the same parameter(s) more than once. For example, four of the Reset Constants frames send two parameters to SetOne. Each sends the name and current value of its Lib constant.

Figure 6-11 shows the Set Pounds routine sending Lib's constant name and value for pounds. (Set Francs, Set Marks, and Set Yen make similar assignments.)

```
; Set Pounds

; send name and value of constant to SetOne
@SetLib.SetOne(''Lb'',Lb)
```

Figure 6-11. Listing for Set Pounds

But rather than acting on the two @item parameters immediately, SetOne ships them off to Lib's GetNum routine (see Figure 6-12). As discussed in Chapter Five, GetNum accepts these parameters for its generic input string. Here, to satisfy the **@inputline's** need for a *default string*, the programmer has formatted the value of the constant as a string with six decimal places.

```
; SetOne

@local(EXEC),
@GetNum("Type constant for  " & @item1,          ;constant name
@business( @item2,6), # NO, # YES, # YES),        ;constant value
EXEC := @item1  &  " := MANY",
@EXEC,
@Currency1.Table
```

Figure 6-12. Listing for SetOne

But SetOne doesn't stop there. It puts **@item1** to work a third time, writing a formula on the fly. (The next section discusses this topic further.)

Because the Table spreadsheet draws its basic data from the Lib constants, the program needs to update Table so that Table takes advantage of the new constant. The @Currency1.Table statement does this by forcing recalculation of Table.

Before continuing, just think about how much code you saved by "recycling" parameters. Without recycling, all four Set *currency* subroutines would have had to make the GetNum call with all its parameters. Still not impressed? What if you had to write this program for a professional currency trader, dealing in 40 or 50 currencies?

SetAll: Writing a Formula on the Fly

The SetAll frame uses a loop and a case statement to get four inputs—one for each currency. The local variable SELECTOR acts as an index to each constant name. Each time through the loop, SELECT loads the name of a constant into the local variable CONST. SetAll then uses CONST three times.

The first time, it places CONST's string (''Lb'') in the prompt string. Thus, the first prompt would say:

Type new constant for Lb

The second and third uses of CONST are quite different; they illustrate how you can ''write a formula on the fly.'' Read the listing in Figure 6-13 carefully before continuing.

```
;SetAll--resets all constants in lib

@local(SELECTOR,CONST,EXEC),

@while(SELECTOR < 4,
   SELECTOR := SELECTOR + 1,
   CONST := @select(SELECTOR,"Lb","Nf","Dm","Yn"),
   @GetNum("Type new constant for " & CONST,        ; const name
      @business(@CONST,6), #NO, #YES, #YES),        ; const value
   EXEC := CONST & " := MANY",          ; build formula on the fly
   @EXEC          ; write new value to constant
),

   @Currency1.Table        ; recalc table to set new values
```

Figure 6-13. Listing for SetAll

Take a look at the default value parameter:

@business(@CONST,6)

The @business function converts @CONST to a string value, demanded by @inputline's syntax for the default value. But why @CONST?

To answer that question, consider the nature of a local variable (CONST is a local variable). Local variables, like normal frames, have a name and a value. What they lack is a *formula area*. You can't select them, press <F2>, and type in a formula. Instead, a local variable's "content area" doubles as its "formula area" (with the same 32,000-character maximum).

To make up for the lack of a formula area, FRED makes a special provision for *local variables containing strings*. By placing an @ in front of a local variable name, you can execute the variable's string as if it were a formula. This makes sense, when you realize that a formula is string without the quotation marks. Currency1 takes advantage of this situation to execute the variable CONST with @CONST.

Follow what happens to @CONST in the loop. The first time through, the expression @CONST executes the string "Lb" (selected by SELECT). This is merely a reference to the Lb formula in Lib. This reference returns the value of the Lb (.8107). On each successive pass through the loop, FRED executes another variable —Nf, Dm, and finally Yn.

Programmers call this technique "writing formulas on the fly" because the formula actually changes during execution ("on the fly"), with the program re-writing its own formula as it recalculates.

Note that FRED recognizes two classes of formulas. The simpler form is a single value, like a numeral. The other form must involve at least one operator or FRED function, like 5+3 or **@business**(6). The difference between these two is that FRED will overwrite the simpler form if told to do so. This is what happens with the "constants" in Lib. FRED will recalculate a formula, but not overwrite it.

As an example, create two frames; label them A and B. In A's formula area, type 5+2 and recalculate it. The result is 7. In B's formula area, write A := A + 1. Recalculate B. Both frames will show the result: 8. Now go back to A; its formula remains unchanged, still 5+2. Change A's formula to just the number 2. Recalculate it.

Now recalculate B. Both frames show 3 as the result. But A's formula has become 3. FRED sees this second form as a constant rather than a formula. With a constant, the value and the formula are always the same.

Notice in Figure 6-13, that SELECTOR was never initialized; you don't see:

```
SELECTOR := 0
```

This is because FRED automatically resets all variables to 0 when recalculating a formula. Initialization overwrites the 0. Because the programmer wanted SELECTOR set to zero, he didn't bother to assign the value.

Why not just write:

```
@business(CONST,6)
```

The reason is that CONST contains a string value ''Lb'' and not a variable named Lb. FRED would see the result of such a formula as:

```
@business("Lb",6)
```

This is no good— ''Lb'' isn't a variable, but Lb is. Move on to the next formula written on the fly and you'll see the same principle at work, but this time with two string elements instead of one:

```
EXEC := CONST & " := MANY"
```

The user has typed in a new conversion constant for a currency, and Lib's GetNum formula has assigned that value to MANY. The question becomes how to get the value from MANY to the appropriate currency variable.

You can't write

```
CONST := MANY
```

because CONST is the name of a local variable and MANY would be assigned to it instead of to the Lb frame in Lib. Nor can you write

```
@"Lb" := MANY
```

because the technique executes local string variables, not strings themselves.

However, because you can concatenate local string variables and strings, you can construct a formula. In this case, the programmer chose to concatenate two strings and place them in the local variable EXEC with:

    EXEC := CONST & " := MANY"

Assuming CONST contained "Lb", Exec would contain the string:

    "Lb" & " := MANY"

When FRED executes @EXEC, he executes the valid formula:

    Lb := MANY

thereby assigning the value in the variable MANY to the variable Lb.

The programmer followed the same rules in the SetOne formula (see Figure 6-12 in the previous section). The statement

    EXEC := @item1 & " := MANY",
    @EXEC,

is different only in its variable name, here @item1. Like CONST, @item1 contains a string representing a constant's frame in Lib. Here too, a string like

    @item1 := MANY

won't execute, so writing a formula on the fly becomes the answer to the question, "How do I assign the value in MANY to a Lib constant?"

Keep the technique of writing formulas on the fly in mind. It can get you out of some sticky programming problems. The following three steps are for writing a formula with more than one element:

1. Create a local variable that you will execute as formula, e.g.,

   @local(EXEC),

2. Concatenate the elements you want in the formula as strings and assign them to the local variable; for example:

   EXEC := CONST & " := MANY"

3. Execute the variable by placing an **@** in front of it:

   @EXEC

Show: The Answer is Strings

The job of the Show formula is to calculate and display the answer. Take a look at Figure 6-14.

   ; Show

   @business(MANY,6) & " " & WITHMONEY & "   buys   " &
   @business(MANY*Look,6) & " " & BUYMONEY

Figure 6-14. Listing for Show

Show does its work by concatenating strings. Because this is a string display, you must format numeric values (MANY and MANY*Look) as string values. The programmer chose **@business** with six decimal places. WITHMONEY and BUYMONEY are string variables so no formatting is necessary.

The operation

```
MANY*Look
```

multiplies the number of units chosen by the conversion factor that Look finds in Table (Chapter Seven focuses on Look and Table). The result of this string is a message like:

```
10.000000 Dollars buys 8.10700 Pounds
```

Generally, it is best to put each activity into its own frame. However, different needs arise in the writing of different programs. You could leave out the Look frame, for example, and write the Look formula into the string. Here is part of the Show string, illustrating this.

```
@business(MANY * @vlookup(INDEX,Table.A2:Table.G6,OFFSET) ,6) &
       "  " & BUYMONEY
```

Note that the Init frame also displays this answer. This is because @GetMany is Init's last call and, therefore, it evaluates to whatever @GetMany evaluates to—in this case, the Show frame. If you wanted, you could move all of GetMany into Init, and eliminate three frames. It comes down to the question of bytes versus well-structured code.

Chapter Seven leads you into the world of tables and lookup functions, and thereby completes the coding of Currency1.

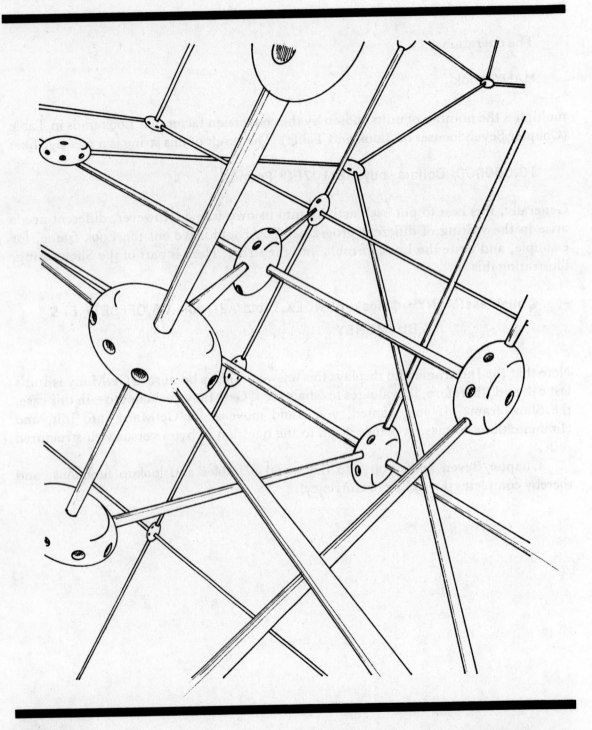

CHAPTER SEVEN
TABLES

A table, such as a spreadsheet, is a two-dimensional array. (You can create a one-dimensional array by holding a spreadsheet to one column or row.) Every language has its own ways of writing to and reading from arrays.

LOOKUP FUNCTIONS AND TABLES

This section looks at how to use the **@vlookup** function to read from a table. (See FRED's region-walking functions for other ways to manipulate table data.)

@vlookup and @hlookup

FRED's two lookup functions are **@vlookup** and **@hlookup**. **@vlookup** works on vertically-oriented tables, **@hlookup** on horizontal tables. That's the only difference. Both take the same three parameters in the same argument. Because Currency1's Table is vertically-oriented, the rest of this chapter speaks in terms of vertical tables and the **@vlookup** function. The syntax for **@vlookup** is:

    @vlookup(index, region, offset)

The *index* and *offset* serve as a pair of pointers. In a vertical table, the index moves *down* the rows, while the offset moves *across* the columns. (In a horizontal lookup, their roles are reversed.)

> **Note:** The positioning of the index determines which lookup function you use. If you put your index numbers down a column, you have vertical lookup; across a row, horizontal lookup.

But on what area of data should these pointers work? The answer is on the area given by the region parameter. In Currency1's Table, the region takes in the entire spreadsheet. This isn't always the case; you may set aside a portion of spreadsheet for a table from which formulas in the rest of the spreadsheet or in a another frame can draw data. The next section examines this in more detail.

The Index Parameter

To see **@vlookup's** parameters at work, take a look at Figure 7-1 showing Currency1's spreadsheet Table and Figure 7-2, showing the Look frame's one-line lookup formula. The index parameter, here the global variable INDEX, serves as the vertical pointer. FRED always aims the index parameter at the *first column* of the region. (An **@hlookup** function goes after the *first row*.)

After getting to the row, FRED looks for a match for the parameter. If he can't find that, he looks for the next number larger than the parameter. This means that, though you may separate numbers in the index row with different increments, you should never put a larger number before a smaller number.

Column C could never be used as the index column because its values follow no particular order. For that reason, the programmer had to create the index column shown in Figure 7-1. What currency would FRED find with an index of 3? Move your finger down column A to 3. Francs. That's all the index does. When combined with the offset, the two point to a cell in the table, a currency conversion factor.

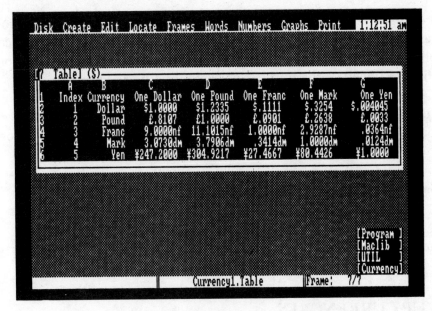

Figure 7-1. Currency1's Table

```
;Look
```

@vlookup(INDEX,Table.A2:Table.G6,OFFSET)

Figure 7-2. Listing for Look

> **Note:** Any time you set up a table with the expectation of reading its data with a lookup statement, design the table with the appropriate lookup function in mind.

The Offset Parameter

In a vertical table, FRED uses the offset to move across the row dictated by the index. (In a horizontal table, he moves down the column given by the index). An index has numbers to work with; what does the offset have? Columns.

FRED calls the leftmost column of the region 0, the next 1, then 2, and so on. Take another look at Figure 7-1. Here, the index column is 0, the Currency column 1, the One Dollar column 2, and so on. Now, with an index of 3 and an offset of 4, what would you find? 3.065408—the number of francs one mark will buy. That's how the table works. To find what one unit of a currency will buy, go to the Currency column 1 and move down it until you find the currency you want to buy. For example, $1.000000 buys $1.000000 (makes sense doesn't it), .810700 pounds, and so on.

> **Note:** The index and offset values for the menu items are derived from this table.

Now that you understand how a lookup function reads a table, it's time to create your own.

SETTING UP CURRENCY1'S TABLE

This section discusses setting up Table in four steps:

1. Basic setup and formatting—typing in column and row labels, aligning and sizing cells, and setting display format.

2. Writing the formulas that read Lib's constants and bringing the @ **nationalize** and tailoring functions into play.

3. Writing the formulas that calculate the conversion factors between currencies (more @ **nationalize**).

4. A bit of cleanup—re-sizing columns and that sort of thing.

Basic Setup and Formatting

Go to the Table spreadsheet you created. It should be seven columns wide and six rows deep. If it isn't go to the Edit menu to subtract columns, the Create menu to add columns. You may want to size the spreadsheet to full-screen width for the time being. Follow the steps below.

1. Type in the column labels:

    Index

    Currency

    One Dollar

    One Pound

    One Franc

    One Mark

    One Yen

2. Select the entire row; press **<F6> <Home>**

3. Right align these labels; press **<Ctrl>-N R**

4. While all columns are selected, expand them all to a width of 12 characters. You can adjust these at cleanup time. For now, press **<F4>** once and **<Rightarrow>** three times (assuming your default column width is nine). Press **<Return>**

5. Size column A down to five characters; press **<Home> <F4>** once each and **<Leftarrow>** four times. Press **<Return>**

6. Type the index numbers 1 through 5 into column A.

7. Type the currency labels into column B:

    -   Dollar
    -   Pound
    -   Franc
    -   Mark
    -   Yen

8. To align all the labels to the right in column B, select the entire column and press **<Ctrl>-N R**

9. To undo the selected area, press <Ctrl>-<Uparrow>

Your Table should resemble the one shown in Figure 7-3.

```
        A         B         C            D           E          F           G
1   Index     Currency  One Dollar   One Pound   One Franc  One Mark   One Yen
2     1       Dollar
3     2       Pound
4     3       Franc
5     4       Mark
6     5       Yen
```

Figure 7-3. Table with Labels and Indices

10. Save your work; press <Ctrl>-<Return>

11. Format the remaining area of the worksheet as Currency format; press <F6> <Ctrl>-<End> <Ctrl>-N C

12. With the area still selected, format it for 4 decimal places; press <Ctrl>-N D 4

13. Save your work again; press <Ctrl>-<Return>

The basics are now in place. In the next section, you'll type in the formulas that read Lib's constants into the spreadsheet.

@nationalize and Constant Formulas

This section introduces the **@nationalize** and tailoring functions by having you enter the formulas that read from Lib's constants. With the constants in place, you can generate a series of formulas across row 2. The numbers they produce correspond to the U.S. dollar equivalent column shown in the daily currency table found in the business section of your local newspaper.

The **@nationalize** function takes two parameters: the type of currency and, optionally, a format (such as **@milli** or **@thousands**).

@nationalize(currency, format)

or

@nationalize(**@pound**, **@milli**)

Framework has three built in currencies that, when written in a spreadsheet or database, display their currency symbols when the display format is Currency (on the Numbers menu):

Currency	Function	Sign
Dollar	@dollar	$
Pound	@pound	£
Yen	@yen	¥

Specify other currencies, like francs or marks, with the **@unit** function. **@unit** takes two parameters—a defining string and a position. The string specifies the defining text, and the position tells Framework whether to put this string before or after the numerals. The position constants are #BEFORE and #AFTER. **@unit** has meaning only when placed within an **@nationalize** statement:

@nationalize(**@unit**(string, position))

or

@nationalize(**@unit**("nf", #AFTER))

Note: The Table would still work if you left out all the foreign currency formatting. Further, you don't even have to size the columns or align the labels. The purpose of Table is to give you, the programmer, a table you can read with ease.

A well formatted table is necessary if you wish to display your currency calculations in the same spreadsheet cell that contains the formulas that format the output.

The Table uses the abbreviations "nf" for New Franc and "dm" for Deutsche Mark. We'll now put these functions to work.

1. Go to Table and position the cursor in cell C2.

2. Type **@nationalize(@dollar**), 1.0000

   Framework immediately recalculates the formula and displays it in dollar currency format.

3. To save yourself from retyping **"@nationalize()"** four more times, copy this statement into cells C3 through C6.

   With the cursor on C2, press **<F8> <Dnarrow> <F6> <Ctrl>-<Dnarrow> <Return> <Return>**

4. Now edit each cell according to the list below:

   C3 **@nationalize(@pound**), Lb

   C4 **@nationalize(@unit("nf", #AFTER**)), Nf

   C5 **@nationalize(@unit("dm", #AFTER**)), Dm

   C6 **@nationalize(@yen**), Yn

   Just as in step 2, each function will recalculate each time you press <Return>

5. Column C should reflect Lib's values. Compare your Table to the one in Figure 7-4. If you find any problems, correct them now.

```
      A        B           C          D         E         F         G
1  Index    Currency   One Dollar  One Pound  One Franc  One Mark  One Yen
2    1       Dollar     $1.0000
3    2        Pound     £.8107
4    3        Franc     9.4200nf
5    4         Mark     3.0730dm
6    5          Yen     ¥247.2000
```

Figure 7-4. Table with Column C Completed

6. Save your work.

The next series of steps sets up the formulas in row 2, the formulas that calculate the U.S. dollar equivalent of each currency.

1. Begin by copying cell C2 into cell D2. Move the cursor to C2 and press \<F8\> \<Rightarrow\> \<Return\>

2. Move the cursor to D2 and edit the formula to read

   @nationalize(@dollar), $C$2/$C3

   The formula says that the U.S. dollar equivalent of a currency equals the dollar divided by the currency per U.S. dollar figure. In this case, the dollar divided by the number of pounds a dollar will buy ($0.8107).

   > **Note:** If you don't understand the use of the dollar sign in specifying cells, see Framework documentation on *absolute cell references*. The dollar signs cause Framework to look at these coordinates in absolute rather than relative terms. They are placed in these formulas to make it possible to copy the formulas accurately.

3. Copy this formula across the rest of the row; press \<F8\> \<Rightarrow\> \<F6\> \<End\> \<Return\> \<Return\>

4. Now edit each formula as shown below by changing the last number in each formula:

   E2 **@nationalize(@dollar)**, $C$2/$C4

   F2 **@nationalize(@dollar)**, $C$2/$C5

   G2 **@nationalize(@dollar)**, $C$2/$C6

When you finish, your Table should resemble the one in Figure 7-5.

	A	B	C	D	E	F	G
1	Index	Currency	One Dollar	One Pound	One Franc	One Mark	One Yen
2	1	Dollar	$1.0000	$1.2335	$.1062	$.3254	$.0040
3	2	Pound	£.8107				
4	3	Franc	9.4200nf				
5	4	Mark	3.0730dm				
6	5	Yen	247.2000				

Figure 7-5. Table after Completing Row 2 Formulas

5. Save your work before continuing. The next section completes the table.

@nationalize and Conversion Formulas

This section shows you how to write the formulas that convert between formulas. They rely on the formulas you created in the last section.

To convert currency A to its value in currency B, the formula multiplies currency A's value in dollars times currency B's value in dollars. Thus, to find how many pounds one franc buys, you multiply the franc's dollar value by the pound's dollar value. In Table, cell F3 bears the formula

@nationalize(@pound),F$2*$C$3

where F$2 is the number of dollars one franc will buy ($ 0.1062) and $C$3 is the number of pounds one dollar will buy ($ 0.8107). Now to the formula, again leveraging your earlier work.

1. Copy D2 to D3; press   \<F8\> \<Dnarrow\> \<Return\>

2. Edit D3's current formula to

   @nationalize(@pound),D$2*$C$3

3. Copy D3 to the cells below it; with D3 selected, press \<F8\> \<Dnarrow\> \<F6\> \<Ctrl\>-\<Dnarrow\> \<Return\> \<Return\>

4. Edit the remaining three formulas as follows:

 D4 @nationalize(@unit("nf", #AFTER)), D$2*$C$4

 D5 @nationalize(@unit("dm", #AFTER)),D$2*$C$5

 D6 @nationalize(@yen),D$2*$C$6

Check your work against Figure 7-6.

	A	B	C	D	E	F	G
			One Dollar	One Pound	One Franc	One Mark	One Yen
1	Index	Currency					
2	1	Dollar	$1.0000	$1.2335	$.1062	$.3254	$.0040
3	2	Pound	£.8107	£1.0000			
4	3	Franc	9.4200nf	11.6196nf			
5	4	Mark	3.0730dm	3.7906dm			
6	5	Yen	¥247.2000	¥304.9217			

Figure 7-6. Table with Column D Completed

5. Save your work.

6. Now copy the four formulas you've just created through the remaining blank cells. Position the cursor on cell D3 and then press <F6> <Ctrl>-<Dnarrow> <F8> <Rightarrow> <F6> <Ctrl>-<End> <Return> <Return>

Check your completed Table against the one in Figure 7-7. Make any necessary corrections.

	A	B	C	D	E	F	G
			One Dollar	One Pound	One Franc	One Mark	One Yen
1	Index	Currency					
2	1	Dollar	$1.0000	$1.2335	$.1062	$.3254	$.0040
3	2	Pound	£.8107	£1.0000	£.0861	£.2638	£.0033
4	3	Franc	9.4200n	11.6196nf	1.0000nf	3.0654nf	.0381nf
5	4	Mark	3.0730dm	3.7906dm	.3262dm	1.0000dm	.0124dm
6	5	Yen	¥247.2000	¥304.9217	¥26.2420	¥80.4426	¥1.0000

Figure 7-7. The Completed Table

7. Save your work.

Cleanup

The Table spreadsheet will work just fine as it is. However, you might want to do the following:

- Display column G (Yen) or even columns C through G in six decimal place format. (Yen quotations often take six places.)
- Re-size some of the columns to make the spreadsheet less wide.

Do as you like once your Table is saved. This is a good time to experiment with spreadsheet formatting.

HOW TO USE CURRENCY1

With Currency1 and Lib on your desktop, make sure that you have a Frames View and that the Show frame is visible. You may also want to put Lib in Frames View with the constants set up so you can view them as you work. It's a good idea to have the spreadsheet in view, too.

Start with a straightforward runthrough of the program:

1. With Currency1 selected, press <F5>. The starter prompt appears at the bottom of the screen.

2. Obey the prompt and press a key. The Choices menu appears.

3. Press **B** to select Buy What.

4. Press **B** for British. The With What menu appears.

5. Buy with dollars. Press **A**

6. The program prompts you for the number of dollars you'd like to spend. If you press 1, Currency1 will calculate the value of one dollar's worth of British pounds. Type **200** and press <**Return**>

7. Your answer appears in the Show frame and the starter prompt reappears:

   200.000000 Dollars buys 162.140000 Pounds

8. Press any key to continue.

9. From the Choices menu, choose Reset Constants; press **R**

10. Say that francs have changed so that a dollar buys 9.00 francs. Press **F**

11. The program now prompts you for the new value of francs. The edit line displays the old value. Type **9** **<Return>**

If your Lib constants and/or your spreadsheet are visible, you can watch the recalculations take place.

12. Press **<Uplevel>** to leave the Reset menu.

13. Press **B** to Buy and **W** to buy West German Marks.

14. Buy with Francs. Press **F**

15. Type **150** and press **<Return>** in response to the prompt. Your answer, based on the new value you entered, appears:

    150.000000 Francs buys 51.216667 Marks

Arbitrage anyone?

The rest is up to you. Take out the newspaper and change all the values. Try calculating in different currencies. Try entering a null amount. Try an exit. Enjoy. And congratulations. In working through these three chapters you've learned a lot about FRED programming. Maybe even more than you realize.

FRAMEWORK

CHAPTER EIGHT

DATA ENTRY

This chapter is the first of three that deal with data entry, databases, and report generation. All three focus on the design and writing of a program named PnL, which records income and expenses and generates expense/income reports and a Profit and Loss statement.

USER-FRIENDLY DATA ENTRY

Chapters Eight, Nine, and Ten demonstrate how you can write an application in FRED that not only gets the job done, but also assists the user every step of the way. Consider the goals of a good data entry system. A good data entry system should do the following:

● Make the next activity obvious

● Minimize typing and, thereby, speed up entry and help avoid errors

● Give the user a chance to correct entry errors

● Relieve the user of file "housekeeping"

Program Overview

PnL accomplishes these goals with menus, editable defaults for every entry, a re-editing option for every field before placing the record in the database, automatic incrementing of check numbers, automatic sorting into date order, automatic restoration of the complete database, and automatic saving of the database when the user quits the program. Take a look at the menu flow chart in Figure 8-1. It gives a simplified picture of the flow of control through the PnL menu system.

PnL takes entries for five profit and loss categories:

> Automotive expenses (Auto)
>
> Photoreproduction expenses (Copies)
>
> Income from a consulting business (Income)
>
> Postal expenses (Postage)
>
> Office supply expenses (Supplies)

Selecting a category (like Auto) automatically sets the selection as the category for the database record. Thereafter, PnL prompts the user for the following:

> Form of payment (How Paid) with a three-part menu (Check, Dollars, Plastic)
>
> Date
>
> Amount
>
> Remarks

Notice that every entry has a default. For example, with payment by check, the last check number is incremented by 1. For the date, the last date entered is repeated. The default for remarks is "none."

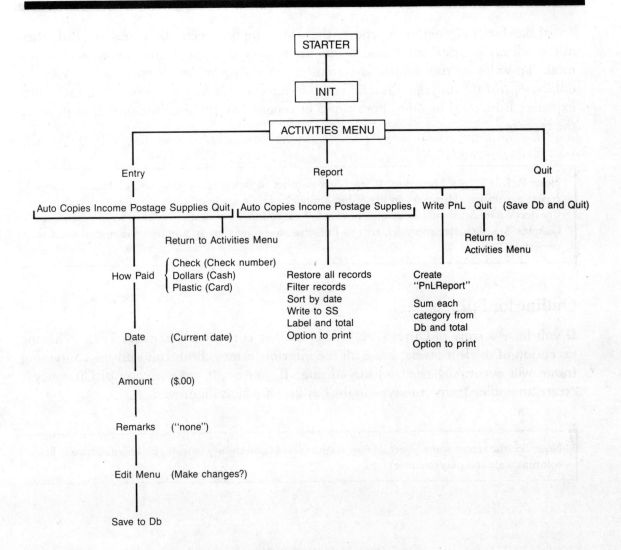

Figure 8-1. The PnL Menu System

Likewise, to generate a report, the user simply selects the category; PnL then automatically queries, sorts, and prints the results on a spreadsheet, complete with a total. To write a Profit and Loss statement, the program totals each category in the database, transferring the numeric result to another spreadsheet which subtracts total expenses from total income. Both types of report give the user the option of printing the report.

Note: PnL is a ''toy'' program. It teaches a number of things about data entry, databases, and report generation. However, in designing a model, certain trade-offs arise; you must weigh how ''perfect'' a model should be against how many subroutines you want to type. The last section of Chapter Ten discusses enhancements to PnL that you might, in an ambitious moment, want to undertake.

Outline for PnL

If you have a copy of Currency1, make another copy and rename it PnL. With the exception of the Init frame, erase all the interior frames. Both Init and the containing frame will eventually need a little editing. If you don't have a copy of Currency1, create an outline frame and type in the outline shown in Figure 8-2.

Note: SS, the report spreadsheet, is four columns wide and twenty rows high. The database is five columns wide and only one row high.

Once you've created the outline, save it.

PnL:
    1 Init (E)
    2 Menus
        2.1 Entry (E)
        2.2 Report (E)
        2.3 Quit (E)
    3 Entry Menu
        3.1 Auto (E)
        3.2 Copies (E)
        3.3 Income (E)
        3.4 Postage (E)
        3.5 Supplies (E)
        3.6 Quit (E)
    4 DoInput
        4.1 GetData
            4.1.1 GetHowPaid
                4.1.1.1 HowPaid
                    4.1.1.1.1 Check (E)
                    4.1.1.1.2 Dollars (E)
                    4.1.1.1.3 Plastic (E)
            4.1.2 GetDate (E)
            4.1.3 GetAmt (E)
            4.1.4 GetRem (E)

Figure 8-2. Outline for PnL
(Continued on following page.)

FRAME WORK

4.2 Edit

    4.2.1 Show

        4.2.1.1 Category (E)

        4.2.1.2 How Paid (E)

        4.2.1.3 Date (E)

        4.2.1.4 Amount (E)

        4.2.1.5 Remark (E)

        4.2.1.6 Save (E)

4.3 Write (E)

5 Report Menu

    5.1 Auto (E)

    5.2 Copies (E)

    5.3 Income (E)

    5.4 Postage (E)

    5.5 Supplies (E)

    5.6 Write PnL (E)

    5.7 Quit (E)

6 Reporter

    6.1 QueryOne (E)

    6.2 Restore (E)

    6.3 Sort (E)

    6.4 WriteOne (E)

    6.5 SS (S)

    6.6 PrintSS (E)

    6.7 MakePnL (E)

Figure 8-2 continued.

7 FINISHED (E)

8 NOTCHECK (E)

9 CHECKNUM (E)

10 Db (D)

Figure 8-2 continued.

The program follows an implicit organization:

I. The Startup Routines

    1. Init

    2. Menus

II. The Input Routines

    1. Entry Menu

    2. DoInput

    3. Lib (not present, yet)

III. The Report Routines

    1. Report Menu

    2. Reporter

IV. The Global Variables

    1. FINISHED

    2. NOTCHECK

    3. CHECKNUM

V. The Database, Db

The program structure is pretty straightforward. Basically, you have menus for inputs and report generation, mediated by a database.

The Starting Touches

Before typing in the menu formulas, enter the formulas for the PnL containing frame and for the Init frame (shown in Figure 8-3). If you already have these frames from Currency1, just make the appropriate modifications. Remember to enter each formula into the *formula entry area* of its frame.

```
PnL:
  ; PnL -- a Profit and Loss calculator and reporter

  ; Print listing routine
  @tm(2),
  @bm(4),
  @po(5),
  @ll(75),
  @fl("PnL Listing"),
  @fc(@date1(@today) & " : " & @time1(@today)),
  @fr(@pn),
  @printreturn,
  @setmacro({Alt-F},PnL.Init)


PnL.Init:
  ; Init

  DoInput.Edit.Show.Date := @today,    ;init date variable

  FINISHED := #FALSE, ; FINISHED is quit flag. TRUE quits

  @keyfilter({Esc},Menus.Quit),    ; Esc set to Exit menu
  @menu(Menus),         ; call 1st menu

  ; check to see if user wants to quit
  @keyfilter({Esc}),               ; turn Esc filter off
  @if(FINISHED, @return(0))    ; if TRUE, back to Starter
```

Figure 8-3. Listings for PnL and Init

> **Note:** If you have a Framework version before 2.0, the above listing will work just fine. If you have a later version, you can simplify things by writing:
>
> ```
> @PnL.Init
> ```
>
> instead of:
>
> ```
> @setmacro({Alt-F}, PnL.Init)
> ```
>
> If you have a version before 2.0, you'll have to press <F5> initially and then <Alt>-F every time you want to run the program. With later versions, pressing <F5> is sufficient. This is similar to the adjustment you made with the fast food program.

SETTING UP THE MENUS

Set up PnL's menus as you set up menus in past chapters; first enter the prompts and then the formulas. Be sure to take advantage of Cut, Paste, and Record to make your formula entry quicker.

Entering Menu Prompts

This section takes you through each menu as it appears in the outline. To enter the prompt, put the outline in frames view and enter each prompt inside its frame, not in its formula area. Size the frames as you go so that each shows all or most of its prompt.

Table 8-1 gives the prompts for items in the Menus menu (also referred to as the "activities menu").

Table 8-1. Prompts for Menus Menu Items

Frame Name	Prompt
Entry	Enter expenses and income
Report	Report categories or P&L
Quit	Leave program and save Db

Table 8-2 gives the prompts for items in the Entry Menu.

Table 8-2. Prompts for Entry Menu Items

Frame Name	Prompt
Auto	Enter Auto expenses
Copies	Enter Copies expenses
Income	Enter Income items
Postage	Enter Postage expenses
Supplies	Enter Supplies expenses
Quit	Return to Activities Menu

Now type in the prompts for the HowPaid menu, displayed in Table 8-3.

Table 8-3. Prompts for HowPaid Menu Items

Frame Name	Prompt
Check	Paid with check
Dollars	Paid with cash
Plastic	Paid with credit card

The Show menu has no prompts. Although its elements bear formulas, these same elements act as variables, storing variables generated by the Input menu. (More on that soon.) Enter the prompts for the Report Menu listed in Table 8-4.

Table 8-4. Prompts for Report Menu Items

Frame Name	Prompt
Auto	Report Auto expenses
Copies	Report Copies expenses
Income	Report Income items
Postage	Report Postage expenses
Supplies	Report Supplies expenses
Write P&L	Generate P&L statement
Quit	Return to Activities Menu

A note on structuring menus: Notice that the Quit item in both the Entry Menu frame and Report Menu frame states "Return to Activities Menu." Unlike the menus in Currency1 (in which the user had to press <Uplevel> to rise to a higher menu level), PnL is structured so that the user can press Q to rise from either the Entry or Report Menu to the activities menu.

FRAME WORK

Compare the two outlines in Figure 8-4. Outline A shows a menu system like that in Currency1. Outline B is a copy of PnL's menu. The difference is that, in Outline B, the activities items (Entry and Report) each contain an **@menu** command to call their respective menus. Outline A, simply has one menu call—to the Menus (activities) menu.

Outline A	**Outline B**
1 Init — **@menu**(Menus)	1 Init — **@menu**(Menus)
2 Menus	2 Menus
2.1 Entry	2.1 Entry — **@menu**(Entry Menu)
2.1.1 Auto	2.2 Report — **@menu**(Report Menu)
2.1.2 Copies	2.3 Quit
2.1.3 etc.	3 Entry Menu
2.2 Report	3.1 Auto
2.2.1 Auto	3.2 Copies
2.2.2 Copies	3.3 etc.
2.2.3 etc.	5 Report Menu
2.3 Quit	5.1 Auto
	5.2 Copies
	5.3 etc.

Figure 8-4. Two Menu Systems

To give you a sharper picture in Figure 8-4, the text shows sample code. But why sample? On to the real thing.

The Menus Menu

As just mentioned, the Menus menu (or Activities menu) calls other menus. Because the Entry and Report menus are called, quitting them with **@quitmenu** takes program execution back to its source—the Activities menu. Type in the formulas for Menus, shown in Figure 8-5.

```
PnL.Menus.Entry:
   @menu(Entry Menu)


PnL.Menus.Report:
   @menu(Report Menu)


PnL.Menus.Quit:
   ; Quit

   ; set flag to true causing exit at init routine
   PnL.FINISHED := #TRUE,
   @setselection("DoInput.Edit"),
   @performkeys("{Ctrl-Uplevel}{Ctrl-Return}"),
   @quitmenu
```

Figure 8-5. Listing for the Menus Menu

Note that before quitting, the Quit item saves the database for you. After quitting, it moves selection to the container frame, PnL.

The Entry Menu

The Entry Menu formulas present the user with the different categories of entries. Choosing a category passes the category name to DoInput, the routine that gets the rest of the input (how paid, date, and so on). In doing so, it recalculates DoInput, causing DoInput to query the user for the rest of the information about the item. Because this menu calls DoInput, DoInput returns control to it, setting the user up for the next entry. Type the Entry Menu formulas in Figure 8-6 into your outline.

```
PnL.Entry Menu.Auto:
  ; Auto

  @DoInput("Auto")


PnL.Entry Menu.Copies:
  ; Copies

  @DoInput("Copies")


PnL.Entry Menu.Income:
  ; Income

  @DoInput("Income")


PnL.Entry Menu.Postage:
  ; Postage

  @DoInput("Postage")


PnL.Entry Menu.Supplies:
  ; Supplies

  @DoInput("Supplies")


PnL.Entry Menu.Quit:
  ; Quit

  @quitmenu
```

Figure 8-6. Listing for Entry Menu

The HowPaid Menu

People could make a programmer's life much easier if they paid for things only with checks. Unfortunately, they also use credit cards and cash. To meet this situation, PnL contains a menu in the middle of DoInput along with two variables, CHECKNUM and NOTCHECK. If you paid with a check, PnL writes a number to CHECKNUM and a #FALSE to NOTCHECK. If you choose Dollars or Plastic, PnL writes the appropriate string to NOTCHECK.

Later routines will check these variables to determine whether to prompt for a check number or continue to the next item, and, when editing a record, whether to show a check number, "Cash," or "Credit Card" as the How Paid default. (More on this in the discussion of the Show menu.) Type in the formulas listed in Figure 8-7.

```
PnL.DoInput.GetData.GetHowPaid:
  ; GetHowPaid

  @menu(GetHowPaid.HowPaid),
  @if(NOTCHECK = #FALSE,
      DoInput.Edit.Show.How Paid := CHECKNUM,
      DoInput.Edit.Show.How Paid := NOTCHECK
  )


PnL.DoInput.GetData.GetHowPaid.HowPaid.Check:
  ; Check

  CHECKNUM := @Integ("Please enter check number",
  (CHECKNUM+1)),
  NOTCHECK := #FALSE,
  @quitmenu


PnL.DoInput.GetData.GetHowPaid.HowPaid.Dollars:
  ; Dollars

  NOTCHECK := "Cash",
  @quitmenu


PnL.DoInput.GetData.GetHowPaid.HowPaid.Plastic:
  ; Plastic

  NOTCHECK := "Card",
  @quitmenu
```

Figure 8-7. Listing for GetHowPaid and HowPaid Menus

FRAME WORK

The Show Menu

Have you ever entered a series of items and then seen that one of them was wrong? Without a way to edit mistakes, making corrections can be difficult and frustrating.

By displaying the Show menu's frames inside the PnL frame (see Figure 8-8), you give the user an opportunity to review entries. If a problem exits, the user can answer the prompt (''Do you wish to make changes (Y or N)'') by pressing ''Y'' (or ''y''). The Show items then become a menu with editable prompts.

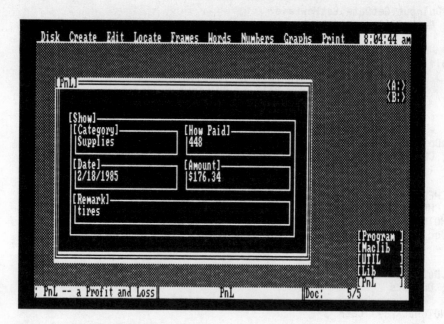

Figure 8-8. The PnL Frame as Interface

As mentioned in Chapter Two, frames can play multiple roles. In Show, they display data and act as menu items. They also act as variables. As you will see when you type in the GetData formulas, GetData stores its results in appropriate Show frames. Even the How Paid item for a particular record ends up in the How Paid frame, by way of NOTCHECK and CHECKNUM.

Type in the listing for Edit (the calling frame) and Show, given in Figure 8-9.

```
PnL.DoInput.Edit:
  ; Edit

  @prompt("Do you wish to make changes (Y or N)?",25),
  @if(@or(@nextkey = {y},@key = {Y}),
         @menu(Edit.Show)
  ),
  @eraseprompt


PnL.DoInput.Edit.Show.Category:
  @String("Change Category",Category)


PnL.DoInput.Edit.Show.How Paid:
  ; Show.How Paid

  @if(NOTCHECK = #FALSE,
      CHECKNUM := @Integ("Change check number",CHECKNUM),

      @String("Change how paid", NOTCHECK)
  )


PnL.DoInput.Edit.Show.Date:
  ; Show.Date

  @Day("Change Date -  Month/Day/Year",Date)


PnL.DoInput.Edit.Show.Amount:
  ; Show.Amount

  @Bucks("Change the amount",Amount)


PnL.DoInput.Edit.Show.Remark:
  ; Show.Remark

  @String("Change the remark",Remark)


PnL.DoInput.Edit.Show.Save:
  ; Show.Save

  @quitmenu
```

Figure 8-9. Listings for the Edit and Show Frames

Perhaps, as you typed, you became curious about frame calls like @Integ. What is it? Where is it? The answer is Lib. The next section (''The New Lib'') covers the following routines in detail:

Bucks

Day

Integ

String

Because PnL has four different types of input, a good library must support this with four ways of filtering input. For the moment, understand that each Show frame calls a particular Lib routine and ships it two parameters: a prompt (for example, ''Change Category'') and a default value (the value currently stored in the Show frame). Before going on to the Lib section, wrap up your menu formula entry with the next section.

The Report Menu

Although the chapter discussing report generation is still two chapters away, you might as well type in its formulas now.

Note: Be sure to type in *three* double quotation marks on either side of each string parameter. This is because each string parameter is part of a database filter formula such as:

    Category = "Auto"

It takes three double quotation marks for just one double quotation mark to appear in the database formula.

Type in the formulas in Figure 8-10.

```
PnL.Report Menu.Auto:
    ; Auto -- Report all auto expenses

    @Reporter("""Auto""")


PnL.Report Menu.Copies:
    ; Copies -- Report all Copies expenses

    @Reporter("""Copies""")


PnL.Report Menu.Income:
    ; Income -- Report all Income expenses

    @Reporter("""Income""")


PnL.Report Menu.Postage:
    ; Postage -- Report all Postage expenses

    @Reporter("""Postage""")


PnL.Report Menu.Supplies:
    ; Supplies -- Report all Supplies expenses

    @Reporter("""Supplies""")


PnL.Report Menu.Write PnL:
    ; Write PnL

    @local(SELECTOR,CONST,STR,CURRENT),

    @Reporter.MakePnL,

    @while(SELECTOR < 5,
        SELECTOR := SELECTOR + 1,
        CONST := @select(SELECTOR,"""Income""","""Auto""",
            """Copies""","""Postage""","""Supplies"""),
        @Reporter.QueryOne(CONST),        ; restore & query db
```

Figure 8-10. Listing for the Report Menu
(Continued on following page.)

```
        ; sum each category & write result to PnLReport
        ; if CONST = Income, write sum to D1
        @if(CONST  = """Income""",
            @put(PnLReport.D1:PnLReport.D1,
                @sum(Db.Amount)),

    ; if CONST <> income, region walk from C4 to C7
            @list(@put(PnLReport.C4:PnLReport.C7,
                    @sum(Db.Amount)),
                @next(PnLReport.C4:PnLReport.C7)
            )    ; end list
        )   ; end if-then-else
),  ; end while

CURRENT := @setselection,
@setselection("PnLReport"),
@performkeys("{F5}"),    ; recalc report
@Reporter.PrintSS("PnLReport"),
@setselection(CURRENT)


PnL.Report Menu.Quit:
  ; Quit

  @quitmenu
```

Figure 8-10 continued.

Now on to the new Lib.

THE NEW LIB

Previous Libs had only to process one kind of input—numeric. PnL, on the other hand, has four kinds of input. Therefore, the new Lib contains four processing routines:

- *Bucks* to process values in currency format (Amount)
- *Day* to process date values (Date)
- *Integ* to process integers (CHECKNUM)
- *String* to process strings (Category, NOTCHECK, and Remark)

The frame labels Bucks, Day, and Integ were chosen because FRED would look on a call to **@currency**, **@date**, and **@integer** as calls to its own built-in functions. Both the GetData and Show frames call on Lib to get user input.

Creating a Lib is an optional programming activity. In this case,the programmer preferred not having to type the pathnames that would become necessary if he stored these routines inside the PnL frame. The trade-off is that you must load two frames onto the desktop instead of just one.

Four Input Routines

The four input routines take two parameters—a prompt string and a default value— and test your input to see if it's valid. If it isn't, an **@while(BOOL** loop, keeps you in the input mode until you type an acceptable value. If valid, the routine returns (**@return**) the value you've entered to the calling routine. The loop keeps you from deleting the default and making a null entry. If you try this, the input routine will come right back again with a default.

If you have a copy of Currency1's Lib, follow the steps below.

1. Make a copy of Lib.

2. Rename the original CurrLib, save it, and delete it from the desktop.

3. Erase the interior frames of the copy (labeled Lib).

4. Inside Lib, create one empty word frame and copy it once.

5. Label the first frame Bucks and the second String.

6. Modify the container frame listing the formula to match the one shown in Figure 8-11.

7. Save Lib.

```
Lib:
   ; Lib

   ; Print listing routine
   @tm(2),
   @bm(4),
   @po(5),
   @ll(75),
   @fl("Listing for PnL Lib"),
   @fc(@date1(@today) & " : " & @time1(@today)),
   @fr(@pn),
   @printreturn
```

Figure 8-11. Listing for the Lib Containing Frame

If you don't have a Lib, follow these steps:

1. Create an outline frame and label it Lib.

2. Delete item 3 and the sublevels under the remaining items.

3. Label the first frame Bucks and the second String.

4. Type the listing shown in 8-11 into the containing (Lib) frame.

5. Save Lib.

Now you're ready to enter the listings for Lib's four input frames. Once you've typed in the listing for Bucks, you'll make two copies of it and modify these appropriately for Day and Integ.

Bucks

Type in the listing for Bucks shown in Figure 8-12.

```
Lib.Bucks:
    ; Bucks -- retrieve a currency value from the user
    ; @item1 - a prompt string
    ; @item2 - the default numeric value
    ; the return value is numeric

    @local(BOOL, NUM, INPUTNUM),
    @if(@iserr(@item2 + 0),
        INPUTNUM := 0,
        INPUTNUM := @item2
    ),
    BOOL := #TRUE,
    @while(BOOL,
        BOOL:= @iserr(NUM :=
            @inputline(@item1,@currency(INPUTNUM,2),
                #NO,#YES,#YES)),
        @if(BOOL=#FALSE, ; #true means there was an error
            BOOL:= @iserr(NUM := @value(NUM))
        )
    ),
    @return(NUM)
```

Figure 8-12. Listing for the Bucks Formula

To complete your Lib formulas, copy the Bucks frame twice. Rename the first copy Day and the second Integ. Bucks, Integ, and Day all start with similar statements. Each performs a test on **@item2,** the default value parameter. Here, Bucks simply adds zero to **@item2.** If addition works (the particular operand isn't that important), FRED knows you've sent him a number. However, if an error results (**@iserr** returns a #TRUE), FRED substitutes a zero as the default value for the user to edit.

Just as in Currency1, this routine goes into a BOOL loop. The programmer sets BOOL to #TRUE so that the loop will run. The loop then tests for an error from

@inputline. If the user makes an erroneous entry, **@iserr** returns a #TRUE. BOOL gets this #TRUE, keeping the loop alive. A valid entry results in **@iserr** and, thereby, BOOL turning #FALSE, ending the loop.

In this case, the routine returns the value of NUM, the local variable that receives the user's input, to the calling formula. And that's it.

Day

Modify the formula already in the Day frame so that it matches the listing in Figure 8-13, and add the additional code in the listing.

```
Lib.Day:
    ; Day -- retrieve a date value from the user
    ; @item1 - a prompt string
    ; @item2 - the default date value
    ; the return value is a date value

    @local(BOOL, STR, INDEX, MONTH, DAY,
            YEAR, LEN, USERDATE),

    ; test for legal input from Show.Date
    @if(@iserr(@sumdate(@item2,1)),
        USERDATE := @today,
        USERDATE := @item2
    ),

    ; get and test user input
    BOOL := #TRUE,
    @while(BOOL,
        BOOL := @iserr(STR :=
            @inputline(@item1,@scientific(USERDATE),
                #NO,#YES,#YES)),
        @if(BOOL = #FALSE, ; #true means an error
            ; Crude test for NUMBERs and '/'
            BOOL := @iserr(@value(STR))
        )
    ),

    ; package user input into @date funct.
    INDEX := 1,
```

```
LEN := @len(STR),
STR := STR & "/0/0", ; Stop values for bogus input

@while(@and( INDEX <= LEN, @mid(STR,INDEX,1) <> "/"),
    MONTH := (MONTH*10) + @value(@mid(STR,INDEX,1)),
    INDEX := INDEX + 1
),
INDEX := INDEX + 1,
@while(@and( INDEX <= LEN, @mid(STR,INDEX,1) <> "/"),
    DAY := (DAY*10) + @value(@mid(STR,INDEX,1)),
    INDEX := INDEX + 1
),
INDEX := INDEX + 1,
@while( INDEX <= LEN,
    YEAR := (YEAR*10) + @value(@mid(STR,INDEX,1)),
    INDEX := INDEX + 1
),
@if(YEAR < 100,
    YEAR := YEAR + 1900
),
@return(@date(YEAR, MONTH, DAY))
```

Figure 8-13. Listing for the Day Formula

The Day formula has two tasks. The first is the same as the other frames—to test the default and get input. The second is to write the date data into the **@date** function. This is an important data entry technique, particularly when you're preparing data for a spreadsheet or database, because you don't want either structure to evaluate 8/27/84 as a number. Nor do you want to send the string ''8/27/84'' to a database (when sorting, a database sees the string ''09/30/84'' as less than ''8/27/84'').

Another reason for preferring dates in function form is that you can manipulate such dates with other Framework functions like **@sumdate**, **@diffdate**, or **@time2**. On the other hand, you're pushing your luck when you ask a user to type

@date(1984,8,27)

every time your program calls for a date entry. Rather than write in computerese, the user wants to type something quick and familiar like:

    8/27/84

This routine lets the user do just that and still end up with the function form in the database and spreadsheet.

Before parsing the date string, Day does some bullet-proofing. Where the **@sumdate** test protects against an improper value being sent to the Day frame, the statement

    STR := STR & "/0/0"

protects against the user entering an improper date, like just the number 6. If the date were December 5th, 1984, STR would carry:

    "12/5/84"

Concatenating the second string turns the date string into:

    "12/5/84/0/0"

If someone types a 6, the string would still look like a date:

    "6/0/0"

Admittedly, this is a crude piece of bullet-proofing. It does not keep you from entering the 13th month or the 32nd of December. If you wish to make such tests, this formula will support your efforts.

Day supplies a final piece of protection just before returning the date formula. Because users often want to shorten "1984" to just "84," Day tests the year and, if necessary, brings it into the twentieth century:

```
@if(YEAR < 100
    YEAR := YEAR + 1900
),
```

To convert the date string into the date function, the Day formula begins with a test and a BOOL loop much like the others. In this case, the test operation is **@sumdate**. If adding one day to the default works, FRED knows he has a date.

After the BOOL loop, the formula proceeds to parse the input (kept in the local variable STR). Each of the three elements of the date—YEAR, MONTH, and DAY—gets its own parsing loop. FRED's primary parsing tool is the **@mid** function. The partial statement

```
@mid(STR,INDEX,1)
```

tells FRED to parse the current date string (STR) by moving the parsing pointer to the nth character (where *n* is the current value of INDEX) and take just 1 character.

This operation takes place in each loop only so long as the INDEX is less than or equal to the length of STR and the found character isn't the "/" (slash). How does the function leap over each slash? By incrementing the pointer before starting the next loop (INDEX := INDEX + 1).

To understand why each **@date** variable is multiplied by ten, look at the following statement:

```
MONTH := (MONTH * 10) + @value(@mid(STR,INDEX,1)),
```

Assume the month is 12. The first time through, MONTH is 0, so the expression evaluates to 1:

```
0*10 + 1
```

The second time through the formula evaluates to 12, like this:

$$1*10+2$$

The next thing the parsing function finds is a slash, so parsing passes on to the DAY variable, where a similar activity takes place.

Once the testing and parsing process has created the three date elements, the formula packages them into an **@date** function and returns the entire function to the calling formula.

Integ

Integ tests for a numeric default and then gets input which it returns as an integer. It's simple to modify the Bucks listing to correspond to the Integ listing in Figure 8-14.

```
Lib.Integ:
    ; Integ -- retrieve an integer from the user
    ; @item1 - a prompt string
    ; @item2 - the default numeric value
    ; the return value is numeric

    @local(BOOL, NUM, INPUTNUM),

    @if(@iserr(@item2 + 0),
        INPUTNUM := 0,
        INPUTNUM := @item2
    ),
    BOOL := #TRUE,
    @while(BOOL,
        BOOL := @iserr(NUM :=
            @inputline(@item1,@integer(INPUTNUM),
                #NO,#YES,#YES)),
        @if(BOOL = #FALSE, ; #TRUE means there was an error
            BOOL := @iserr(NUM := @value(NUM))
        )
    ),
    @return(@int(NUM))
```

Figure 8-14. Listing for the Integ Formula

String

String is the simplest of the Lib frames. It only makes one test. The **@isna** function returns a #TRUE when a value is not available (#N/A!). Basically, String keeps the user from deleting the default string and pressing a <Return> (which would enter a #N/A!) by replacing #N/A! with a single space character.

As with the Day frame, String does not provide total bullet-proofing. In a professional level program, a programmer would want to limit Remark and other strings to a given number of characters (or do you want the Great American Novel written in the Remark field?). Type in the formula for String, given in Figure 8-15.

```
Lib.String:
  ; String -- retrieve a string from the user
  ; @item1 - a prompt string
  ; @item2 - the default string value
  ; the return value is a string

  @local(STR),
  @if(@isna(STR := @inputline(@item1,@item2,#NO,#YES,#YES)),
      STR := " "
  ),
  @return(STR)
```

Figure 8-15. Listing for the String Formula

PROCESSING INPUT

By this time, you have typed in most of the formulas that handle processing (Show menu and Lib formulas). Typing in these last three listings completes the data entry portion of PnL.

DoInput

The DoInput formula drives both the GetData and Show formulas. Type it in from Figure 8-16.

```
PnL.DoInput:
    ; DoInput

@Reporter.Restore,
DoInput.Edit.Show.Category := @item1,          ; assign category
@DoInput.GetData,              ; get input for DB
@DoInput.Edit,                 ; go to edit input routine
@DoInput.Write                 ; write entries into DB
```

Figure 8-16. Listing for DoInput

The first statement,

```
@Reporter.Restore
```

calls a routine you'll see in Chapter Nine. In short, Restore throws out the *working set* of records and summons all records into the database.

Following restoration, DoInput assigns the current category name, shipped to it by selecting a category for entry, to the Show.Category frame, where the frame plays the role of a variable.

Next, DoInput calls the GetData routines to get the remaining four pieces of information needed to complete an expense/income record. With the information in hand, the program calls up Edit, giving the user the chance to make corrections. Finally, DoInput calls the Write formula, which writes the new data into the database. (Chapter Nine, describing the database, discusses the Write formula.)

GetData

Like DoInput, GetData calls a series of routines. Each routine gathers a different piece of information from the user. Type in the listing, shown in Figure 8-17. As the listing shows, GetData calls the remaining four items to get the information needed to complete a record:

● The GetHowPaid menus

● The GetDate routine

- The GetAmt routine

- The GetRem routine

```
PnL.DoInput.GetData:
   ; GetData

   @GetData.GetHowPaid,
   @GetData.GetDate,
   @GetData.GetAmt,
   @GetData.GetRem
```

Figure 8-17. Listing for GetData

Because you've already typed in the GetHowPaid menus, all you need to do now is type in the remaining three routines. See Figure 8-18. Note that each routine calls a Lib routine and assigns the result to the appropriate Show frame. This concludes the discussion of the data entry component of PnL. It's now time to discuss storing data in Db, PnL's database.

```
PnL.DoInput.GetData.GetDate:
   ; GetDate

   DoInput.Edit.Show.Date := @Day
       ("Date of transaction (Month/Day/Year)?",
       DoInput.Edit.Show.Date)


PnL.DoInput.GetData.GetAmt:
   ; GetAmt

   DoInput.Edit.Show.Amount :=
   @Bucks("The amount of money?",.00)


PnL.DoInput.GetData.GetRem:
   ; GetRem

   DoInput.Edit.Show.Remark :=
   @String("Any remarks?","none")
```

Figure 8-18. Listing for GetData Routines

FRAMEWORK

CHAPTER NINE

THE DATABASE

This chapter presents the Framework database from a programmer's viewpoint and shows you how to set up the PnL database, Db.

INTRODUCING THE DATABASE

The Framework database supports all the functions you normally expect from a database. This chapter looks in detail at the database's structure, with particular attention paid to the following:

- Describing fields and records, and defining formulas for fields
- Writing data into a database under program control
- Querying or ''filtering'' records
- Sorting records
- Restoring all database records after filtering

The Framework database frame differs from other types of frames in that it dedicates itself completely to managing data. For example, when you write a formula in the database border's formula area, FRED assumes you've written a database *filtering formula*, not a general purpose formula. Therefore, he tries to apply it to each current record to decide whether or not to filter it.

A formula for another purpose, such as reading from a spreadsheet, will confuse FRED and cause problems, the character of which depends on what the formula is trying to do. However, like a spreadsheet frame, you can treat a database frame like a data structure (a "hot" array) in which you can reach the data by filtering and sorting.

Database Structure

Within the containing frame, a Framework database contains two elements: a *field name row* (above the double line) and *data area* below it. Each row in the data area is a *record*. Each record comprises one or more *fields*. Each column in the record, in turn, is a *field*. You name each field by typing a *field name* into the field name row. To make this clearer, you will type in the field names for PnL's database, Db.

Put your Db frame in Forms View (press <F10>) and shrink it so that only the label row and first data row show. Then position the cursor in the left corner of the label row. Type the following labels, pressing <Tab> between each label to move to the next cell.

Category   How Paid   Date   Amount   Remark

Now size the fields, according to Table 9-1. Simply go to each label, press <F4> and then <Rightarrow> the appropriate number of times (default column width is 9).

Table 9-1. Db Field Sizes

Field Name	No. of Characters
Category	11
How Paid	10
Date	12
Amount	13
Remark	10

When you finish, your database should look like the one in Figure 9-1.

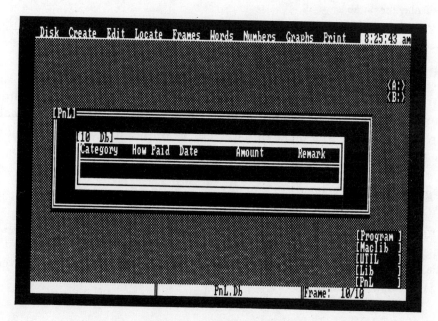

Figure 9-1. The Database with Field Labels

FRAME WORK

> **Note:** You can shrink database fields to a zero width. This is handy for hiding sensitive or (from the user's standpoint) irrelevant data.

You may think that a database with only one record or row has limited utility. You're right. However, the stragegy for entering records into the database under program control calls for adding a row to the database each time you want to enter a record. There is more on this below, in the "Writing Records to a Database" section.

> **Note:** In a database frame, pressing <F10> does not switch to Outline View. Rather, it switches between Table View and Forms View of a record. Keep this in mind when you write your own database applications. PnL displays the Show frames to tell the user the status of each entry and does not display the database at all.

Database Formulas

In the introduction to this chapter you read that a formula placed in the database border works only as a query or *filter formula*. A typical formula uses a logical operator to compare a field name to a piece of data. For example, to extract only those records whose Category is Auto, you would write the filter formula

        Category = "Auto"

in the formula area of the database border and then recalculate. Note that in searching for a string, you must supply quotation marks. Otherwise, FRED thinks you're talking about a variable. Here's a numeric example. To see all the amounts entered that are less than $100.00, you would enter:

        Amount < $100

As you will see, you can enter such formulas under program control.

The Framework database also supports two other types of formulas: the label or *defining formula* and the *local formula*. A local formula applies only to the cell in whose formula area it resides. PnL's database has no local formulas. It does, however, take advantage of defining formulas.

A defining formula, written in the formula area of a field label, applies itself to every piece of data belonging to the field label in question. For example, you might want to generate sales tax figures from a Sales field. In this case, you might enter the following formula behind the Sales Tax label (assuming the sales tax is six percent):

    Sales Tax := Sales * 6%

Note: Framework supports certain symbols applied to numbers. For example, you can type

        Amount < $100

instead of

        Amount < 100

or

        Sales * 6%

instead of

        Sales * .06

to make your formulas easier to understand and enter.

Db's defining formulas have a slightly different task; each formula enters the current value for its field, found in the appropriate Show menu frame. When recalculated, each formula checks to see if there is an empty field to write data into. Because the formula that causes the recalculation has just created an empty row, there always is.

The "Writing Records to a Database" section, below, discusses this mechanism in more detail. For now, place the cursor on the first and only data row in the database, and remove the entire row; type:

<Ctrl>-E R Y

With the one row deleted, you won't accidentally recalculate one of the defining formulas and place trash into the data area.

Now place the cursor on the Category field and enter each listing in Figure 9-2 in the formula area of its field name. Because of the similarity of these formulas, you can speed up your own data entry by "cutting" the first formula, "pasting" it into the other formula areas, and then modifying it.

```
PnL.Db.Category:
   Category := @if(Category = #N/A!,
               DoInput.Edit.Show.Category,
               Category    ; if other, give own value
              )


PnL.Db.How Paid:
   How Paid  := @if(How Paid = #N/A!,
               @if(@isnumeric(DoInput.Edit.Show.How Paid),
                   @integer(DoInput.Edit.Show.How Paid),
                   DoInput.Edit.Show.How Paid
               ),
               How Paid    ; if other, give own value
              )


PnL.Db.Date:
   Date := @if(Date = #N/A!,
           DoInput.Edit.Show.Date,
           Date    ; if other, give own value
          )


PnL.Db.Amount:
   Amount := @if(Amount = #N/A!,
             DoInput.Edit.Show.Amount,
             Amount  ; if other, give own value
            )
```

```
PnL.Db.Remark:
    Remark := @if(Remark = #N/A!,
            Do Input.Edit.Show.Remark,
            Remark        ; if other, give own value
        )
```

Figure 9-2. Listings for Db's Defining Formulas

Because How Paid can store either an integer or a string, the How Paid formula tests for a number. If it finds a number, it puts it into string integer format to cause automatic left alignment of the number. Check numbers, like telephone numbers and ZIP and area codes, are not arithmetical entities and behave better in a database when entered as strings.

To enable you to edit database entries once they're in the database, each formula includes an ELSE, the field's name. In other words, if the item is not available, write it in. If an item is available, let it be itself.

WRITING RECORDS TO A DATABASE

If you've written more than a handful of programs, you know you can usually find more than one way to accomplish a given task. In developing PnL, two ways of writing records to the database were tried. The first way was with a series of **@get-@put-@next** statements. Unfortunately, this method took longer and longer as PnL entered each new record into Db because the routine had to read through each field, looking for an empty row. To speed things up, the thinking was turned inside-out: Why not have Db *read* in the records, instead of having another frame *write* them in? Thus were born the defining formulas you just typed in.

This section looks at how the reading activity was accomplished with an emphasis on how Framework databases respond to defining formulas and recalculations. Assume that DoInput (see Figure 8-16) has done all its work—restoring the database and getting the user's inputs and edits. Execution arrives at the Write frame. Type in Write's brief listing, shown in Figure 9-3, before continuing. (That's a numeral ''1'', not the letter ''I'' following the ''R'' in the listing.)

```
; Write
@setselection("Db"),
@performkeys("{Dnlevel}{Ctrl-C}R1{Return}{F5}"),
```

Figure 9-3. Listing for Write

Because Write is preparing to create a new row in the database, the first thing it does is select the database and get into it. Note that the program could not have been written:

```
@setselection("Db.Category"),
```

and eliminated the {Dnlevel} because the above statement would not have worked on a database with no records (as this one is before you make your first entry). True, you could keep one blank record in the database, but this can create other problems when counting records, sorting, and retrieving. It's better to keep it clean. Also note that Framework can add a row when the cursor is in the field label area; the cursor needn't be in the data area.

With positioning accomplished, Write proceeds to create one row by going to the Create menu choice ''Rows / Records: Add'' and entering the argument ''1'' with:

```
{Ctrl-C}R1{Return}
```

When Framework creates the new row, the cursor moves into it. Write must tell the defining formulas (the ones you typed behind the field labels) to recalculate, so it concludes by ''typing'' the <F5> key.

When you work with defining formulas, keep two rules in mind. First, Framework will recalculate only the *selected record(s)*. In this case, it's a blank record, so you don't have to worry about the procedure either messing up previous data or taking a lot of time. Second, when Framework recalculates a record, it looks to the field label of the current field for a defining formula. If a formula is present, it writes the data demanded by the formula. If no formula is present, Framework moves on to the next field.

Consider Db in light of these two rules. In the first field, the defining formula says, if the field is blank (it is) read in whatever's in the DoInput.Edit.Show.Category frame. So Framework writes in the last category the user selected. Regardless of whether a formula is present, Framework then moves to the next field and repeats these same steps. Thus, it reads in data from the Show "variable" frames.

This is a quick and efficient way of getting data into a database. Once you've got data in your database, you'll probably want to retrieve it. That's the subject of the next section.

FILTERING A DATABASE

To retrieve records from a database, you must apply a filtering formula to the database. The formula effectively retrieves those records that match the description given in the filter formula.

Framework does not actually retrieve records—it *hides* the records that do not match the formula. Filtering works only on the records not currently hidden. This might be all records or just a working set. If you filter the working set for records it doesn't contain, the database will return no records.

This means two things. First, you can filter by steps, taking the working set of a working set, and so on. Second, if you want to search all records in the database, you should first restore all records. PnL's Db has no need to filter working sets, but it does need restoration before each filtering activity.

Retrieving Records

PnL generates two types of reports. The first type is a report on one of the five entry categories. This report shows the following for the chosen report category:

How the item was paid for

The date of each transaction

The amount paid

The sum of all amounts paid

The second type of report is a summary labeled PnLReport. It displays:

Total income

Totals for each expense category

A subtotal for all expenses

The resulting income before taxes

Chapter Ten discusses the writing of both types of report. The remainder of this chapter shows how PnL retrieves the data to write these reports.

The retrieval process begins when the user selects the Report menu and chooses a report category. If the user chooses Auto, the following formula goes into effect:

```
@Reporter("""Auto""")
```

This calls the Reporter frame and ships it the argument in parentheses. As mentioned in Chapter Eight, the extra double quotation marks are needed to include a pair of quotation marks in the string.

Figure 9-4 shows the flow of control from the Report Menu to the option of printing the current report.

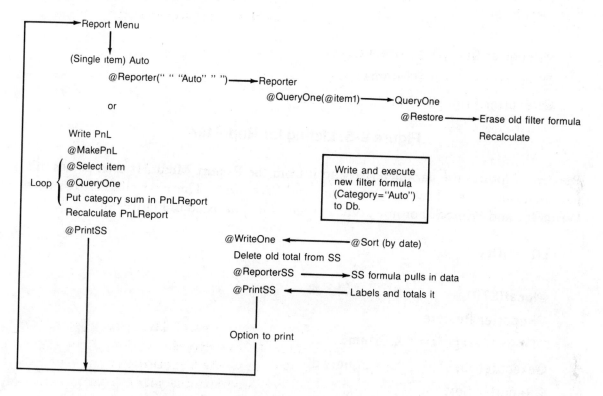

Figure 9-4. Flow of Control for a Report

Before reading about Reporter, type in its formula, given in Figure 9-5.

```
; Reporter

@Reporter.QueryOne(@item1),
@Reporter.WriteOne(@item1),
@Reporter.PrintSS("PnL.Reporter.SS")
```

Figure 9-5. Listing for Reporter

Reporter captures the parameter sent to it from the Report Menu. It then passes this parameter on to two frames, QueryOne and WriteOne. The next chapter discusses WriteOne and PrintSS. For now, type in QueryOne, as listed in Figure 9-6.

```
; QueryOne

@local(STR),
@Reporter.Restore,
STR := "Category = " & @item1,
@execute(Db,STR),          ; query db
@Reporter.Sort
```

Figure 9-6. Listing for QueryOne

QueryOne stands at the heart of the record filtering process. The first thing it does is restore the database so that the filtering process will act on *all* database records. It then moves on to incorporate the category parameter into a string to be executed as a formula by the **@execute** command.

    @execute takes two parameters: a frame name and a formula. Given these, **@execute** writes the formula to the frame and executes it. If the destination frame already has a formula, **@execute** over-writes it.

Here, given that the chosen expense category is Auto, **@execute** writes the formula

    Category = "Auto"

into the formula area of Db's border and immediately executes the formula. The result: All the records whose Category is Auto become the working set. This formula will remain in effect until the next restore operation. To get the "feel" of filtering and sorting, the section "Handling the Database" below has you perform both of these activities by hand.

With the appropriate records selected, QueryOne sorts them into ascending date order by calling Sort. The stage is set for report generation.

Sorting

Besides accepting, storing, and returning (filtered) data, the Framework database can *sort* data. You can sort data into either ascending (smallest value at the top) or descending (greatest value at the top) order.

FRED does not have a built-in sort function (like an "@sort"). Rather, you sort with the Locate menu, either by hand or through an **@performkeys** statement. Sorting takes three steps:

1. Select the field you want to sort.

2. Go to the Locate menu with <Ctrl>-L

3. Type either A for Ascending or D for Descending order.

To illustrate sorting in a program, PnL sorts its working set by date in ascending order. Go to the Sort frame in your PnL outline and enter the formula in Figure 9-7.

```
PnL.Reporter.Sort:
  ; Sort

  ; sort records into ascending date order
  @setselection("PnL.Db"),
  @performkeys("{Dnlevel}{Rightarrow}{Rightarrow}" &
  "{Ctrl-L}a{Ctrl-Home}{Uplevel}")
```

Figure 9-7. Listing for PnL's Sort Formula

The Sort formula selects the database and then jumps the cursor down into the field name area and moves to the Date field. Then the **@performkeys** statement goes to the Framework Locate menu, does an ascending sort, and jumps back out to the database border. It exits through <Ctrl>-<Home> to ensure that the next access to the database will enter in the Category field, where filtering and writing begin. (You'll have a chance to sort a database by hand in the "Handling the Database" section below.)

What do you do when you want to sort more than one field? For example, what if you wanted your working set sorted by date in ascending order, and then by Amount in descending order. In such a case, you sort the least significant field first (Amount) and then the most significant field (Date). Framework doesn't limit the number of fields you can sort in this way.

Sorting brings up an interesting question: In what order does the database normally keep its data? Basically, elements reside in the order they are entered. If you sort and save, the sorted order takes over. If you retrieve a working set and then restore all the records to the database, the working set records will be on top, in whatever order they appeared, with the remaining records in the order they had before you pulled out the working set.

Note: If you need to develop a database in which the order of entry is important, create a numbering field. Increment the value in the numbering field by one for each new record you enter. Then, to sort the database back into entry order, perform an ascending sort on the numbering field.

Restoring the Database

Each time you call for a report, QueryOne writes a filter to Db. Therefore, before writing to or retrieving from Db, you must erase this filter and recalculate the database to bring out all records hidden by the previous filter. The Restore formula is simplicity itself. Type it in from the listing in Figure 9-8.

```
; Restore--erase db filter formula
; and bring up full set of records

@setselection("PnL.Db"),          ; restore all recs
@performkeys("{F2}{F6}{Ctrl-End}{Del}{Return}{F5}")
```

Figure 9-8. Listing for Restore

Restore selects Db and then enters the Db border formula area, selecting and deleting all text. The formula ends with an <F5> to recalculate the database, restoring all records.

> **Note:** In this program the programmer chose to restore first and then filter. You can just as easily restore the database immediately after processing the filtered information.

Another way to restore a database is to write the #TRUE constant as the filter formula. The #TRUE formula matches all of the records, so none remains hidden. To accomplish this, you could write:

```
@execute(PnL.Db, #TRUE)
```

MAKING DATABASE ENTRIES

Now that you've typed in all the formulas necessary for making entries (you'll complete the reporting portion of the program in the next chapter), take it for a test spin.

Test Entries

Note that How Paid needs a numeric value in CHECKNUM before the Get Data.HowPaid.Check formula can work. Go to CHECKNUM's *formula area*, type 444, and press <Esc> to leave.

Before entering data, make sure the five Show frames are visible inside PnL; then select PnL. If you have a Framework version earlier than 2.0, press <F5><Alt>-F to begin. If you have a later version, just press <F5>

Immediately, the activities menu appears. Press **E** to choose Entry. Once the Entry menu appears, follow the prompts at the bottom of the screen and type in the records shown in Figure 9-9. In this first run, edit your selections only if you have to.

If one of the dates or other categories looks like it will require a lot of editing, don't edit—just type. If you start typing before you begin editing, the first character typed will throw out the default. In fact, you don't even have to type "1985"; "85" will do the trick. Lib's Day formula will make up the difference. Also, you don't have to type in all the zeroes after the decimal point. Your entry routines automatically put numbers in currency format.

Category	How Paid	Date	Amount	Comment
Auto	445	3/4/85	189.96	tuneup
Postage	446	3/4/85	20.00	stamps
Copies	Dollars	3/18/85	5.00	none
Income	5055	3/14/85	500.00	client A
Copies	Plastic	2/28/85	93.45	forms

Figure 9-9. Five Initial Entries

Now enter an additional record to which you will have to make a correction:

| Auto | 448 | 3/7/85 | 176.34 | tires |

When you are offered the chance to edit your entries, change the check number in the last entry to 447, and save the correction.

> **Note:** There are no entries for Supplies. When you come to the Report chapters, you'll see how the SS and Write PnL formulas handle this problem.

Once you have finished, press **Q** twice to quit and save your database. That's all there is to it. In the next section, you'll examine the database with its new entries.

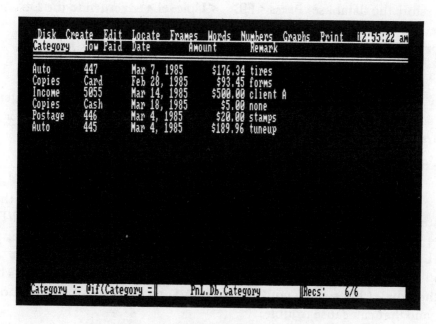

Figure 9-10. Portrait of a Database

Handling the Database

PnL is designed so that the user won't have to deal directly with the database. However, for the purposes of maintenance and curiosity, the database remains available. Here's how to get into the database: select Db and press <F9>

To give yourself a better idea of what will be happening under program control, try a filter, a restoration, and a sort. Follow these steps.

1. Return to Forms View; press <F9> <Uplevel>

2. To see only records for Auto, press <F2> and type **Category = "Auto"** <Return>

3. Take another look at the database; press <F9> and you'll see Auto's working set.

4. Now restore the database. Press <F9> <Uplevel> to return to the Db's border. Delete the formula and recalculate; press <F2> <F6> <End> <Del> <Return>

   Take a look at the results; press <F9>

5. Finally, sort the database into ascending date order: Move the cursor over to the Date column (it doesn't matter whether you're on the field name or in the data area) and issue the ascending sort command; press <Ctrl>-L A

6. Leave the database; press <F9> <Uplevel>

A couple of notes: If you need to edit records in the database, you must edit them in the appropriate form; that is, Formula Edit (<F2>) for numbers and Label/Field Edit (<Space>) for strings (including check numbers). Dates are a special case; you must edit them by re-writing them with the **@date** function.

If you must delete a record from the database, don't just delete the characters; remove the row. Otherwise, you'll find blank records floating around in your database, and that can cause trouble.

Turn to the next chapter to see your database at work.

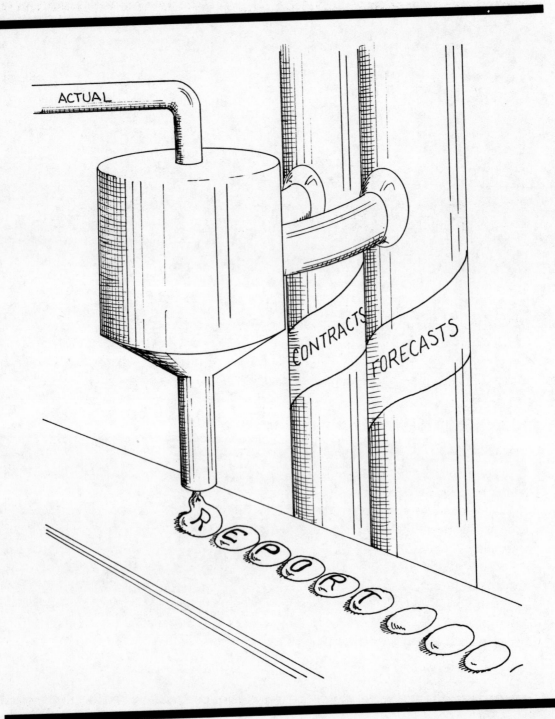

ASHTON·TATE

FRAMEWORK

CHAPTER TEN

REPORT GENERATION

This chapter illustrates two ways of generating reports: the basic reporting of an individual income/expense category and the writing of a profti and loss statement. Once you finish this chapter, you will have completed your PnL program and have plenty of ideas for enhancements.

REPORT STRATEGIES

PnL follows two different strategies for its two different report types. To write a report for a single category, the Report functions retrieve the appropriate records from the database and then write them into the spreadsheet named SS. SS carries a series of formulas that pulls the data into the spreadsheet with an **@get-@put-@next** group of formulas before summing and labeling the results with an **@performkeys** statement.

To write the Profit and Loss statement, a different strategy is used. PnL creates a spreadsheet on the fly and writes the sum of each category directly to the spreadsheet. The sum formula works directly on the database working set, rather than on the figures assembled in a spreadsheet. A permanent spreadsheet is used for category reports because the user would probably want to look at these often.

Why take the extra time to create a spreadsheet on the fly? On the other hand, why store a few K worth of spreadsheet for a P&L statement, which users demand less often? There's no reason why you couldn't create category spreadsheets on the fly and have a fixed P&L. Or have both spreadsheets fixed or both created on the fly. Much of how you set up a report depends on how your clients use your software.

More options? Instead of writing data into spreadsheets with **@get-@put-@next** statements, you could transfer the data with an **@performkeys** statement that "presses" Framework's Copy key (<F8>). Try the different strategies yourself and see what works best in your programming efforts. Now on to writing a report.

WRITING AN EXPENSE REPORT

The SS spreadsheet contains a lengthy formula that does the work of retrieving data from Db's working set and summing its amounts. Before setting up SS, set up the two formulas that "surround" the spreadsheet formula: WriteOne and PrintSS.

The WriteOne Formula

Type in the formula for WriteOne, shown in Figure 10-1.

```
; WriteOne


@setselection("PnL.Reporter.SS"),          ; select ss
@performkeys("{F9}{Del}{Ctrl-Home}"),        ; delete Total
@PnL.Reporter.SS(@item1)          ; send category to SS
```

Figure 10-1. Listing for WriteOne

This formula does two things: it deletes the previous report total and then passes the category parameter (like " " "Auto" " " to SS, where the actual reporting begins.

A little background on the deleting strategy will be helpful here. SS clears the data from the last report with the **@fill** function. **@fill,** however, cannot overwrite formulas. This is a problem because the SS formula writes an **@sum** formula to add all the amounts for the current category. The solution to the problem relies on Framework's ability to remember the last spreadsheet cell in which the cursor resided. To take advantage of this, WriteOne zooms the spreadsheet frame open. This action automatically places the cursor on the cell from which it exited the last time you worked with the spreadsheet. The formula then "presses" <Del> and positions the cursor for writing data by performing a <Ctrl>-<Home>. At this point, everything is ready for SS's formula to do its work.

The PrintSS Formula

When PnL has finished generating a report, it calls PrintSS to give the user the option of printing the report or continuing (returning to the Report menu). Type in PrintSS's formula, shown in Figure 10-2.

```
; PrintSS

@local(STR),
@eraseprompt,
@prompt(" Press <Return> to print;   " &   " any other key to continue ",10),
@if(@nextkey = {Return},
  @list
  STR := " @print(" & @item1 & ")",
  )
),
@return(0)
```

Figure 10-2. Listing for PrintSS

The **@print** function prints a document or frame under program execution. The **@printreturn** statement in PnL's border formula area has nothing do with this. **@printreturn** stops the Print menu from hunting through the entire program looking for print parameters.

@print takes one parameter—the name of the frame or document you want to print. Here, because the name could be either "SS" or PnLReport (the name of the Profit and Loss report), the programmer placed an **@item1** as the name. **@item1** will contain the appropriate label, depending on which frame is calling PrintSS. As in Currency1, the situation calls for a formula on the fly, so the programmer has concatenated the **@print** function and **@item1** into a variable (STR) for execution.

Regardless of whether the user chooses to print, the **@return** function containing a dummy argument returns execution to the calling frame.

Setting up SS

Before discussing SS's formula, set up the SS spreadsheet. This process includes:

Typing in the column labels

Setting column widths

Formatting two columns for currency display

Positioning the cursor for **@WriteOne**

Follow the steps below to perform these tasks.

1. Type in the four column labels:

    How Paid   **Date**   **Amount**   **Total**

2. Align Amount and Total to the right; press <Ctrl>-NR

3. Size each column as follows:

> How Paid—17 characters
>
> Date—11 characters
>
> Amount—12 characters
>
> Total—14 characters

4. Now to put columns C and D in currency format. Move the cursor to cell C2 and press <F6> <Ctrl>-<End> <Ctrl>-NC <Uparrow> <Dnarrow> <Rightarrow> <Uplevel>

5. With your spreadsheet formatted and its entry position set, save your work.

THE SPREADSHEET FORMULA

The spreadsheet formula performs five tasks:

> Clearing the data from the last report
>
> Setting up report labeling strings (like "Auto Expenses")
>
> Writing the working set of data onto the spreadsheet
>
> Labeling the report
>
> Totaling the expenses

The Formula

Figure 10-3 contains the listing for the SS formula. Type it in, studying it as you go along. The remainder of the chapter discusses each of the tasks in the formula.

```
PnL.Reporter.SS:
  ; SS -- a Report spreadsheet

  @local(CT,STR,NAME),

  ; strip off extra quotes
  NAME := @mid(@item1,2,@len(@item1)-2),

  ; setup expense string
  @if(NAME <> "Income",
      NAME := NAME & " Expense"
  ),

  ; clear previous report
  @fill(SS.A2:SS.C20, " "),

  ; if working set empty, print message
  ;  else get data from Db and write it in
  @if(@count(Db.Amount) = 0,
      ; then -- write in category and 0 total
      @list(@performkeys("{Dnarrow}" & NAME &
            "{Tab}{Ctrl-2}{Rightarrow}0{Return}"),
          @return(0)
      ),
      ; else -- get data from working set
      @while(@get(Db.How Paid:Db.Amount) <> #Null!,
          @put(SS.A2:SS.C20, @get(Db.How Paid:Db.Amount)),
          @next(SS.A2:SS.C20),
          @next(Db.How Paid:Db.Amount),
          CT := CT + 1     ; CT is number of items written in
      )
  ),

  ; move to the line below last expense line
  STR := "@setselection(" & """SS.A"
      & @integer(CT/3+2) & """)",
  @STR,

  ; write expense category and sum amounts
  STR := "@performkeys(""" & NAME &
      "{Tab}{Rightarrow}{Rightarrow}@sum(" &
      "SS.{Uparrow}{Leftarrow}{Uparrow}:" &
      "SS.{Uparrow}{Ctrl-" &
      @integer(CT/3-1) & "}{Uparrow})" & "{Return}"")",
  @STR
```

Figure 10-3. The SS Formula

Initialization Tasks

The SS formula has two initialization tasks beyond declaring local variables: setting up the strings that will label the spreadsheet and clearing the previous data from the spreadsheet. Setting up the strings takes two steps. First, because the string comes in with three quotation marks ("""Auto"""), you must strip two quotation marks from each end. The following statement does just that:

```
NAME := @mid(@item1,2, @len(@item1)-2),
```

Here, with **@item1** as its string, **@mid** positions its pointer after the second character, and assigns to NAME the length of **@item1** less 2, thus removing the final two quotation marks. The resulting string has just one set of quotation marks surrounding the category label ("Auto" instead of """Auto"""").

To provide an accurate label for the spreadsheet, you need to state that an item is an expense. That's true of four of the categories, but not of Income. Therefore, the program concatenates the string " Expense" (note the space before the word) to the NAME variable only when the value of NAME is not the string "Income":

```
@if(NAME <> "Income",
    NAME := NAME & " Expense"),
```

If the value of NAME is "Auto", it appear as "Auto Expense" when printed on the report.

An **@fill** statement clears the information written by the previous report by writing a space character into each cell in the range A2 to C20:

```
@fill(SS.A2:SS.C20, " "),
```

The starting point is A2 so that you don't fill the column labels. The formula doesn't include column D, the Total column. DoOne erases that figure with a <Del>.

Getting the Data

The task of getting the data into the spreadsheet poses one question: What if a category has no records? For example, perhaps you haven't spent any money on postage. If you write a null working set into the spreadsheet, it will bring in the field labels and then total them as zero. Still accurate, but a little sloppy.

The solution is to test the database for the number of Amount entries, with **@count** (the test is performed on Amount, because **@count** only works on numeric entries) as shown in Figure 10-4.

```
@if(@count(Db.Amount) = 0,
    ; then -- write in category and 0 total
    @list(@performkeys("{Dnarrow}" & NAME &
        "{Tab}{Ctrl-2}{Rightarrow}0{Return}"),
    @return(0)
    ),
```

Figure 10-4. Testing for Zero Db Items

The formula tells FRED that if the count is 0, write in a label and give the total as 0. Then quit the SS formula with a **@return**. The third part of the formula—the ELSE statement—tells FRED to get the data. See Figure 10-5. Basically, this **@while** loop tells FRED to test the database to see if any records remain. If there are, the next record found is put in the next available spreadsheet cell. Once that task is completed, FRED advances two pointers—one to get the next record and one to mark the next available spreadsheet cell.

The last statement in the loop increments to a counter (CT). Later statements will use the value stored in this counter as an index to direct the movement of the cursor. The next statement, "Indexing: Random Access in a Spreadsheet," explains this.

```
; else -- get data from working set
@while(@get(Db.How Paid:Db.Amount) <>  # Null!,
   @put(SS.A2:SS.C20, @get(Db.How Paid:Db.Amount)),
   @next(SS.A2:SS.C20),
   @next(Db.How Paid:Db.Amount),
   CT := CT + 1        ; CT is number of items written in
)
),
```

Figure 10-5. Getting the Data

Indexing: Random Access in a Spreadsheet

In the original design of PnL, the program stacked all the reports together on the spreadsheet for a final report. However, this presentation contained too much detail and lacked a clear summary, so it was changed. The present form of Write PnL generates a nice, clean summary, but the SS formula still contains two examples of random access to spreadsheet cells through *indexing*.

Indexing is a technique whereby the one or two variables are substituted for the usual coordinates. Thus, these variables or indices drive cursor movement, instead of navigational keys like <Dnarrow> and <Ctrl-Uparrow>.

The string-oriented nature of both cases of indexing demand writing a formula all on the fly. Take a look at Figure 10-6, a listing for the statements that position the cursor for writing the report label.

```
; move to the line below last expense line
STR := @setselection("&"""SS.A"
  & @integer(CT/3+2) & """)",
@STR,
```

Figure 10-6. Moving to the Sum Row

Here, instead of an arrow key move, the statement sets the cursor position through **@setselection**. In this case, column is not a question, so "A" is stated outright. The question is how many rows to move the cursor. Because CT counts all the entries from the database, dividing CT by three (the number of columns that **@get** draws from) yields the number of rows of data written.

To get the correct row number, the formula adds two to this count—one for the label row and one to get the cursor down to the first row below the data. If you wanted to have a blank row between the data and the total line, you could add three.

In the second-to-last line of Figure 10-7, a value is supplied to a <Ctrl>-key combination. Because typing <Ctrl>-3 <Uparrow> moves the cursor up three cells, the value of CT less one row is applied to specify the exact range of cells that **@sum** takes as a parameter. This technique can come in handy when you're trying to deal with closely packed blocks of data.

```
; write expense category and sum amounts
STR := "@performkeys(""" & NAME &
  "{Tab}{Rightarrow}{Rightarrow} @sum(" &
  "SS.{Uparrow}{Leftarrow}{Uparrow}: " &
  "SS.{Uparrow}{Ctrl-" &
  @integer(CT/3-1) & "}{Uparrow})" & "{Return}"")",
@STR
```

Figure 10-7. Performing the @sum Operation

As with the fast food example, keystrokes that type in the data and create the formula are recorded and then transferred to SS with Cut and Paste for editing (notice the presence of the NAME variable).

> **Note:** Sometimes, turning a series of macro keystrokes into a formula on the fly can become a bit complicated. A good way to determine if you've broken the keystrokes up into a legal string is to Cut and Paste the formula into a test frame. When you can make the proper string appear, you've got it. Just Cut and Paste the tested formula back into your program and make necessary adjustments, like assigning the string to a local variable.

You now have all the frames necessary to generate a category report. Try one. It should resemble the report shown in Figure 10-8. You'll have to wait until after the next section, ''The Profit and Loss Statement,'' before you can select the Write PnL menu item.

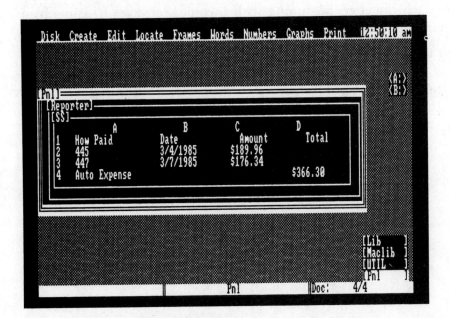

Figure 10-8. A Typical Category Report

This concludes the discussion of the SS formula. In the next section, you will set up the routines necessary for creating PnLReport, the Profit and Loss summary.

THE PROFIT AND LOSS STATEMENT

Reports on individual expenses are an important part of bookkeeping and accounting. Ultimately, however, the accountant wants to see a summary—The Profit and Loss statement. Generating this statement, a spreadsheet with the title PnLReport, begins when you select the Write PnL menu item. This selection sets a series of formulas in motion. In brief, PnL does the following things to write the Profit and Loss statement:

- Creates, labels, and formats a spreadsheet named PnLReport

- Takes each category, beginning with Income, retrieves it, sums its amount, and transfers the amount to the spreadsheet.

- Offers the user the option to print the resulting report

Figure 10-9 shows a typical PnLReport, generated by Write PnL.

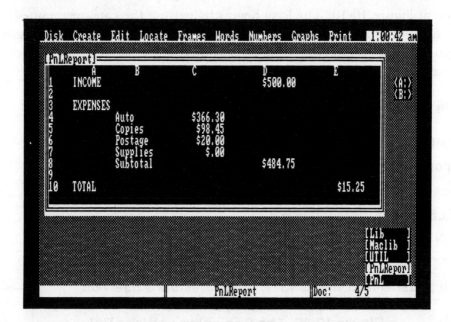

Figure 10-9. A Typical PnLReport Spreadsheet

The Write PnL Formula

After declaring its local variables, Write PnL calls MakePnl, the formula which creates and sets up the PnLReport spreadsheet. From that point on, an **@while** loop does most of Write PnL's work.

Figure 10-10 shows the beginning of Write PnL and the start of the loop. The loop itself performs three tasks:

- Selecting each category name in a stated order

- Restoring and retrieving the category's data from Db

- Region-walking that data into the appropriate cell

Take a look at Figure 10-10. The loop begins by getting the category name (packaged to ship in filter formula form) with an **@select** statement. The loop ships the name (assigned to CONST) off to QueryOne, the same routine called by Reporter to restore the database, execute the filter formula, and sort the working set.

```
; Write  PnL

@local(SELECTOR,CONST,STR,CURRENT),
@Reporter.MakePnL,
@while(SELECTOR < 5,
   SELECTOR := SELECTOR + 1,
   CONST := @select(SELECTOR,"""Income""","""Auto""",
     """Copies""","""Postage""","""Supplies"""),
   @Reporter.QueryOne(CONST),          ; restore & query db
```

Figure 10-10. The Beginning of Write PnL

With the working set ready, the loop can proceed to extract data from it. Figure 10-11 shows the second part of the loop. Because the Income total does not sit neatly in the same region with the expense statements, region-walking is needed to find out which category the program is currently writing. As labeling category reports showed, FRED is up to the task of dealing with exceptions. Figure 10-11 shows an **@if** test for category, similar to the test for labeling.

```
; sum each category & write result to PnLReport
; if CONST = Income, write sum to D1

@if(CONST = """Income""",
  @put(PnLReport.D1:PnLReport.D1,
    @sum(Db.Amount)),

; else (CONST <> income), region walk from C4 to C7
    @list(@put(PnLReport.C4:PnLReport.C7,
      @sum(Db.Amount)),
      @next(PnLReport.C4:PnLReport.C7)
    )         ; end list
  )           ; end if-then-else
),            ; end while
```

Figure 10-11. Region-Walking Data into PnLReport

Here, the results of the test tell FRED in which region to write the sum of the category's amount. If the category is Income, he puts the sum of Income amounts at D1. If the test finds a non-Income category, he puts the amount in the appropriate cell in the region C4 to C7.

Note: This **@get-@put-@next** block is written in Write PnL because if it were written as a subroutine and called, Write PnL would re-initialize the region-walking pointer every time it came back to the subroutine. The subroutine would place the Income amount correctly, but would write all the expense amounts at C4. Keep this principle in mind when writing region-walking routines.

Notice in Figure 10-11 that you don't need to write all the amounts out onto a spreadsheet and sum them there. Instead, you can apply the **@sum** function to the numeric category you want to add in the working set. Here, the statement sums the amount with:

@sum(Db.Amount)

Unlike the SS formula, this formula doesn't need to make any special provision for a category with no record. **@sum**(Db.Amount) returns a zero from a null working set.

Once the loop has written PnLReport, Write PnL still has a certain amount of cleanup to do. First, it must recalculate PnLReport so that the expense subtotal and final totals reflect the figures just written in. Figure 10-12 shows the cleanup routines.

@setselection, when not carrying a parameter, returns the current cursor position. Thus, you save the current position by storing it in a local value named CURRENT. This way, after the cleanup is done, the cursor can be returned to its position prior to the cleanup. The last statement actually does this, by making CURRENT **@setselection**'s parameter.

```
CURRENT := @setselection,
@setselection("PnLReport"),
@performkeys("{F5}"),          ; recalc report
@Reporter.PrintSS("PnLReport"),
@setselection(CURRENT)
```

Figure 10-12. Write PnL ''Cleanup'' Statements

The cleanup begins by selecting PnLReport. You have to select a frame before you can recalculate it. Also, selecting the frame makes it visible to the user who may want to study it or print it. Once the user has had the opportunity to print the report, Write PnL's work is done, and so it selects the pre-cleanup cursor position.

> **Note:** In the current form of the program, you should either save or delete PnLReport after quitting PnL. Although you can have more than one PnLReport on the desktop, FRED will work only with the first PnLReport it comes to. The program will overwrite the first PnLReport, leaving the second PnLReport (the more recently created of the two) without any data. This is true not only of PnLReport but of any frames bearing the same name.

You have only one more formula to write before you can write a Profit and Loss statement—MakePnL.

The MakePnL Formula

The MakePnL statement is mostly one long macro. To create this macro the first time, Record was fired up and several shots were made at creating PnLReport. When the macro was right, Cut and Paste were used to move the resulting string into the MakePnL report frame. After a tad of editing, the frame was ready to create a complete spreadsheet on the fly.

> **Note:** One error occurs during the setup of the spreadsheet. Framework does not like to perform an arithmetic operation when no operands are present. The error constant #VALUE! (which means that the reference value is incorrect) disappears when Write PnL recalculates PnLReport. If you wanted to avoid this, you could write a zero into each of the referenced locations before writing the formula.

To type in the MakePnL report frame, begin by entering the frame label and the first statement shown. Then, with MacLib on your desktop, do the following:

1. Select the PnL border.

2. Press \<Alt\>-\<F2\> to invoke the Record macro.

3. Select a macro letter that has no other significance to start the Record process, and type the \<Alt\>-letter combination.

4. With the exception of the quotation marks and the ampersands, press each of the keys represented in MakePnL. As you work, you will get a slow-motion view of all the things that go into creating this particular spreadsheet. If you make a mistake, correct it (you can always edit the mistake and your recovery measures later). If you get into trouble, cancel the record process, delete the incomplete frame, and start over.

5. When you've finished, complete Record by typing your <Alt>- letter combination.

6. Delete the frame you created during the Record process. If you want, test your work by typing the <Alt> key combination.

7. Go into the formula area of the macro letter in MacLib, select the entire string, and invoke the Cut macro.

8. When the cutting procedure is complete, leave MacLib and return to the formula area of Write PnL.

9. Position the cursor and type the Paste macro.

10. When Paste has finished its work, edit the string in accordance with the one in Figure 10-13.

```
PnL.Reporter.MakePnL:
  ; MakePnL

  @setselection("PnL"),
  @performkeys("{Ctrl-C}w5{Return}h10{Return}s{F3}" &
      "{Uparrow}{Uparrow}{Return}{F4}{Dnarrow}{Return}" &
      "PnLReport{Return}{Dnlevel}INCOME{Tab}{Rightarrow}" &
      "{F6}{Ctrl-End}{F4}{Ctrl-6}{Rightarrow}{Return}" &
      "{Ctrl-N}C{Ctrl-Home}{Dnarrow}{Dnarrow}" &
      "EXPENSES{Return}{Ctrl-Dnarrow}TOTAL{Tab}" &
      "{Uparrow}{Uparrow}Subtotal{Return}{Uparrow}" &
      "Supplies{Return}{Uparrow}Postage{Return}{Uparrow}" &
      "Copies{Return}{Uparrow}Auto{Return}{Ctrl-Dnarrow}" &
      "{Ctrl-2}{Rightarrow}{F2}@sum({Uparrow}{Leftarrow}" &
      ":{Uparrow}{Ctrl-4}{Uparrow}){Return}{Ctrl-End}" &
      "{F2}{Uparrow}{Ctrl-Uparrow}{Leftarrow}-{Uparrow}" &
      "{Ctrl-Dnarrow}{Return}{Return}{Ctrl-Home}{Uplevel}")
```

Figure 10-13. Listing for MakePnL

Having entered the string that creates PnLReport, notice the statement that precedes the string:

@setselection("PnL"),

Without this instruction, the program would create the PnLReport frame *inside* the PnL frame. This kind of thing can be dangerous to your other routines and create referencing problems. Beyond that, by placing PnLReport outside the program frame, you give the user the opportunity to delete, rename, or save PnLReport independently of its parent program, PnL.

With the Report portion of the PnL program complete, run it. Generate reports for each category, including Supplies, which has no records. Be sure to select Write PnL to see the summary work at handling a category with zero records. Then add new entries and generate more reports. The next section discusses possible enhancements to PnL.

ENHANCEMENTS

This section suggests enhancements to the PnL application that make it more than an elaborate toy program. These include:

More expense categories

More fields

More reports

More report information

More bomb-proofing

Dynamic sizing of SS

A Menu following Report—Print, Save, Delete, Graph

Print parameters

Graphing of PnLReport

The chance to print and/or save the entire database

Autosave

Memory checking

More expense categories. If you really wanted to have a professional system, you'd have a complement of other categories such as Entertainment, Utilities, Rent, Travel, Dues, Equipment, Maintenance, Salaries, and so on. You could also link in depreciation routines.

> **Note:** With larger menus, you'll eventually duplicate first letters on one or more categories (Taxes, Telephone, Travel). This will force the user to select with an arrow key and press <Return> to choose a category. As an alternative, you might do away with a menu of categories and have the user type in the expense name or an abbreviation. You can bomb-proof this entry by comparing it to a database list of acceptable entries. Such a database could also translate an abbreviation (like ''Ph'' for ''Phone'') into a single-word entry.

More fields. What other information do you or your client want? Purchase order numbers? Invoice numbers? Vendor information? Vendor billing dates?

More reports. You might want to add a submenu under Report Menu containing ''Report by Category'' and ''Report by Date.'' With Report by Date, the user could specify a date range and get a report of all expenses alphabetically by category. With more fields, you could also have reporting by vendor, by purchase order number, and so on.

More report information. Would you or your client like to know and compare current expenses with the budget for each category, by amount or by percent?

More bomb-proofing. Currently, the Edit menu lets a user type in anything for Category and How Paid. To keep a user from making up categories, misspelling, or otherwise doing things that would mess up data retrieval, you could compare any entry in these categories to an acceptable set of entries.

Dynamic spreadsheet sizing. In a very short time, the number of expenditures in many categories will exceed 20 rows. To overcome this problem, you could store a small, one-line spreadsheet. Then, by counting the number of entries in the working set, you could expand the spreadsheet accordingly.

A Menu following Report. Such a menu could offer the user several options: Delete, Rename, Print, Save, or Graph the current report.

Print parameters. You could add headers and/or footers and specify margins in the PrintSS formula.

Graphs. There could be a graph option (as mentioned) or you could generate them automatically at report time.

Print and/or save the entire database. Some people like massive backup procedures. You could include a database dump (in alphabetical and date order) to the printer or to a disk file outside of PnL. Such a file could be either an ASCII file or a Framework frame (see the **@writetextfile** and **@writeframefile** functions).

Autosave. Although PnL automatically saves the database when you quit the program, it has no provision for saving during entry time, which, given a lot of expenses, could become extensive. You can protect the user's work by creating a counter to keep track of the number of entries made and automatically saving the database every set number of records (for example, one, five, or ten).

Memory Checking. As long as you're doing Autosave, building in memory checking routines is a good idea. Check to see if the user has enough working memory to load in the program and the current database with **@memavail**. While you're doing Autosave, check to see if enough disk space remains. Perhaps you could start issuing warnings when only 1K is left. Ultimately, large databases may call for a way to break up the database into smaller files and perform overlays at report time. See Chapter Thirteen ("Memory Management") for details on how to write FRED overlays.

Any more ideas? You're the programmer—have at it.

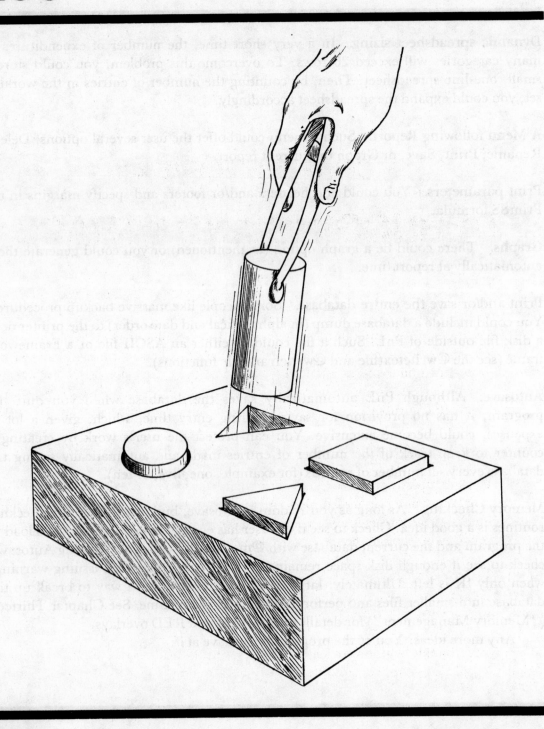

CHAPTER ELEVEN

DEBUGGING AND @TRACE

When you stop to think about it, programmers only become interested in debugging for one reason: A program doesn't work as the programmer expected it to. Does the program not work at all? Does it hum along for a while and then whirr off in hyperwarp to an electronic Never Never Land? Or do you get unexpected ouput (strings instead of numbers, incorrect numbers, etc.)?

THE ART OF DEBUGGING

FRED offers the programmer considerable debugging assistance. This chapter discusses basic debugging techniques with an emphasis on FRED's **@trace** function. Debugging a program begins with isolating where things went wrong. This means working your way through the three steps that comprise any computer program:

- Input
- Processing
- Output

Debugging usually begins with checking your input. This is one of the reasons this book has placed so much emphasis on bullet-proofing input statements. Don't be

FRAME WORK

unfair to your programs—don't expect alchemy. If you're taking invalid input, the best you can expect from a program is gracefully executed trash.

If you can verify that input has gone well, the next place to look is processing. If you can't find it there, you have but one place to check—the output code.

How do you isolate and check each of these elements? The answer is debugging technique—applying **@trace** to selected areas of code, assigning out variables so you can watch their progress as the program runs, putting in stops, setting up your program frames like a control panel, and breaking out a portion of code and testing it in its own frame.

If this answer seems vague, there's a good reason. While debugging demands logic, as writing code does, it also calls on the programmer to work from intuition and experience. Debugging is as much an art as it is a science. The most any book or teacher can do is supply you with the tools.

@trace AND TRACEKIT

The FRED function **@trace** records every step of a program as the program executes. In this section, you will learn about **@trace** and its companion utility, Tracekit, by debugging a simple program, Bug.

About @trace

@trace's syntax demands that you turn it off or on. When on, you must supply the name of a word frame to send **@trace's** results to. For example:

    @trace(View, # ON)

View is the frame to which **@trace** will send its results when you recalculate your program. The #ON turns **@trace** on. When you finish running the program, you select the View frame and press <F9> to find out what's happened.

When you turn **@trace** on, it works system-wide. **@trace** keeps on recording, recalculation after recalculation, until you turn it off. For example, if you were to turn **@trace** on in a program called Pro 1, **@trace** would record Pro 1. If you then recalculated a program called Pro 2, **@trace** would record it, sending the output to the same frame as it did for Pro 1. Room permitting, the receiving frame would then contain information about the recalculation of both programs. **@trace** doesn't stop recording recalculations until you turn it off as follows:

> **@trace**(# OFF)

An **@trace** receiving frame can contain only 32,000 characters, the maximum number of characters for any Framework frame. Because large programs can meet this limit rather readily (especially if you re-run the program without turning trace off and clearing the receiving frame first), it's best to trace portions of programs.

In its receiving frame, **@trace** shows every value assignment, the value output of functions, subroutine calls, and even **@trace** being turned on and off. The section "Bug: A Bad Program Going Good" shows you how to run a program with **@trace** on. First, look at **@trace**'s companion utility Tracekit.

Tracekit

Tracekit is a four-part frame that includes frames for the following tasks:

- Turning **@trace** on
- Turning **@trace** off
- Viewing the results of **@trace** ("trace stream")
- Clearing the trace stream frame

Tracekit is, in essence, a trace control panel. You can find it in the Lib frame supplied on your Framework Utility disk. To get a copy of Tracekit on your desktop, follow these steps:

1. If you have another file labeled Lib on your desktop, save it, if necessary, and then delete it from the desktop.

Note: If you already have a file named Lib on your storage disk, change the desktop Lib's name to something else (like FWLib) before saving.

---

2. Put the Utilities disk in your drive and bring Lib onto your desktop.

3. Go into Lib and select Tracekit.

4. Copy Tracekit to the desktop (select Lib's border before pressing <Return>).

5. Delete Lib from the desktop.

6. Put Tracekit into Frames (not Outline) View, and save it for later use.

7. Move Tracekit into the upper-left corner of your desktop, ready for "Bug."

   Each frame inside of Tracekit is like a button. You "push" each button by selecting and recalculating. Thus, to turn trace on you move into the Tracekit frame, select trace on and press <F5>. Similarly, to turn trace off, you select and recalculate trace off. To clear the last "listing" from trace stream, you select and recalculate the "clean" frame. Tracekit makes it unnecessary to plant **@trace** commands in the program, unless you want to get down to a fairly low level.

Bug: A Bad Program Going Good

To see **@trace** at work, type in the program named Bug, *exactly* as it appears in Figure 11-1. The eagle-eyed reader may detect the problem even while entering the program, but don't let that ruin the fun of seeing a bug at work and the joy of squashing it.

```
Bug:
; Bug

@local(CT,NAME,STR),

NAME := @inputline("Your name please"),
CT = @len(NAME),

@while(CT > 0,
    STR := STR & @mid(NAME,CT,1),
    CT := CT - 1
),

NAME & " spelled backward is " & STR
```

Figure 11-1. Listing for Bug

Size the frame and move it so that your desktop resembles the one in Figure 11-2.

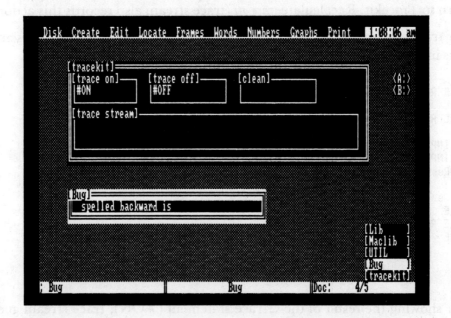

Figure 11-2. A Desktop with Tracekit and Bug

Looking over the listing, you can see that Bug's purpose is to get input, a name, and by parsing the name with **@mid** to spell the name backwards. Recalculate Bug and respond to the prompt by typing the name "jo." The output shows that Bug succeeded in keeping the name you typed, but failed to process and output the name spelled in reverse. Bug shows

> jo spelled backward is

Time to trace the program. Follow these steps:

1. Go to Tracekit and recalculate the *trace on* frame (trace stream immediately reflects this).

2. Recalculate Bug and type "jo" again. The result is the same.

3. Return to Tracekit. Recalculate *trace off* (trace stream also records this action).

4. Select trace stream and press **<F9>** to see **@trace**'s results. It should resemble the results in Figure 11-3.

```
TRACE Result: #ON
LOCAL
LOCAL Result: 0
SET
     INPUTLINE
     INPUTLINE Result: "jo"
SET Result: "jo"
LEN
LEN Result: 2
WHILE
WHILE Result: #FALSE
TRACE
```

Figure 11-3. The Results of the First Trace

After showing the result of the **@trace** statement (# ON), trace stream goes on to state that it encountered an **@local** statement. The "Result: 0" means that local variables were declared and initialized to a value of zero. So far, so good.

@trace records every assignment statement with SET. The first SET statement recorded is:

NAME := **@inputline**("Your name please"),

Here, **@inputline**'s result is what you typed, "jo," as is the result of assigning that input to NAME.

The next operation, **@len**, is correct. The length of the string "jo" is 2. But wait! Where's the SET statement? After all, the program does assign the length of NAME to the counter variable (CT), so that CT can drive the loop. Hmmm. Take a look at the loop.

It fails immediately, indicating that its test condition (CT > 0) failed the first time. This means that CT was 0 (FRED's initial value for a local variable) or less. In other words, everything points to a problem in the Bug statement that assigns string length to CT. Take another look at it:

    CT = @len(NAME),

The operator! This isn't BASIC; FRED assigns values with ":=", not with "=". Edit your assignment statement accordingly. Now recalculate Tracekit's *clean* frame and *trace on* frame to record the next run. Recalculate Bug, and type "jo" as your input string. This time, everything should work correctly. Output is as expected—jo spelled backwards is oj.

Turn trace off and take a look at the new program flow shown in Figure 11-4 with its added comments.

```
TRACE Result: #ON
LOCAL
LOCAL Result: 0
SET                    NAME := @input...
    INPUTLINE
    INPUTLINE Result: "jo"        your entry
SET Result: "jo"
SET                              CT := @len...
    LEN
    LEN Result: 2                @len(NAME)
SET Result: 2
WHILE
    SET                          STR := STR & @mid...
        MID
        MID Result: "o"          @mid(NAME,CT,1)
    SET Result: "o"
    SET                          CT := CT -1
    SET Result: 1
    SET                          second pass thru loop
        MID
        MID Result: "j"
    SET Result: "oj"
    SET
    SET Result: 0
WHILE Result: #FALSE
TRACE                            CT not > 0
                                 turn trace off
```

Figure 11-4. The Results of the Second Trace

Sound logical practice demands reading through an **@trace** listing starting with the first line, so that you can verify each step as correct before continuing to the next. Nonetheless, the first thing the programmer noticed the moment he looked at the first set of results was that the loop failed without doing anything.

His own experience drew him directly to the assignment line, where he saw the problem. However, before correcting it, he went to the top and read down to the problem, just to be sure no other problems existed. Yes, eyesight and insight play important roles in debugging.

Although this bug was easier to find than most, it's not any sillier than most. If you've had much experience with programming, you can probably recount numerous occasions, when, finding a bug, you threw up your hands and uttered something like ''How could I've done *that*?'' Well, you did. Everyone does. Be thankful for things like **@trace** that help you find such problems, even if you blush slightly when you find them. One FRED programmer spent an hour debugging a routine, testing, trying different things, until he saw that instead of a statement like:

```
TOTAL := @Calc.NewNum
```

he had written:

```
TOTAL := Calc.NewNum
```

Just as there's a big difference between the logical operator ''='' and the assignment statement '':='', there's a big difference between storing a value and storing a recalculated value. One **@** sign is all it took.

Tracing Portions of a Program

As mentioned earlier, if you turn **@trace** on, you turn it on system-wide. Although, you can place an **@trace** statement somewhere in the middle of a subroutine, if you press <Return> or otherwise recalculate the frame, you will turn **@trace** on, causing it to record everything from the start of the program until it encounters an **@trace** off statement. Therefore, to ensure that you record only the desired portion of a program, turn **@trace** off at the beginning of the program, on for the portion you want, and then off again at the end of the portion.

For example, if you wanted to record only the loop portion of Bug, you would put @trace statements in as shown in Figure 11-5.

```
Bug:
    ; Bug
    @trace(#OFF),
    @local(CT,NAME,STR),

    NAME := @inputline("Your name please"),
    CT := @len(NAME),
    @trace(tracekit.trace stream,#ON),
    @while(CT > 0,
        STR := STR & @mid(NAME,CT,1),
        CT := CT - 1
    ),
    @trace(#OFF),
    NAME & " spelled backward is " & STR
```

Figure 11-5. Tracing the Loop Portion of Bug

Figure 11-6 shows the results of this trace.

```
Disk  Create  Edit  Locate  Frames  Words  Numbers  Graphs  Print   1:14:53 am
TRACE Result: #ON
WHILE
    SET
        MID
        MID Result: "o"
    SET Result: "o"
    SET
    SET Result: 1
    SET

        MID
        MID Result: "j"
    SET Result: "oj"
    SET
    SET Result: 0
WHILE Result: #FALSE
TRACE

                        tracekit.trace stream      Char:   1/1
```

Figure 11-6. Results of Tracing the Loop

You can also follow a similar procedure for tracing two or more portions at a time. Just turn **@trace** off and on as appropriate.

Note: This example takes advantage of the trace stream frame on the desktop. Without Tracekit, you just create an empty/word frame, label it, and send the results to it.

OTHER DEBUGGING TECHNIQUES

Thanks to the flexibility of the FRED language, the programmer can exercise a fair degree of creativity in ferreting out bugs. Common techniques include assigning out variables and breaking statements into component pieces for analysis in test frames. This section leads you into some of these possibilites.

Assignment

The basic idea behind assignment as a debugging tool is straightforward. You set up frames through which you can read the state of variables as the program recalculates. This technique offers several options you can initiate individually or harness together:

● Inserting assignment statements into the program
● Setting up your program frames like a control panel, so you can watch changing values
● Changing local variables to global variables so you can watch their values during development and debugging of a program
● Placing **@nextkey** statements to stop the program until you press the key

For example, say that you wanted to watch **@mid** parsing NAME. You could write an assignment statement, sending each result of each parsing act to a desktop frame labeled VAL. Sometimes operations move too quickly to analyze, so you might want to add a one second pause.

Take a look at the listing for Bug with an assignment statement in Figure 11-7. If you want to modify your own version of Bug to see this assignment in action, create a frame named VAL and position it where you can see it when the program runs. Then just run the program.

```
Bug:
   ; Bug
@local(CT,NAME,STR),

   NAME := @inputline("Your name please"),
   CT := @len(NAME),

   @while(CT > 0,
       STR := STR & @mid(NAME,CT,1),
       VAL := STR,        ; write STR to VAL
       @beep(20,100),   ; pause 1 second
       CT := CT - 1
   ),

   NAME & " spelled backward is " & STR
```

Figure 11-7. Bug with Assignment Lines Inserted

A similar technique for watching STR at work would be to remove STR as a local variable and make it a global variable by renaming VAL to STR. As Figure 11-8 shows, this procedure calls for two other modifications: initializing STR to erase the previous string, and leaving a space character and deleting the space character after "is" in the final string. Try this one as well.

```
Bug:
   ; Bug
@local(CT,NAME),

   NAME := @inputline("Your name please"),
   CT := @len(NAME),
   STR := " ",        ; init STR with a space

   @while(CT > 0,
       STR := STR & @mid(NAME,CT,1),
       @beep(20,100),   ; pause 1 second
       CT := CT - 1
   ),

   NAME & " spelled backward is " & STR
```

Figure 11-8. Bug with STR Converted to a Global Variable.

These are a few techniques for variable watching. Put them to work as your debugging requires. Sometimes, however, it's not all that easy to debug based on a variable, particularly if the variable is "hidden" in a formula written on the fly. This is the subject of the next section.

Debugging a Formula Written on the Fly

The problem with variables in formulas written on the fly is that if you include a bug, the error pops up for the whole statement (like @EXEC), instead of in the string. To create a bug and learn how to debug it, create a frame called Fly, and type in its listing as shown in Figure 11-9.

```
; Fly


@local(EXEC),
EXEC := @inputline("Type a formula"),
@EXEC
```

Figure 11-9. Listing for Fly

Now try it out. Recalculate Fly and type 5+2<Return> to see the result, 7. Fine. Now, type an invalid formula: 5+2/0<Return>

Fly returns the "Cannot divide by 0" on the bottom of the screen and #DIV/0! inside its own frame. When you press <F2> to see the source of the error, the cursor rests on the "EXEC" portion of @EXEC. When you have a long formula, that can mean a lot of study, unless you can isolate the point in the formula where the error occurs. Here's one strategy for tackling this type of situation: Create a frame labeled Flea, and then modify Fly's listing to correspond with the one in Figure 11-10.

```
; Fly

@local(EXEC),
EXEC := @inputline("Type a formula"),
@setformula(Flea, EXEC),
@Flea
;@EXEC
```

Figure 11-10. Modified Listing for Fly

Basically, you've disabled **@EXEC** with a semicolon and, through **@setformula**, written the formula to Flea. Because **@setformula** writes the formula to a frame, you can examine all the formula's elements by checking the referenced frame.

> **Note:** Because **@setformula** overwrites any formula currently in the referenced frame, you can use this method for repeated tests.

With the modifications in place and Flea on your desktop, recalculate Fly and enter the same formula: **5+2/0 <Return>**. Besides the #DIV/0! message in the two frames, the bottom line of the screen displays:

    Called function returned with an error

This is one of FRED's most valuable error messages, because it leads you to the place where the bug hides. If you have a series of subroutine calls, each subroutine will give this message. Just follow the error messages to the problem.

For example, with Fly still selected, press **<F2>** and you'll see the cursor sitting on the Flea. Follow that clue. Press **<Esc>** and select Flea.

Press **<F2>** to see the formula you typed. Here's the error message and the cursor right on the problem—the zero operand. In essence, that's how you isolate problems in formulas written on the fly, even fairly complex ones.

CHAPTER TWELVE

COMMUNICATING WITH THE OUTSIDE WORLD

So far, this book has only looked at interactions among Framework files. But there is also an outside world which wants to send data to Framework in foreign formats—and wants data back in formats it can understand. And then you have DOS next door with its many capabilities. How do you open that door? This chapter discusses the issues such questions pose and offers some solutions.

INPUT: CONVERTING NON-FRAMEWORK FILES

Suppose you wanted to check DOS to find out the status of the NumLock key. Or capture a DOS screen. Or bring in a file written in a non-Framework format. FRED gives you access to such input.

Talking with DOS

There are a number of reasons for checking the status of the <NumLock> key in a FRED program. You may want to warn the user to turn it off before exiting the data entry portion of a program. Or you might want to check to see if a printer is "out there'' before continuing with an **@print** routine. A simple assembly language routine would enable you to do such things. At the appropriate time you can call the routine with FRED's **@run** function.

@run takes two parameters, a reference to a frame where you want to deposit the output from a program (and the command line to invoke your program), and the name of a program you're calling:

    @run(LockOn, "Num.Exe")

When FRED encounters this statement, he will go out to DOS, load and execute Num.Exe, and return the program's screen output to the LockOn frame.

Figure 12-1 gives the listing for an 8088 assembly language program, Num.Exe.

```
stack      segment    stack
           dw 256 dup (?) ; declare stack for local usage
stack      ends
cgroup     group      cseg
cseg       segment    byte public
assume cs:cgroup
numlock?           proc      near
      num state              equ       20h
      ; call the rom keybd routine to get keybd status flag
      mov        ah,2
      int        16h
      ; test returned byte (in AL) to see if numlock is set
      and        al,num state    ; is the num state bit set
      jz         not numlock
      mov        ax,1            ; it is set
      jmp        qnumlock?
not numlock:
      mov        ax,0            ; it is not set
qnumlock?:
      mov        ah,4Ch ; return AL as status (1=numlock ON)
      int        21h
      ret
numlock?           endp
cseg  ENDS
      END        numlock?
```

Figure 12-1. Listing for Num.Exe

This program tests the keyboard status flag for the status of the <NumLock> key and loads the result into AL. A DOS interrupt sets this value as the number the program will return. Figure 12-2 shows LockOn's formula for interpreting this value.

```
; LockOn

@if(@run(LockOn, "Num.Exe")=1,
    @prompt("Please press<NumLock>to continue",22)
)
```

Figure 12-2. Listing for LockOn

How did communication take place between the FRED program and the language program? Num.Exe is designed to supply a single piece of information—the state of <NumLock>. The mechanism that returns this information is the *error level number* that DOS allows a program to set. Any number between 0 and 255 is an acceptable error level number.

To set this error level, the error level number (0 for <NumLock> off, 1 for <Numlock> on) is placed into the AL register, the DOS command selection value (4C hex) is placed into the AH register, and an interrupt (21 hex) is generated to start the DOS routine executing. See your DOS technical reference manuals for explanations of the various DOS interrupt routines.

All FRED functions return a value. The value of the **@run** function is either the error level set by the program (if no DOS errors occurred) or the DOS error number (if a DOS error occurred). Test the returned number with the **@isabend** function to differentiate between these two results. The value of **@isabend** returns a #TRUE when a DOS error value is present.

Note: You can add "command line" options to programs like Num.Exe as a way of sending input to the program. The reader might wish to enhance this program by sending Num.Exe a parameter to alter the state of <NumLock>, as well as returning its current state.

Beyond calling assembly language programs, you can also run and capture DOS routines with **@run**. DOS possibilities range from things as simple as generating and reading in a disk directory (see the next section) to running batch files.

Capturing DOS Screen Output

You do a lot of things with DOS, from converting file formats to pulling in information. This section shows you how to enlist the **@run** function in pulling a DOS directory into a Framework frame.

This program takes two frames: GetDir contains the formula, and MyDir receives the DOS text characters. Figure 12-3 contains the listing for GetDir.

```
; GetDir
@run(MyDir, "a:\Command.com /c dir a:")
```

Figure 12-3. Listing for GetDir

Again, you can see the **@run** command with its first argument, the name of the receiving frame. Instead of an "Exe" program, the second argument has two parts. First, the formula summons the DOS Command.com file. You *must summon* this program before executing any DOS or batch commands. In this case, the pathname is only the drive designation followed by the backslash, a complete pathname.

After naming the file, the /C option is include to tell DOS to treat the next instructions as if they were typed at the keyboard. Finally, the standard directory command is issued, naming drive A as the drive to read. You can follow this model in capturing any kind of DOS screen output.

Note: Any screen output that is accomplished with DOS commands will be placed in the named frame because it is output to the screen. However, the first time that a program bypasses DOS to write to the screen, FRED will stop recording the output. Most versions of BASIC, for example, take over the screen immediately, thereby nullifying your efforts.

Reading in Non-Framework Text Files

This section discusses two approaches to importing text files into the Framework environment. The first is a file prepared by another application—a text file filled with ASCII characters. The second is the case in which another language builds up a text file at FRED's bidding.

In the first instance, you need only issue a Disk menu Get File by Name command as the following statement does.

```
@performkeys("{Ctrl-D}ga:Memo.txt{Return}"),
```

This statement captures a text file named Memo.txt. The Disk menu Get File by Name command automatically wraps a ''foreign'' file in a frame and brings it to the desktop.

In the second instance, FRED runs a program that builds up a text file. When the file is ready, FRED brings it onto the desktop. One way to name this file is to ''hardwire'' the output file name into the program.

For example, say your program, named Bildfile.exe, always generates the name Summary.txt. Your FRED statement might look like this:

```
@run(Toss, "BildFile.exe"),
@performkeys("{Ctrl-D}ga:Summary.txt{Return}"),
```

Here, Toss represents the mandatory parameter—a frame name that will receive BildFile's screen output, if any. Most converter programs don't output to the screen, so this frame could end up blank. When BildFile finishes its work, the **@performkeys** statement goes out and brings Summary.txt to the desktop.

Another way to name an output file is to write the external program so that it looks for parameters, like an input file name and an output file name. The syntax is almost the same, except that here, you supply BildFile with two parameters:

```
@run(Toss, "BildFile.exe InFile OutFile"),
@performkeys("{Ctrl-D}ga:OutFile{Return}"),
```

> **Note:** The next section contains an actual example of parameter passing in a program that sends parameters to the Framework utility program Trans123. Also, see the Diskutil.fw program on the Framework Utilities disk for a FRED program that performs many DOS tasks—copying disks, formatting, etc.—for more examples of interacting with DOS.

Importing text files is straightforward enough. But what about files that remain in a non-text file format, a format generated by another application?

Reading Files in Foreign Formats

What if you have a spreadsheet or database created in Lotus's 1-2-3 application? Or a VisiCalc spreadsheet in DIF format? How do you get it (values, labels, and formulas) into Framework format? The answers lie on the Framework Utilities disk: Trans123.exe and Trandif.fw.

As its extension indicates, Trans123 is not a FRED program. Because 1-2-3 files can take a large amount of memory, you should normally run Trans123 in DOS only. To do this, get into DOS and type the command line string:

    Trans123 <Return>

Respond to Trans123's four questions for the following:

   The name of the 1-2-3 file

   The name of the converted file (it can be the same)

   The number of rows in the 1-2-3 file

   The number of columns in the 1-2-3 file

> **Note:** You can send default values for the last three items by pressing <Return>.

With its questions answered, Trans123 converts the 1-2-3 file into a Framework spreadsheet. To work with the new file, follow these steps:

1. Bring the Framework file to the desktop.

2. Select cell A1.

3. Type **\<F6\> \<Ctrl\>-\<End\> \<Ctrl\>-N W** to force redisplay of values.

4. Select the spreadsheet frame and recalculate it.

5. Save the new file in its recalculated state.

> **Note:** As Trans123 itself warns, Trans123 does not translate macros. If you have any circular references, you should set their initial values through an assignment formula on the spreadsheet.

You can execute Trans123 with an **@run** statement, if the spreadsheet is not too large and you have enough memory. Figure 12-4 shows a program, named Get123, that goes to a small (5-row by 4-column) spreadsheet named Profit.wks and renames it Profit1.fw. Once Trans123 has converted Profit.wks, the program brings it onto the desktop and recalculates.

```
; Get123

@run(Pf, "b\Trans123.exe b:\Profit.wks b:\Profit1.fw 5 4 "),
@performkeys("{Ctrl-d}gb:\Profit1.fw{Return}"),
@setselection("Profit1.a1"),
@performkeys("{F6}{Ctrl-End}{Ctrl-n}w{Ctrl-Home}{F5}{Uplevel} "),
@performkeys("{Ctrl-Return}"),
```

Figure 12-4. Listing for Get123

Note: This program demands at least one other frame, PF, to satisfy **@run**'s syntax. After running, Get123, PF will contain all the text written by Trans123. If you have a version of Framework prior to 2.0, you will need to have a third frame to assign a macro key to Get123 and then invoke the program through that macro key. Also, DOS has been directed to a particular disk and path by specifying the ''B:'' designation. Without a designation, FRED looks to the default disk and pathname.

DIF stands for *Data Interchange Format*. Software Arts, Inc. created DIF so that different applications could share data. A typical example involves shipping data from a VisiCalc spreadsheet to a plotting program. Another example is a VisiCalc user sending you VisiCalc data in DIF format. TransDIF is the utility that converts these files into Framework format.

Because TransDIF is a FRED program, you will need to bring it and the DIF file you want to convert to the Framework desktop. To run TransDIF, follow these steps:

1. Recalculate TransDIF; press **<F5>**
2. Follow the prompt and press **<Space>** to continue.
3. Type in the name of the DIF file.

That's it. TransDIF will do all the work right before your very eyes.

Note: TransDIF supports only files that were written out in DIF format according to the specifications published by DIF's creators, Software Arts, Inc. This means two things. First, files converted to DIF by specifications other than those propounded by Software Arts, Inc. may not work at all or may yield curious results (like switching rows for columns, columns for rows). Second, it means that DIF programmers can modify TransDIF to support extensions to DIF.

The subject of converting data among different applications raises the questions of how to prepare Framework data for other applications, the subject of the next section.

OUTPUT: CONVERTING FRAMEWORK FILES TO TEXT FILES

This section takes up the subject of how to convert Framework documents, spreadsheets, and databases into text files. The key function for writing out Framework files is **@writetextfile.** This section discusses how to prepare the different types of frames for **@writetextfile.**

Writing Word Frame Text Files

Converting a word frame to a text file is fairly simple. You apply it as a parameter to the **@writetextfile** function:

> **@writetextfile**("BobMemo.txt",Memo to Bob)

This statement converts the text in the frame Memo to Bob to a text file named BobMemo.txt which FRED will save to the default directory. That's it.

Note: The "txt" extension is optional. You could also have prefixed the new filename with a pathname. The filename must conform to DOS conventions.

A word frame converted by **@writetextfile** has certain characteristics:

- It contains just characters with no attributes (like bold type).
- It puts an EOL at the end of each line.
- It contains no frame information except the frame name.

You can easily import such a file into a wordprocessing application or transmit it to another computer through a modem. Databases are just as easy to convert.

Delimited Databases

When you convert a database to a text file, **@writetextfile** automatically converts text strings and dates in the database into delimited, quoted strings. Field names are included. Numerals remain numerals. **@writetextfile** writes just one record per line. Take a look at the simple database in Figure 12-5. (If you want to try this, just create a three-column, four-row database and remember to type the dates in with the **@date** function.)

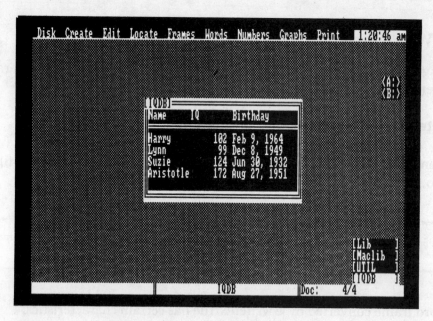

Figure 12-5. The IQDB Database

To convert this database into a text file, you need a one-line program. Create an empty/word frame and label it Writer. Type the following formula into Writer's formula area.

@writetextfile("DbTest",IQDB)

This formula converts IQDB into a textfile named DbTest and saves DbTest on the default storage location.

Recalculate Writer. Then retrieve DbTest from disk. Your results should look like those in Figure 12-6.

```
"Name","IQ","Birthday"
"Harry",102 ,"Feb 9, 1964"
"Lynn",99 ,"Dec 8, 1949"
"Suzie",124 ,"Jun 30, 1932"
"Aristotle",172 ,"Aug 27, 1951"
```

Figure 12-6. The DbTest Text Frame

Delimited entries are important because they make it possible for you to ship Framework database entries to dBASE II and dBASE III for further processing. If you need to transport dBASE II or dBASE III files to a Framework database, look into the **@dbasefilter** function.

The Framework text database file can become an important instrument for writing out text versions of Framework spreadsheets, the next topic.

Text Spreadsheets

If you apply **@writetextfile** directly to a spreadsheet, the result will look just like the spreadsheet from which the numbers were taken, including the spacing between the columns. But it's all text, including the space characters that separate the columns.

As an example, fill a spreadsheet full of random numbers between 1 and 1000. Follow these steps:

1. Create a three-column, four-row spreadsheet and name it RanDumb.

2. In cell A1, you write the formula

   @int(@rand∗1000)+1

3. Copy this formula throughout the spreadsheet by pressing <F8> <F6> <Ctrl>-<End> <Return> <Return> <Ctrl-Home>

4. With the numbers ready, edit Writer's formula to

@writetextfile(''Rands'',RanDumb)

and recalculate it.

5. Retrieve the Rands file. It resembles Figure 12-7.

801	619	890
306	876	54
32	200	872
189	250	492

Figure 12-7. The Rands Spreadsheet Text File

Well enough. But what if you need to hand those numbers off as delimited strings for further processing? That takes a four-step process:

1. Remove the formulas from the spreadsheet, leaving only values.

2. Create a database with the same dimensions as the spreadsheet.

3. Copy the spreadsheet cells into the database.

4. Write the database out with **@writetextfile**.

The quickest way to remove formulas while keeping their numbers is to write a macro formula, shown in Figure 12-8. Type this formula into the formula area of Randumb. The essence of this formula is that it enters a cell's formula area, deletes the formula, points to itself, and brings its own value into the formula area by ''pressing'' the pound sign (#), instead of <Return>.

```
RanDumb:
   ; RanDumb
   ; remove formulas, keep numbers

   @local(NUM COLS, NUM ROWS, COL, ROW),
   NUM COLS := @value(@inputline("How many columns")),
   NUM ROWS := @value(@inputline("How many rows")),
   ROW := 1,   ; initialize row counter
   @setselection("RanDumb.A1"),   ; put cursor in first cell

   @while(ROW <= NUM ROWS, ; test for number of rows completed
       COL := 1,  ;initialize number of columns for each loop pass
       @while(COL <= NUM COLS, ; test for columns completed
           ; go in and convert formula to number
           @performkeys("{F2}{F6}{Ctrl-End}{Return}{Del}" &
               "{Uparrow}#{Esc}{Rightarrow}"),
           COL := COL +1    ; increment column counter
       ),      ; end col loop
       ROW := ROW +1,       ; increment row counter
       @performkeys("{Home}{Dnarrow}") ; setup for next pass
   ),      ; end row loop

   @setselection("RanDumb")    ; return cursor to frame
```

Figure 12-8. Formula for Converting Formulas to Numbers

If you have a Framework version prior to 2.0, you'll need to create an **@setmacro** frame to call RanDumb. Put this formula in a frame labeled Go:

@setmacro({Alt-F},RanDumb)

With Go selected, press <F5> <Alt-F>

If you have version 2.0 or later, just recalculate RanDumb when you're ready. Admittedly, you could perform this function by hand, by turning the line that does the formula-to-number conversion into a single keystroke macro. That would be fine for a 12-cell spreadsheet, but would you want to do that a hundred times? Or a thousand times?

If you haven't done so already, recalculate the formula. When it has finished its work, only numbers will remain in the spreadsheet. Jump into RanDumb and move the cursor over the cells. No formulas, just numbers.

Now all you need to do is copy these numbers into a three-column by four-row database. If you still have a copy of IQDB around, make a copy of it, rename the copy RandDB, and erase all its contents. From IQDB's frame, press: **<Dnlevel> <Ctrl>-<Home> <F6> <Ctrl>-<End> <Del> <Ctrl>-<Home>**

To copy the numbers from the spreadsheet into the database, follow these steps:

1. Select the spreadsheet and press **<Dnlevel> <Ctrl>-<Home> <F6> <Ctrl>-<End> <F8>**

2. Press **<Uplevel>** and select RanDb.

3. Press **<Dnlevel> <Dnarrow> <Return>** to complete the copy.

To write RanDb out as a text file named RandText, modify Writer as follows:

    @writetextfile("RandText",RandDb)

Recalculate it. To conclude, bring RandText onto the desktop. Figure 12-9 shows a sample, based on the version of RanDumb shown above in Figure 12-7.

""	,""	,""
801	,619	,890
306	,876	,54
32	,200	,872
189	,250	,492

Figure 12-9. The Contents of the RandText Text File

If you want, you can jump in and delete the first row of null strings which were written because no field names exist in R and DB.

The examples in this brief view of building and writing text files should provide you with plenty of ideas when you need to do this sort of thing for real. For example, you could link the four steps you've taken here into a single program that would automate the whole process. As you can see, FRED has plenty of power for these assignments.

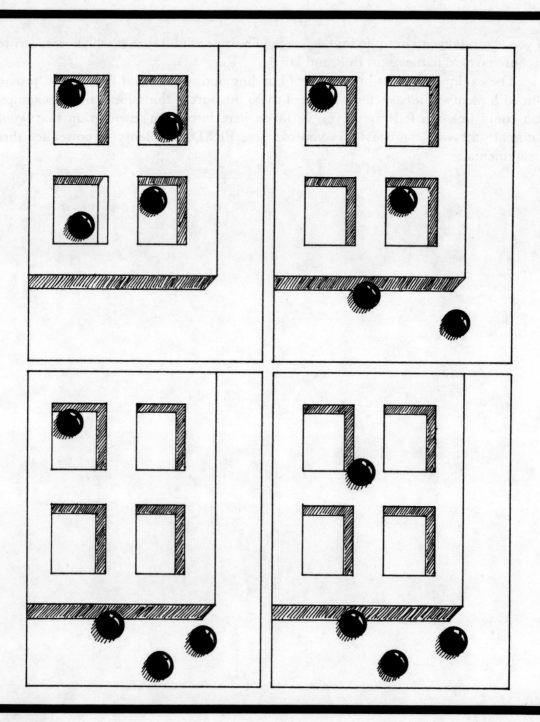

CHAPTER THIRTEEN

MEMORY MANAGEMENT

This chapter illustrates memory management technique with a program named Chain. It also illustrates the basic principles involved in writing a program to consolidate spreadsheets through overlays. Memory management becomes necessary when you have more data than your machine has memory. Imagine trying to consolidate expense report spreadsheets from a hundred regional sales offices, for example.

CHAINING A SERIES OF PROGRAMS TOGETHER

Take a look at the listing for Chain in Figure 13-1. Chain acts as an overlay manager, bringing in one program at time and executing it. The largest amount of memory needed equals the memory taken by Chain plus the amount taken by the largest program in the chained series.

   The key to running a program chain is to have each program in the series (except for the last program) assign the next program to Chain. For example, Program 1 might have line like:

```
Chain:="Program2"
```

The user initializes the whole process by responding to a prompt for a program name. This user initialization step means that Chain can drive different sets of programs; it isn't "hardwired" for any specific set of programs.

```
Chain:
  ; Chain
  ; Chain is a driver for bringing a series of individual
  ; programs into memory one at a time. When each program
  ; ends, it assigns the next step to the Chain frame,
  ; for example: Chain := "Step 7"
  ; As each program expires, Chain deletes it, and frees
  ; up memory for the next program.

@printreturn,
@local(PREVPGM, EXEC),

  ; Initialize Chain by getting first program.
Chain := @inputline("What program do you wish to run"),
@while(PREVPGM <> Chain,
    @echo(#OFF),
    ; Load in requested program.
    @performkeys("{Ctrl-D}g" & Chain & ".fw{Return}"),
    @echo(#ON),
    PREVPGM := Chain,
    EXEC := "@" & Chain,      ; Build formula to execute
                              ; program.
    @EXEC,                    ; Execute program.

    ; Execution returns to Chain so delete requested program.
    @setselection("PREVPGM"),
    @performkeys("{Del}"),
    @memavail          ; Free up deleted memory.
),                      ; Loop to the next entry in the chain.

"Finished"
```

Figure 13-1. Listing for Chain Program

One of the most important statements any overlay program can issue is **@memavail**, seen here at the bottom of the loop. **@memavail** flushes the *undo buffer* so that all memory absorbed by this buffer becomes available to the next program. Until flushed, the undo buffer holds the contents of the deleted program, just in case you want to undo it.

> **Note:** **@memavail** clears the undo buffer so that it can return the amount of available memory. This comes in handy for seeing if the user has enough memory available to load a frame.

You needn't reserve Chain for a series of memory-consuming programs. You can put Chain to work to drive any series of programs.

OVERLAYS AND SPREADSHEET CONSOLIDATION

This section discusses a scenario for spreadsheet consolidation. The elements include:

- 100 spreadsheets to consolidate—SS1 through SS100
- A Consolidation spreadsheet—SSC
- Cell formulas in SSC, each of which looks for data from one cell out of all the cells in all 100 spreadsheets
- A chaining program to drive the whole process—DoConsol

For the purposes of this discussion, the contents of the 100 spreadsheets don't matter. What does matter, however, are SSC's formulas and the driver program, DoConsol. Take a look at a typical formula in an SSC cell, here, cell K12. K12's one job is to get data from one cell, J14, in one spreadsheet, SS76.

```
@if(@iserr(SS76.J14),
   SSC.K12,
   SS76.J14
)
```

What this formula says is, if a reference to cell J14 in spreadsheet SS76 results in an error (probably because SS76 isn't in memory yet), cell K12 in spreadsheet SSC should keep its present value. Otherwise, suck in the value found at SS76.J14. Here, K12 represents just a call to a particular spreadsheet and a particular cell within that spreadsheet. All of SSC's data-retrieval formulas will make similar, specific references.

The program that drives the overlay process will have a loop to choose each successive spreadsheet by *indexing* through an **@select** statement. For a cell indexing model, see the SS formula in the PnL program, Chapter Ten. In outline, the loop, which resembles the loop in Chain, looks like this:

1. Select next spreadsheet

2. Load the spreadsheet

3. Recalculate SSC with **@SSC**

4. Delete the spreadsheet

5. Flush the undo buffer

When the loop recalculates SSC, it changes only those cells which make reference to current spreadsheet. The rest of the cells, because they do not make reference to the current spreadsheet, will retain their values.

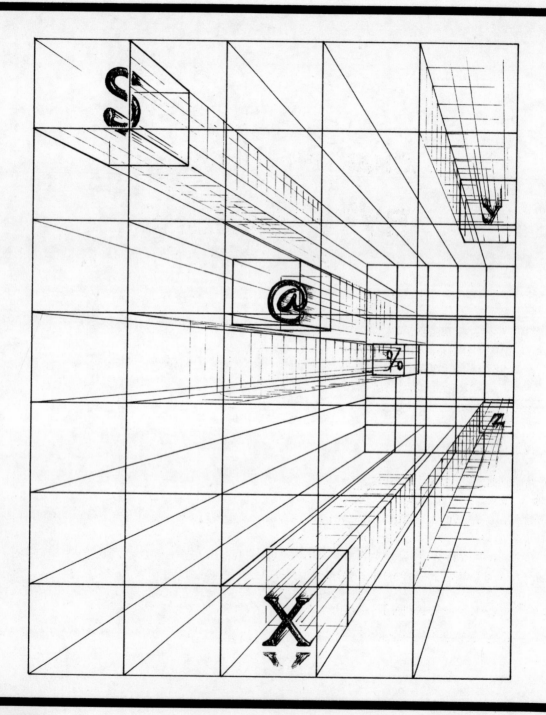

ASHTON · TATE

FRAMEWORK

CHAPTER FOURTEEN

BYTE-SAVERS

This chapter addresses the question of how to save bytes through two techniques: cutting the number of bytes taken by a graphics screen and abbreviating some common but lengthy Framework functions. Both are helpful for shrinking the amount of space a frame takes on disk. Abbreviation leaves more working memory when working with large programs.

SAVING GRAPHS

When you save a graph, you save every bit that goes into painting the graph on the screen. The larger the graph, the more bits, and the more disk space taken by the graph frame. With graphs, the way to save bytes is to save the graph frame without the graph in it, but with its graphing formula ready to go when you recalculate the frame. To see how this works, you'll need to create a simple spreadsheet (the data for graphing) and a graph frame with an **@drawgraph** formula. Follow the steps below:

1. Create a four-row by four-column spreadsheet and label it ABC1984.

2. Fill in all the data shown in Figure 14-1, except the Net numbers in the last row.

3. Type the following formula into cell B4 and copy it into cells C4 and D4:

B2-B3

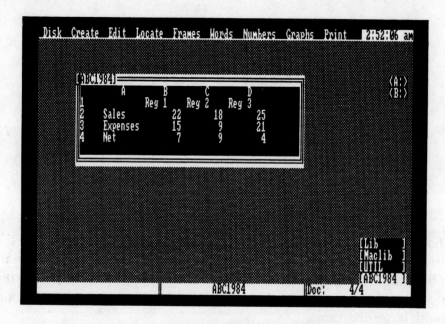

Figure 14-1. ABC1984 Spreadsheet

4. Create an empty/word frame and label it ABC Graph.

5. Go into the formula area of ABC Graph, and type in the formula in Figure 14-2.

```
; ABC Graph

; @return(" "),
@drawgraph(ABC1984.B2:ABC1984.D4,
    # ROW,
    # BAR,
    "ABC Company 1984 Regional Report",
)
```

Figure 14-2. Listing for ABC Graph

6. When you've finished typing in the formula, recalculate the ABC Graph frame. A graph, similar to the one in Figure 14-3, appears immediately.

Note: The printed version has a larger title and may be more accurate than what you see on your screen.

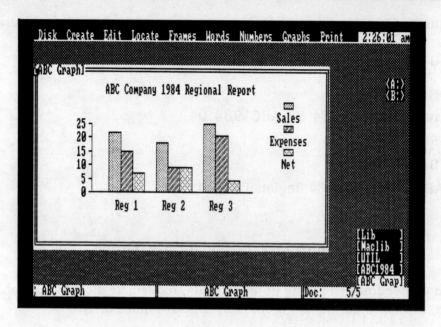

Figure 14-3. ABC Graph Displayed

> **Note:** FRED can draw a graph only in an empty frame or a frame currently occupied by a graph. Short of writing an **@execute** or similar formula to place an **@drawgraph** formula, the **@drawgraph** won't work if written in a spreadsheet or database frame or cell.

ABC Graph's **@drawgraph** formula fills all the mandatory parameters—area to be graphed, orientation, and type of graph—and adds the first of the optional parameters, a graph title. The key to saving a "null" graph is the **@return** statement, currently commented out. Follow the next set of steps to save a "null" graph:

1. Enable the **@return** function by going into the formula area and deleting the semicolon which precedes the **@return** function.

2. Recalculate the frame. A single space character (**@return**'s parameter) replaces the graph.

3. Go back into the formula area and re-insert the semicolon in front of **@return**.

4. To leave the formula area, press **<Esc>**, *not* <Return>. (Pressing <Return> would recalculate the frame, drawing the graph again.)

5. Save the blank ABC Graph frame and delete the ABC Graph from the desktop.

6. To see the graph once again, bring ABC Graph back to the desktop. It's still blank.

7. Now recalculate it. Your graph reappears.

That's all there is to it. In this case, you saved about 2K. With the graph on the screen, ABC Graph takes 3K. Without it, 1K. Not bad for a relatively small graph.

When you enable and recalculate the **@return** function, **@return** yields only a space character as a value for the whole frame. Execution goes no further. The programmer chose a space character because FRED will overwrite text characters. It will not, however, over-write numbers.

ABBREVIATED FUNCTION NAMES

In a long program, you can save yourself quite a few bytes by *abbreviating function names*. For example, instead of typing "**@performkeys**" or "**@setselection**" or "**@eraseprompt**" dozens of times each, you could type "**@p**" or "**@s**" or "**@e**," respectively.

The key is to put the actual functions in a desktop Lib, even the Lib your application draws on. To see the principle behind abbreviations in action, abbreviate the function **@beep**. Perform the following steps.

1. Create an outline frame and an empty/word frame.

2. Name the outline frame Lib and the word frame Noise.

3. Go into the outline and label the "1" frame as B.

4. Go into B's formula area and write this formula:

   @beep(@item1, @item2)

   Leave B and Lib.

5. Go into Noise's formula area and type the following formula:

   @B(100,100)

6. Recalculate Noise and a low-pitched, one-second beep sounds.

In effect, you have called a frame named B, and shipped it two parameters. **@beep** in the B frame picked these parameters up and sounded the tone. In essence, that's how any abbreviation works.

Be aware of several caveats attached to creating abbreviations. First, those functions which take simple strings or numeric values make the best candidates for abbreviation.

Second, avoid functions which change the state of a program, like **@local**. **@local** changes the state of its frame by creating local variables. **@local** in a library would create the variables in the library frame, not in your subroutine frame. Also avoid functions with more than one possible evaluation, like **@if**. What you look for from **@if** is an evaluation of the #TRUE part *or* the #FALSE part. A library version of **@if** would cause evaluation of *both* parts.

Third, if you choose to abbreviate a function like **@prompt**, which takes an optional argument, remember to always pass both parameters, or create tests that will allow the function to work if you omit any of the optional parameters.

Note: A function bearing **@item** parameters will fail if you send it a number of arguments other than what it expects.

Fourth, to be on the safe side, create a single-frame test of any function you want to abbreviate (as you did with **@beep**) to make sure it will work.

Finally, if what you really want to do is avoid typing ''**@performkeys**'' 43 times, consider setting up a macro, like <Alt>-P to do the work for you. Take a look at the **@performkeys** macro shown in Figure 14-4 (created in a few seconds with the Record macro).

Note: Typesetting restrictions necessitated breaking the macro into two concatenated strings. You needn't concatenate a ''real life'' macro.

@performkeys("{Ctrl-W}b @performkeys{Ctrl-W}n(""""),"

& "{Ctrl-3}{Leftarrow}")

Figure 14-4. An @performkeys Macro

If you install this macro in MacLib and press <Alt>-P, you'll see

@performkeys(""),

with the cursor on the second double quotation mark. This is just another way to say, if you have a task to perform, Framework and FRED have the tools.

APPENDIX A
Key Names
in FRED

Figure A-1 illustrates the proper key names for the non-alphanumeric keys available for use in your FRED programs. Curly braces must surround non-alphanumeric keys and key combinations that include non-alphanumeric keys (for example, {Ctrl-C} when used in **@performkeys**). FRED ignores capitalization, but it is best to remain consistent throughout your programs. The spelling of key names can never be altered; hyphens, where indicated, cannot be omitted.

Control-Key Combinations

{Ctrl-Uplevel}   {Ctrl-End}
{Ctrl-Dnlevel}   {Ctrl-Pgup}
{Ctrl-Uparrow}   {Ctrl-Pgdn}
{Ctrl-Dnarrow}   {Ctrl-Return}
{Ctrl-Rightarrow}   {Ctrl-Backspace}
{Ctrl-Leftarrow}   {Ctrl-Del}
{Ctrl-Home}

There are 46 possible Alt-key combinations:

{Alt-A} ... {Alt-Z}   {Alt-F1}...{Alt-F10}
{Alt-0}...{Alt-9}

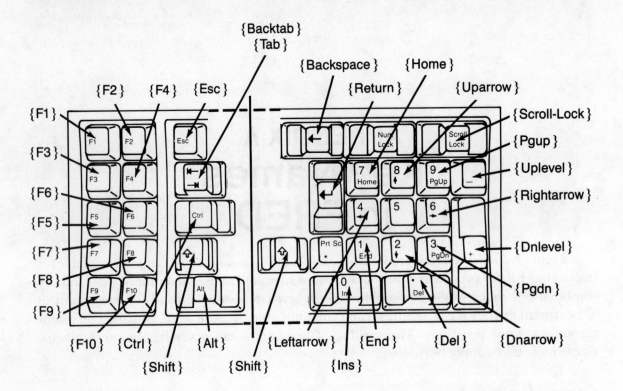

APPENDIX B

ASCII TABLE

Binary	Hex	Decimal	Character	Code	Symbol	Description
00000000	00	0		^@	NUL	Null
00000001	01	1	☺	^A	SOH	Start of Heading
00000010	02	2	☻	^B	STX	Start of Text
00000011	03	3	♥	^C	ETX	End of Text
00000100	04	4	♦	^D	EOT	End of Transmission
00000101	05	5	♣	^E	ENQ	Enquiry
00000110	06	6	♠	^F	ACK	Acknowledge
00000111	07	7	•	^G	BEL	Bell
00001000	08	8	◘	^H	BS	Backspace
00001001	09	9	○	^I	SH	Horizontal Tabulation
00001010	0A	10	◙	^J	LF	Line Feed
00001011	0B	11	♂	^K	VT	Vertical Tabulation
00001100	0C	12	♀	^L	FF	Form Feed
00001101	0D	13	♪	^M	CR	Carriage Return
00001110	0E	14	♫	^N	SO	Shift Out
00001111	0F	15	✳	^O	SI	Shift In
00010000	10	16	►	^P	DLE	Data Link Escape
00010001	11	17	◄	^Q	DC1	Device Control 1
00010010	12	18	↕	^R	DC2	Device Control 2

DEVELOPER'S HANDBOOK

FRAME WORK

Binary	Hex	Decimal	Character	Code	Symbol	Description
00010011	13	19	‼	ˆS	DC3	Device Control 3
00010100	14	20	¶	ˆT	DC4	Device Control 4
00010101	15	21	§	ˆU	NAK	Negative Acknowledge
00010110	16	22	▬	ˆV	SYN	Synchronous Idle
00010111	17	23	↨	ˆW	ETB	End of Transmission Block
00011000	18	24	↑	ˆX	CAN	Cancel
00011001	19	25	↓	ˆY	EM	End of Medium
00011010	1A	26	→	ˆZ	SUB	Substitute
00011011	1B	27	←	ˆ[	ESC	Escape
00011100	1C	28	∟	ˆ₁	FS	File Separator
00011101	1D	29	↔	ˆ]	GS	Group Separator
00011110	1E	30	▲	ˆ ˆ	RS	Record Separator
00011111	1F	31	▼	ˆ	US	Unit Separator
00100000	20	32				
00100001	21	33	!			
00100010	22	34	"			
00100011	23	35	#			
00100100	24	36	$			
00100101	25	37	%			
00100110	26	38	&			
00100111	27	39	'			
00101000	28	40	(			
00101001	29	41	)			
00101010	2A	42	*			
00101011	2B	43	+			
00101100	2C	44	,			
00101101	2D	45	–			
00101110	2E	46	.			
00101111	2F	47	/			
00110000	30	48	0			
00110001	31	49	1			
00110010	32	50	2			
00110011	33	51	3			

Binary	Hex	Decimal	Character	Binary	Hex	Decimal	Character
00110100	34	52	4	01010110	56	86	V
00110101	35	53	5	01010111	57	87	W
00110110	36	54	6	01011000	58	88	X
00110111	37	55	7	01011001	59	89	Y
00111000	38	56	8	01011010	5A	90	Z
00111001	39	57	9	01011011	5B	91	[
00111010	3A	58	:	01011100	5C	92	\
00111011	3B	59	;	01011101	5D	93	]
00111100	3C	60	<	01011110	5E	94	^
00111101	3D	61	=	01011111	5F	95	_
00111110	3E	62	>	01100000	60	96	`
00111111	3F	63	?	01100001	61	97	a
01000000	40	64	@	01100010	62	98	b
01000001	41	65	A	01100011	63	99	c
01000010	42	66	B	01100100	64	100	d
01000011	43	67	C	01100101	65	101	e
01000100	44	68	D	01100110	66	102	f
01000101	45	69	E	01100111	67	103	g
01000110	46	70	F	01101000	68	104	h
01000111	47	71	G	01101001	69	105	i
01001000	48	72	H	01101010	6A	106	j
01001001	49	73	I	01101011	6B	107	k
01001010	4A	74	J	01101100	6C	108	l
01001011	4B	75	K	01101101	6D	109	m
01001100	4C	76	L	01101110	6E	110	n
01001101	4D	77	M	01101111	6F	111	o
01001110	4E	78	N	01110000	70	112	p
01001111	4F	79	O	01110001	71	113	q
01010000	50	80	P	01110010	72	114	r
01010001	51	81	Q	01110011	73	115	s
01010010	52	82	R	01110100	74	116	t
01010011	53	83	S	01110101	75	117	u
01010100	54	84	T	01110110	76	118	v
01010101	55	85	U	01110111	77	119	w

Binary	Hex	Decimal	Character	Binary	Hex	Decimal	Character
01111000	78	120	x	10011010	9A	154	ü
01111001	79	121	y	10011011	9B	155	¢
01111010	7A	122	z	10011100	9C	156	£
01111011	7B	123	{	10011101	9D	157	¥
01111100	7C	124	¦	10011110	9E	158	₧
01111101	7D	125	}	10011111	9F	159	ƒ
01111110	7E	126	~	10100000	A0	160	á
01111111	7F	127	⌂	10100001	A1	161	í
10000000	80	128	ç	10100010	A2	162	ó
10000001	81	129	ü	10100011	A3	163	ú
10000010	82	130	é	10100100	A4	164	ñ
10000011	83	131	â	10100101	A5	165	Ñ
10000100	84	132	ä	10100110	A6	166	ª
10000101	85	133	à	10100111	A7	167	º
10000110	86	134	å	10101000	A8	168	¿
10000111	87	135	ç	10101001	A9	169	⌐
10001000	88	136	ê	10101010	AA	170	¬
10001001	89	137	ë	10101011	AB	171	½
10001010	8A	138	è	10101100	AC	172	¼
10001011	8B	139	ï	10101101	AD	173	¡
10001100	8C	140	î	10101110	AE	174	«
10001101	8D	141	ì	10101111	AF	175	»
10001110	8E	142	Ä	10110000	B0	176	░
10001111	8F	143	Å	10110001	B1	177	▒
10010000	90	144	É	10110010	B2	178	▓
10010001	91	145	æ	10110011	B3	179	│
10010010	92	146	Æ	10110100	B4	180	┤
10010011	93	147	ô	10110101	B5	181	╡
10010100	94	148	ö	10110110	B6	182	╢
10010101	95	149	ò	10110111	B7	183	╖
10010110	96	150	û	10111000	B8	184	╕
10010111	97	151	ù	10111001	B9	185	╣
10011000	98	152	ÿ	10111010	BA	186	║
10011001	99	153	ö	10111011	BB	187	╗

Binary	Hex	Decimal	Character	Binary	Hex	Decimal	Character
10111100	BC	188	╝	11011110	DE	222	▎
10111101	BD	189	╜	11011111	DF	223	▄
10111110	BE	190	╛	11100000	E0	224	α
10111111	BF	191	┐	11100001	E1	225	β
11000000	C0	192	└	11100010	E2	226	Γ
11000001	C1	193	┴	11100011	E3	227	π
11000010	C2	194	┬	11100100	E4	228	Σ
11000011	C3	195	├	11100101	E5	229	σ
11000100	C4	196	─	11100110	E6	230	μ
11000101	C5	197	┼	11100111	E7	231	τ
11000110	C6	198	╞	11101000	E8	232	Φ
11000111	C7	199	╟	11101001	E9	233	θ
11001000	C8	200	╚	11101010	EA	234	Ω
11001001	C9	201	╔	11101011	EB	235	δ
11001010	CA	202	╩	11101100	EC	236	∞
11001011	CB	203	╦	11101101	ED	237	ø
11001100	CC	204	╠	11101110	EE	238	ε
11001101	CD	205	═	11101111	EF	239	∩
11001110	CE	206	╬	11110000	F0	240	≡
11001111	CF	207	╧	11110001	F1	241	±
11010000	D0	208	╨	11110010	F2	242	≥
11010001	D1	209	╤	11110011	F3	243	≤
11010010	D2	210	╥	11110100	F4	244	⌠
11010011	D3	211	╙	11110101	F5	245	⌡
11010100	D4	212	╘	11110110	F6	246	÷
11010101	D5	213	╒	11110111	F7	247	≈
11010110	D6	214	╓	11111000	F8	248	°
11010111	D7	215	╫	11111001	F9	249	·
11011000	D8	216	╪	11111010	FA	250	·
11011001	D9	217	┘	11111011	FB	251	√
11011010	DA	218	┌	11111100	FC	252	ⁿ
11011011	DB	219	█	11111101	FD	253	²
11011100	DC	220	▄	11111110	FE	254	■
11011101	DD	221	▐	11111111	FF	255	

DEVELOPER'S HANDBOOK

INDEX

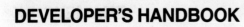

SURVEY

Thank you for purchasing an Ashton-Tate book.
Our readers are important to us. Please take a few moments to provide us with some information so that we can better serve you.

Name: _____

Company Name: _____

Address: _____

City/State: _____ Zip: _____

Country: _____ Date: _____

1) How did you first learn about this publication?
- 21-1 ( ) Someone who saw or bought it
- -2 ( ) Software dealer or salesperson
- -3 ( ) Hardware dealer or salesperson
- -4 ( ) Advertising
- -5 ( ) Published review
- -6 ( ) Computer store display
- -7 ( ) Computer show
- -8 ( ) Book store
- -9 ( ) Directly from Ashton-Tate

2) Where did you purchase this publication?
- 22-1 ( ) Directly from Ashton-Tate™
- -2 ( ) From my Dealer
- -3 ( ) Computer show
- -4 ( ) Book store

3) Have you purchased other Ashton-Tate books and publications?
- 23-1 ( ) Yes 23-2 ( ) No
  If Yes, please check which ones:
- 23- 3 ( ) *Everyman's Database Primer/ dBASE III*
- - 4 ( ) *Advanced Programmer's Guide/ dBASE III & dBASE II*
- - 5 ( ) *dBASE II for Every Business*
- - 6 ( ) *dBASE II Programmer's Companion*
- - 7 ( ) *Framework: An Introduction*
- - 8 ( ) *Framework: On-the-Job Applications*
- - 9 ( ) *Framework: A Programmer's Reference*
- -10 ( ) *Through the MicroMaze*
- -11 ( ) *Introduction to UNIX System V*
- -12 ( ) *Exploring Pascal*
- -13 ( ) *BASIC Booster Library*
- -14 ( ) *Special Effects Library*
- -15 ( ) *MacPack: Creative Activities with MacPaint and MacWrite*
- -16 ( ) *Ashton-Tate Quarterly*

4) What type of software programs are you using now?
- 24- 1 ( ) Accounting
- - 2 ( ) Spreadsheet
- - 3 ( ) Word Processing
- - 4 ( ) Other (Please specify) _____
  _____

5) What type of software programs are you interested in?
- 25- 1 ( ) Academic/Scientific
- - 2 ( ) Agriculture
- - 3 ( ) Building
- - 4 ( ) Business
- - 5 ( ) Financial
- - 6 ( ) Health Care
- - 7 ( ) Home/Hobby
- - 8 ( ) Insurance
- - 9 ( ) Membership/Registry
- -10 ( ) Professional
- -11 ( ) Real Property
- -12 ( ) Software Utilities
- -13 ( ) Spreadsheet
- -14 ( ) Integrated

6) Whom are you purchasing the book for?
- 27-1 ( ) Business
- -2 ( ) Self

7) What make and model computer do you use?
- 28-1 _____

8) Do you expect to purchase other software programs during the next 12 months? If so, what type?
- 29-1 ( ) Accounting
- -2 ( ) Sales
- -3 ( ) Inventory
- -4 ( ) Other (Please specify)_____
  _____

9) What subjects would you like to see discussed?
- 30-1 _____
  _____
  _____

10) How can we improve this book?
- 31-1 _____
  _____
  _____

11) What is your primary business?
A. Computer Industry
- 32-1 ( ) Manufacturing
- -2 ( ) Systems house
- -3 ( ) DP supply house
- -4 ( ) Software
- -5 ( ) Retailing
- -6 ( ) Other _____
B. Non-Computer Business
- 33-1 ( ) Manufacturing
- -2 ( ) Retail trade
- -3 ( ) Wholesale trade
- -4 ( ) Financial, banking
- -5 ( ) Real estate, insurance
- -6 ( ) Engineering
- -7 ( ) Government
- -8 ( ) Education

(continued)
- 34-1 ( ) Military
- -2 ( ) Health services
- -3 ( ) Legal services
- -4 ( ) Transportation
- -5 ( ) Utilities
- -6 ( ) Communications
- -7 ( ) Arts, music, film
- -8 ( ) Other _____

12) What is your position and title? Please check one in each list
POSITION
- 35- 1 ( ) Data processing
- - 2 ( ) Engineering
- - 3 ( ) Marketing/Advertising
- - 4 ( ) Sales
- - 5 ( ) Financial
- - 6 ( ) Legal
- - 7 ( ) Administration
- - 8 ( ) Research
- - 9 ( ) Operations/production
- -10 ( ) Distribution
- -11 ( ) Education
- -12 ( ) Other _____
TITLE
- 35-13 ( ) Owner
- -14 ( ) Chairperson
- -15 ( ) President
- -16 ( ) Vice President
- -17 ( ) Director
- -18 ( ) Manager
- -19 ( ) Dept. head
- -20 ( ) Programmer
- -21 ( ) Other _____

13) How many employees are in your company?
- 36-1 ( ) Less than 10
- -2 ( ) 10 to 25
- -3 ( ) 26 to 100
- -4 ( ) 101 to 300
- -5 ( ) 301 to 1,000
- -6 ( ) over 1,000

14) I would like to remain on your mailing list.
- 37-1 ( ) Yes 37-2 ( ) No

38-1 I'd like to purchase additional copies of the current edition of this book at $24.95 plus $3.00 handling.

☐ My check is enclosed
My MasterCard/Visa card number is:

_____

Expiration date _____

Signature _____

BUSINESS REPLY MAIL

FIRST CLASS   PERMIT NO. 959   CULVER CITY, CA

POSTAGE WILL BE PAID BY ADDRESSEE

ASHTON·TATE ■ ™

10150 WEST JEFFERSON BOULEVARD
CULVER CITY, CALIFORNIA 90230

TABLE OF FIGURES

CHAPTER FOUR: KEYFILTERS

CHAPTER FIVE: LIBRARIES

CHAPTER SIX: MENUS

TABLE OF TABLES

ASHTON-TATE ■™ PUBLISHING GROUP

901 South La Cienega Boulevard,
Inglewood, CA 90301, (213) 642-4637

ORDER FORM

FORM OF PAYMENT:

☐ Check   ☐ MasterCard   ☐ VISA

TITLE	Quantity	Price Each	Total Price	TITLE	Quantity	Price Each	Total Price
Advanced Programmer's Guide Featuring dBASE II and dBASE III		28.95		Framework: On-the-Job Applications		19.95	
Application Junction (1985 version)		29.95		Get Connected: A Guide to Telecommunications		24.95	
BASIC Booster Library for the Apple® Macintosh		29.95*		IBM PC Public Domain Software, Volume I		24.95	
BASIC Booster Library for the IBM® PC		29.95*		Introduction to UNIX™ System V		17.95	
Data Management for Professionals		15.95		MacBASIC Programming		24.95	
dBASE II® for Every Business		19.95		MACPACK: Creative Activities with MacPaint and MacWrite		15.95	
dBASE II for the First-Time User		19.95		Personal Computing and C		19.95	
dBASE II Guide for Small Business		24.95		Personal Financial Management		29.95*	
dBASE II Progammer's Companion		29.95*		Soft Words, Hard Words: A Common-Sense Guide to Creative Documentation		14.95	
dBASE III™ for Every Business		19.95		Special Effects Library for the Apple IIc and Apple IIe		29.95*	
dBASE III™ for Sales Professionals		29.95*		Special Effects Library for the Commodore 64™		29.95*	
dBASE III Trail Guide		29.95*		System Design Guide Featuring dBASE II		18.50	
Everyman's Database Primer Featuring dBASE II		19.95		The Illustrated dBASE II Book		16.95	
Everyman's Database Primer Featuring dBASE III		19.95		The Reference Encyclopedia for the IBM Personal Computer		69.95	
Exploring Pascal: A Compiler for Beginners		39.95*		Through the MicroMaze: A Visual Guide from Ashton-Tate		9.95	
Framework: A Developer's Handbook		24.95		Through the MicroMaze: A Visual Guide to Getting Organized		9.95	
Framework:™ An Introduction		15.95		Up and Running: Adventures of Software Entrepreneurs		15.95	
Framework: An Introduction to Programming		24.95		User's Guide to dBASE II		15.95	
Framework: A Programmer's Reference		24.95					

*book/disk package.

Name: _____

Company: _____

Address: _____

City: _____ State: _____ Zip: _____

Phone: ( ) _____

SHIPPING CHARGES
(U.S. Domestic)

Books are mailed book rate and take 3-4 weeks to arrive.

Up to $20 . . . $2.00
$20.01 to $30 . . . $3.00
$30.01 to $40 . . . $4.00
$40.01 to $50 . . . $5.00
$50.01 to $60 . . . $6.00
Over $60 . . . $7.00

MERCHANDISE TOTAL	
SHIPPING CHARGE (See Chart)	
SUBTOTAL	
CA SALES TAX 6½% (Residents Only)	
ORDER TOTAL	

Thank You For Your Order

||||||

NO POSTAGE
NECESSARY
IF MAILED
IN THE
UNITED STATES

ASHTON·TATE ™

10150 WEST JEFFERSON BOULEVARD
CULVER CITY, CALIFORNIA 90230